T0301997

The Nature and Method of Economic Sciences

The Nature and Method of Economic Sciences: Evidence, Causality, and Ends argues that economic phenomena can be examined from five analytical levels: a statistical descriptive approach, a causal explanatory approach, a teleological explicative approach, a normative approach, and finally, the level of application.

The above viewpoints are undertaken by different but related economic sciences, including statistics and economic history, positive economics, normative economics, and the 'art of political economy'. Typically, positive economics has analysed economic phenomena using the second approach, causally explaining and often trying to predict the future evolution of the economy. It has not been concerned with the ends selected by the individual or society, taking them as given. However, various new economic currents have emerged during the last 40 years, and some of these do assign a fundamental role to ends within economics. This book argues that the field of positive economics should adapt to deal with the issues that arise from this. The text attempts to discern the nature of economic phenomena, introducing the different approaches and corresponding economic sciences. It goes on to analyse the epistemological characteristics of these in the subsequent chapters, as well as their disciplinary interrelations.

This book is a valuable resource for students and scholars of the social sciences, philosophy, and the philosophy of economics. It will also be of interest to those researching political economy and the development of economic thought.

Ricardo F. Crespo is Professor at the IAE Business School, Universidad Austral, Argentina, and at the Philosophy Department, Universidad Nacional de Cuyo, Argentina. He is also a Researcher at CONICET (Argentina's National Council of Scientific and Technical Research).

Routledge INEM Advances in Economic Methodology

Series Editor: Esther-Mirjam Sent, the University of Nijmegen, the Netherlands.

The field of economic methodology has expanded rapidly during the last few decades. This expansion has occurred in part because of changes within the discipline of economics, in part because of changes in the prevailing philosophical conception of scientific knowledge, and also because of various transformations within the wider society. Research in economic methodology now reflects not only developments in contemporary economic theory, the history of economic thought, and the philosophy of science, but it also reflects developments in science studies, historical epistemology, and social theorizing more generally. The field of economic methodology still includes the search for rules for the proper conduct of economic science, but it also covers a vast array of other subjects and accommodates a variety of different approaches to those subjects.

The objective of this series is to provide a forum for the publication of significant works in the growing field of economic methodology. Since the series defines methodology quite broadly, it will publish books on a wide range of different methodological subjects. The series is also open to a variety of different types of works: original research monographs, edited collections, as well as republication of significant earlier contributions to the methodological literature. The International Network for Economic Methodology (INEM) is proud to sponsor this important series of contributions to the methodological literature.

Economics and Performativity
Exploring Limits, Theories and Cases
Nicolas Brisset

A Structuralist Theory of Economics
Adolfo García de la Sienra

Amartya Sen and Rational Choice
The Concept of Commitment
Mark S. Peacock

The Nature and Method of Economic Sciences
Evidence, Causality, and Ends
Ricardo F. Crespo

For more information about this series, please visit: www.routledge.com/Routledge-INEM-Advances-in-Economic-Methodology/book-series/SE0630

The Nature and Method of Economic Sciences

Evidence, Causality, and Ends

Ricardo F. Crespo

Routledge
Taylor & Francis Group

LONDON AND NEW YORK

First published 2020 by Routledge

2 Park Square, Milton Park, Abingdon, Oxon OX14 4RN
605 Third Avenue, New York, NY 10017

Routledge is an imprint of the Taylor & Francis Group, an informa business

First issued in paperback 2021

Publisher's Note

The publisher has gone to great lengths to ensure the quality of this reprint but points out that some imperfections in the original copies may be apparent.

British Library Cataloguing-in-Publication Data
A catalogue record for this book is available from the British Library

Library of Congress Cataloging-in-Publication Data
Names: Crespo, Ricardo F, author.
Title: The nature and method of economic sciences:
evidence, causality, and ends/Ricardo F. Crespo.
Description: Abingdon, Oxon; New York, NY: Routledge, 2020. |
Series: Routledge INEM advances in economic methodology |
Includes bibliographical references and index.
Identifiers: LCCN 2019050360 (print) | LCCN 2019050361 (ebook)
Subjects: LCSH: Economics–Philosophy. | Economics–Methodology. | Economics.
Classification: LCC HB72 .C7384 2020 (print) | LCC HB72 (ebook) |
DDC 330.01–dc23
LC record available at https://lccn.loc.gov/2019050360
LC ebook record available at https://lccn.loc.gov/2019050361

ISBN: 978-1-138-32052-9 (hbk)
ISBN: 978-1-03-217362-7 (pbk)
DOI: 10.4324/9780429453236

Typeset in Bembo
by Newgen Publishing UK

Contents

Illustrations

Figures

Tables

Foreword

Ricardo Crespo's 2017 book, *Economics and other disciplines: Assessing new economic currents*, investigated 'reverse imperialism' and how economics has been influenced by what it has imported from other social sciences compared to what it has exported to them. At the heart of this investigation is the question of what economics is since how it is influenced by its place in social science depends on how this question is answered. Crespo, however, does not answer the question, as have many others who seek to identify the one single thing that defines and distinguishes economics from the other social sciences. He begins with the subject matter of economics – 'the economy' – and emphasizes that it has a number of different meanings that can be examined in quite different ways. What we rather need to identify, then, are a number of different economic sciences in their distinct yet complementary roles and forms. Understanding economics' place in the larger world of social science begins with understanding the complexity and interconnections of economics' diverse types of investigation.

Economists themselves, however, often proceed as if their projects of research were independent of one other. Perhaps an economist takes the ends of economic action as given, and practices a positive economics built around instrumentally rational, utility maximizing individual behaviour. This likely ignores that people's ends are also an object of economic investigation, and that how they may vary affects behaviour. It also closes off what other social sciences may teach us about economic behaviour. Or perhaps an economist specializes in managing data and statistics that form the body of evidence underlying economic theories. What those theories may claim is not one's responsibility; indeed, assembling evidence calls for neutrality regarding what theorists argue. Nor are the possible influences of other sciences on economics one's concern when one's domain is data and statistics.

For Crespo, that there are these different economic science pathways only constitutes a dilemma for economics if one's ambition is that economics be seen as single science with a univocal meaning and definition. Not only does this miss how the different economics sciences work together in different ways, but it misses how the diversity of their investigations produces versatility and openness in economic investigation. Thus Crespo rejects Jack Hirschleifer's imperialist view that economics constitutes 'the universal grammar of social science' because this also eliminates the issue of how economics in its multiple forms influences and is influenced by other social sciences. Economics, that is, needs to be seen as a pluralistic activity because its subject matter is plural and multidimensional.

The important contribution this book makes, then, is that it lays foundations for a richer and more realistic conception of economics as a complex kind of investigation of the multifaceted world we occupy. Perhaps it is to be expected that the emergence of economics in its relatively short 200-year history since Adam Smith would have left us searching essential meanings rather than attending to multiple meanings. Crespo's message, however, is that we will find our 'essential' meanings in the latter.

John B. Davis
University and University of Amsterdam

Acknowledgements

There is a story behind every book. The story behind this book goes a long way back. I put forward the first general ideas at a seminar held at the University of Buenos Aires (4 September 2014) and at a seminar organized by the Centre for Humanities Engaging Science and Society (CHESS) at Durham University (15 October 2014). I got valuable audience feedback, including from Nancy Cartwright, Julian Reiss, Tim Thornton (he also commented the paper on his blog: http://inthespaceofreasons.blogspot.com/2014/10/), Juan Pedro Garcés, and Erin Nash. I also received helpful remarks on a previous version from Harold Kincaid and on a corrected version from Rich Cameron and María Cerezo. A new version was presented at the INEM 2015 Conference in Cape Town, South Africa, on 20–22 November 2015. These ideas were eventually put down on CHESS Working Paper No. 2016–02, Durham University, in February 2016, under the title 'Causality, teleology and explanation in social sciences' (http://dro.dur.ac.uk/20006/1/20006.pdf). I am very grateful for all these contributions and I want to express my special note of thanks to the anonymous reviewers.

I wish to extend particular gratitude to John B. Davis. During the last months of 2017, we worked together over email to turn my book idea – which developed the notions contained in the previous mentioned papers – into a formal proposal. The book proposal was submitted in January 2018 to Routledge and was approved in March. John has then completely read, revised, and commented on the entire book manuscript, providing extensive and excellent feedback and contributing relevant central ideas. My debt to John, however, goes far beyond this particular collaboration. John – along with Marcel Boumans – has not only supervised my PhD thesis, which I eventually defended at the University of Amsterdam, but has revised many of my previous books and articles and is always willing to take the time to answer my emails asking for his advice.

I also want to thank Daniel Heymann for his comments on Chapter 3, Marcel Boumans on Chapter 4, Juan José Llach on Chapters 10 and 11, and Karsten Steuber on Chapter 7. They have all provided useful comments and insights. I shared my book idea with Uskali Mäki, who warned me that some relevant concepts needed revision. I discussed every stage of the writing process with my students of Philosophy of Economics at the Master program in

Economics at the University of Montevideo: they contributed interesting and challenging questions and comments.

The topics covered in several chapters of this book have been presented at seminars and conferences and have been enriched with useful comments from attendees. I presented a previous version of Chapter 1 at the 16th International Congress on Logic, Methodology and Philosophy of Science and Technology (Prague); of Chapter 3 at the LIII Annual meeting of the Argentine Association of Political Economy (La Plata, Argentina); of Chapter 7 at a seminar held by IAE Business School; of Chapter 8 at the XXV Conference on Epistemology of Economic Sciences, University of Buenos Aires, and of Chapter 10 at a seminar organized by the National Academy of Economic Sciences (Argentina). I am grateful for the input offered by Aki Lehtinen, Gonzalo Carrión, Eduardo Scarano, Sandra Visokolskis, Alberto Müller, Juan Carlos de Pablo, and Sina Badiei.

Andy Humphries at Routledge has enthusiastically supported this book project, and Anna Cuthbert and Emma Morley have diligently managed the process. Mariana Donadini and Carmen Bordeu revised the style. Leigh Westerfield has carefully edited the whole book. Anitta Benice attentively accomplished the publishing process. However, I am solely responsible for any shortcomings and oversights. Finally, Liliana Luchi and Fernanda Cid at IAE Business School's library efficiently handled my bibliography demands.

I must acknowledge the use of some conceptual elements drawn from previously published work. Specifically, from Chapters 2, 3, and 6 of *Philosophy of the Economy. An Aristotelian Approach*, Springer, Dordrecht, 2013; Chapter 5 of *Theoretical and Practical Reason in Economics. Capacities and Capabilities*, Springer, Dordrecht, 2013; Chapter 3, last section, of *Economics and Other Disciplines. Assessing New Economic Currents*, Routledge, London, 2017; 'Models as Signs as Good Economic Models', *Estudios Económicos*, XXIX (N.S.), 58, 2012, pp. 1–12; 'Abduction in Economics', coauthored with Fernando Tohmé, *Synthese,* 2013, 190/18, pp. 4215–4237; 'Two Conceptions of Economics and Maximization', *Cambridge Journal of Economics*, 2013, 37, pp. 759–774; 'The Common Good and Economics', *Cuadernos de Economía*, 2016, 39, pp. 23–33; 'Liberal Naturalism and Non-Epistemic Values', *Foundations of Science*, 2019, 24/2, pp. 247–273. I appreciate the permissions granted to use part of these materials when it proved necessary, and I am also grateful to the anonymous reviewers of these published parts of the book, who offered valuable advice.

I also want to convey my sincere gratitude to the academic institutions where I work for their support in my endeavours: IAE Business School (Universidad Austral, Argentina); School of Philosophy, National University of Cuyo (Mendoza, Argentina), and Argentina's National Scientific and Technical Research Council (Consejo Nacional de Investigaciones Científicas y Técnicas, CONICET, by its initials in Spanish).

Lastly, it is only fair that my deepest gratitude goes to my family, to whom I dedicate this book. It would not have been possible without their support.

Buenos Aires and Mar del Plata, 22 September 2019

Abbreviations

CA	Capability Approach
EH	Economics of Happiness
EUT	Expected Utility Theory
HDI	Human Development Index
HDR	Human Development Report
RCT	Rational Choice Theory
UNDP	United Nations Development Program

1 Introduction

I completed my undergraduate studies in economics in the 1970s. We used to read and study the recent articles of journals such as *JPE*, *AER*, and *EJ*. Today, when I look back on those articles, I realize how much economics has evolved. On the one hand, positive economics has become increasingly specialized. Current micro- and macroeconomics bear little resemblance to their 1970s counterparts. Asymmetrical information; industrial organization; new developments in game theory, econometrics and uncertainty management; rational expectations; and dynamic stochastic general equilibrium are all revamping economics.

On the other hand, valuable inputs from other sciences are enriching economic approaches, such as the contributions from psychology that have led to behavioural and happiness economics, or the influence of experimental sciences on experimental economics and of neurology on neuroeconomics, as well as the sociological and anthropological notions on identity, reciprocity, gifts, norms, and institutions used in economic theory developments, or the borrowings from ethics that paved the way for capability and civil economy approaches. Indeed, while during the second half of the twentieth century – and still today – economics has been exporting its 'logic' to other social sciences – a tendency that has been called 'economic imperialism' – we are witnessing today a slow opposite process that shifts away from the application of a narrow economic logic to other human behaviours and the reduction of the economic viewpoint to that rationale. In this so-called 'reverse imperialism', other sciences export categories and concepts to economics and economic life. Thus, a 'mainstream pluralism' consisting of different approaches that draw elements from different sciences outside economics emerges and fuels an internal process in economics (Davis 2008, 2011). Bruno Frey and Matthias Benz (2004: 68) assert that the time has come for a change in direction, with new emphasis placed on *importing* insights from other sciences rather than on *exporting* the logic of economics. This advice stems from the failure of economic rationality to explain some 'abnormal' behaviours (as behavioural economics has shown) and its failure to predict the course of economic affairs (as is patently evident). It also derives from the inadequacy and 'unnatural' nature of the economic logic when trying to explain non-economic behaviours (legal, political, religious, family, ethical), in which other criteria apply (i.e. justice, the common good, relation with God, love, a conception of the good, respectively).

The trends producing the new developments in positive economics and the reverse imperialist currents seem divergent. On the one hand, positive economics, following the paradigmatic notion of economics defined by Lionel Robbins – 'the science which studies human behavior as a relationship between ends and scarce means which have various applications' (1935: 15) –, takes the ends of economic actions as given, subsuming them into an unanalysed scale of consistent preferences, and considers the optimal allocation of means in order to maximize the achievement of the former – to reach the 'highest' possible 'indifference curve'. On the other hand, the new reverse imperialist currents try to uncover the contents of preferences, looking for the psychological, sociological, and ethical motivations of economic actions – that is their underlying ends.

This divergence in tendencies and the proliferation of visions and approaches to economic phenomena, together with the multiplication of economic and/ or financial – global or local – crises, are signs of the seemingly unstable and disjointed character of economic science, which require a deep reflection about its nature and method. A 2019 call for papers for a conference on 'the soul of economics', motivated by discussions on the status of economics since the 2007–2008 global financial crisis, points to some questions about the components of this soul: theoretical foundations, the nature of models, the role of empirical analysis, the new research programs. Many years ago, Benjamin Ward's 1972 book *What's Wrong with Economics?* failed to provide a clear therapy to correct what was wrong. In this book, instead of criticizing contemporary economics, I will try to craft a proposal for economics including different perspectives.

In this unstable scenario, in order to build a useful proposal, we urgently need philosophy. It is similar to an orchestra conductor who combines all instruments to create one harmonious melody. Philosophy can guide the process by suggesting what the role of each discipline is and how they should interact and fulfil their separate roles. We need a renewed investigation of the nature and method of economic science.

This consideration has compelled me to investigate the notion of the subject matter of economic science, the economy. I have concluded that 'economy' has different but related meanings. This multiplicity of meanings creates multiple kinds of economic sciences to appropriately deal with them. In my research, I have found that the logic concept of 'analogy' is useful to deal with this multiplicity. Analogical terms have different related meanings, one being the 'focal' or primary meaning to which the other derivative meanings refer and are connected.[1] Aristotle used 'healthy' as an example: the focal meaning of healthy relates to a healthy human body; derivative meanings refer to healthy foods, sports, medicines, plans and so on (cf. *Metaphysics* IV, 2, 1003a 32ff).[2]

'Economy' does not have a univocal but an analogical meaning, and economics is not a homogeneous science: there are several economic sciences – or one economic science only in a wide sense, with a broad scope. There are different but related meanings of economy and, consequently, different but related approaches to economic phenomena, different kinds of economic sciences with their own adequate methods, and different aims and roles: both economy and economic science are analogical concepts. This means that there are different economic sciences, but that they are complementary; they can be integrated in some way. They have something in common: dealing with economic phenomena.[3]

As we will see, the conclusion of Chapter 2 is that we can distinguish two principal meanings of the economy: one points at the end of satisfying human material needs, and the other indicates a way to accomplish this satisfaction by allocating disposable means to maximize the attainment of our ends. 'Economic theory' should deal with the second notion of the economy, as positive economics does today, but it should also understand and consider different ends that influence economic phenomena but are not included in 'preferences', as will be explained in Chapters 3 and 7.

However, the economic sciences do not end with economic theory. History is *magistra vitae* and expands our horizons. Similarly, the history of economic thought enriches our notion of economy, of economic sciences, and of their methods. Not surprisingly, then, I have found interesting insights about all these topics in old economists. I particularly base my thinking about the economic sciences on John Stuart Mill, Carl Menger, and John Neville Keynes. As I explain in Chapter 3, their ideas on these topics lead us to distinguish the following as different parts of economic science – understood in broader terms or as different economic sciences:

- statistics and economic history, which *describe* and provide detailed information needed by economic theory;
- economic theory, which *explains* economic causes (positive economics) and *interprets* or *understands* the reasons or final causes underlying economic phenomena;
- normative economics, which *prescribes* ideals or the ends of economic activity;
- the art of economics or applied economics, which *designs* policies to achieve those ideals and *implements* them.

Let me expand on the explanation of the second discipline, economic theory. The economy comprises a set of human and social phenomena ultimately built on certain human actions directed to the satisfaction of human needs. People perform conscious actions under the guidance of reason. They use reason to decide what ends to pursue and how to implement ways of achieving them. The first mentioned use of reason has been called practical reason and, the second, technical or instrumental reason. We cannot perform any conscious action without both uses of reason.[4] Ends or reasons trigger the use of means to achieve those ends. There is no conscious action without defining ends – a function of practical reason – and without determining the way of using means – a function of instrumental reason. Reason performs both tasks. This is very well expressed by Amartya Sen: 'reason has its use not only in the pursuit of a given set of objectives and values [instrumental reason], but also in scrutinizing the objectives and values themselves' [practical reason] (2002: 39).

As noted, positive economics takes ends as given. It interprets economic actions as being guided by an instrumental maximizing logic which is a subcategory of instrumental rationality and through which it efficiently applies means to achieve those ends. Or else it assumes that economic agents should behave in this maximizing way. That is, some economists hold that maximizing logic is descriptive, while others believe it is normative, depending on their view of maximizing logic – a point that I will discuss later. Instrumental rationality concerns the way of allocating means (resources) in order to achieve a given set of predetermined ends (preferences). Though not necessarily, it could also strive for 'maximization', that is, for allocating means in a way that achieves the maximum of ends: this is instrumental maximizing rationality. French sociologist Raymond Boudon argues that there is a psychological tendency, albeit not a logical implication, to consider instrumental rationality as a maximizing rationality (2004: 47). Here lies the difference between pure technical thinking (allocation only) and positive economics thinking (the most efficient allocation). The issue for positive economics is to know how to better achieve the desired given ends. It looks for the 'efficient' or driving cause of the desired result.

However, considering reason only in this instrumental role is not enough. We cannot only take means into account because they are triggered by ends or reasons for acting, classically called 'final causes'. Ends and means mutually interact. The idea of ends as given produces a truncated view of action. 'Acting on such radically truncated judgments would be crazy', asserts Elizabeth Anderson (2005: 8). This is the reason why I have previously described the roles of economic theory as the *explanation* – looking for or determining efficient causes of action – and the *understanding* – ascertaining the final causes – of economic actions.

On the other hand, reverse imperialist currents seek to identify the drivers or ends of economic actions. The focus is on knowing the ends, 'reasons' or 'final causes' of economic actions. In a previous book, *Economics and Other Disciplines. Assessing New Economic Currents* (Routledge 2017), I explored whether these new reverse imperialist currents actually tackle the issue of ends. I concluded that some of them do indeed deal with ends. This is relevant because dealing with ends broadens the perspective of analysis of economic phenomena, thus going beyond instrumental maximizing logic. There are ends whose satisfaction, even optimization, does not imply maximization.[5] At the same time, some of these new currents entail a broader conception of economics than the Robbins definition. In fact, some of them call for a rebirth, in some respects, of the old political economy held by classical economists such as Adam Smith. For example, happiness was a topical subject in classic economic theory, and Sen makes constant references to Smith. Smith's science of Political Economy combines a plethora of motivations driving economic decisions and actions – psychological, sociological, ethical, and historical – that were not explicitly considered in Robbins' economics. They are supposedly included in preferences, but their heterogeneity prevents their conflation under this single category (I will develop this conclusion in Chapters 3 and 7).

In Robbins' economics, preferences remain unexamined; they are just preferences, regardless of their content. Consequently, from this perspective, using statistics and determining efficient causes prove enough, since economics only aims at explaining the efficient causes and does not seek to understand the reasons of economic actions. However, today, a complementary and prior question arises: which ends trigger the actions for those causes? That is, which are the final causes or intentions that lie behind economic phenomena? Some of the new reverse imperialist currents, in fact, attempt to enter the 'black box' of ends by considering the psychological, sociological, cultural, ethical, and even biological motivations of actions. This new question about ends increases the task of economic theory. It must now 'understand' or 'interpret' the ends or reasons, or the final causes, also called *teloi* – and then proceed to look for the so-called teleological explanations of phenomena.

Let us look at an example of an attempt to consider ends in economics. To this purpose, Sen draws on an old approach to economic issues. In his book *Ethics and Economics*, he states that economics has stemmed from two different origins. One of them is an ethics-related tradition that dates back to Aristotle (Sen 1987: 2–4). For Sen, '[t]his "ethics-related view of social achievement" cannot stop the evaluation short at some arbitrary point like satisfying "efficiency". The assessment has to be more fully ethical and take a broader view of "the good"' (1987: 4). He mentions Adam Smith, John Stuart Mill, and Karl Marx as later members of this tradition. The other origin is engineering related, and Sen characterizes it as follows:

> This approach is characterized by being concerned with primarily logistic issues rather than with ultimate ends and such questions as what may foster 'the good of man' or 'how should one live'. The ends are taken as fairly straightforwardly given, and the object of the exercise is to find the appropriate means to serve them. Human behaviour is typically seen as being based on simple and easily characterizable motives.
>
> (1987: 5)

Sen argues that while the ethical and engineering-related origins are complementary, modern economics leans towards the latter, thus impoverishing economics (1987: 7). Accordingly, he recommends reconsidering the ethical origin, which takes an array of non-economic (non-maximizing) motivations of economic actions into account. In contrast, the engineering-related tradition, taking ends as given, implicitly subsumes all possible motivations into a formal concept of utility that should be maximized allocating the available means in the best possible way.

But why is it necessary or appropriate to conceive economic theory as encompassing both traditions? Why not leave the traditional 'division of labour' to economists (dealing with the issue of optimally assigning means to given ends) and let individuals or politicians decide about ends? Why is the 'integration' position preferred to the 'division of labour' position?[6] My answer is that apart from epistemological reasons that will be explained in this book (not all motivations can be grouped under a homogeneous unique category), there is an important practical reason: because integration could be a way for overcoming the tensions or conflicts between the proposals of the engineering-related tradition – possibly unethical – and the ethical-related tradition. In my country, Argentina, we use the term *grieta* – the crack – to refer to a fracture between rational economic arguments and 'irrational' attitudes of impoverished, ignorant people who, unable to afford their basic living expenses, vote for populist, often corrupt politicians who give unrealistic promises only to eventually deepen poverty (I will come back to this problem in Chapter 10). This 'crack' does not help improve people's well-being. Aside from efficiency, other factors need to be considered: if ends remain unanalysed, it will not be possible to detect if any human good is threatened by an efficient allocation of means. For example, it has been argued that, in some cases, tolerance of a low level of corruption proves more cost-effective than trying to completely prevent it. But this is not ethical.[7] Philip Nel (2019) finds that under poor institutional conditions, some kinds of bribery are associated with an increase in the relative income share of the poorest 40 per cent, mitigating income inequality. However, he does not intend to justify bribery. He clarifies: 'the paper does not condone or promote bribery/corruption in any form or manner' (2019: 17). At the same time, an ethically driven behaviour must be compatible with resource availability. All in all, complementation or integration of different approaches will prove necessary.

The new currents in economics implicitly advocate for a broader and more integrated conception of the social sciences. We need different approaches in order to work together. Integration may help us understand – through behavioural, institutional, or happiness economics – modes of conduct which are supposedly defined as 'abnormal' by the rational choice theory, that is the standard decision theory of contemporary positive economics. To achieve this end, economic theory should increase its scope and dare to deal with the ends of action, hence analysing a fuller set of motivations behind economic actions. In a practical science such as economics, excessive specialization can have a negative impact. The ample view was the stand adopted by classical economists. We need to refashion and recover their ideas.

Coming back to the above-mentioned classification of economic sciences, it can be deduced that there are five compatible levels or approaches involved in economic science:

a)   a statistical and historical *descriptive* level
b)   a *causal efficient explanatory* level
c)   a *teleological explicative* or *understanding/interpretive* level
d)   a *normative* level
e)   the formerly called *art* of Political Economy

The idea of this book is that, far from being incompatible, these levels are complementary: economic phenomena require a multilevel approach provided by the above-mentioned sciences: statistics, economic history, economic theory (explaining and understanding), normative economics, and the 'art of political economy' (as called by Neville Keynes).

Consequently, this book has various aims. In my previous book, I argue that reverse imperialist currents should be integrated into a new conception of economic science that assimilates insights from biology, neurosciences, psychology, sociology, politics, and ethics. In this book, I will propose integrating these currents with positive economics and establishing a link between the different economic sciences. However, there is a tension between recognition of the different economic sciences and their potential integration. What kind of integration would that be? When we search for a positive definition of this integration, we come across general notions that have not already been agreed upon (and who knows if they will ever be).

Integration is not the 'unity of the science ideal' as understood by logical empiricists or positivists in a reductionist way, usually physicalist. Neither is the mentioned reductionist 'economic imperialist' position. Jack Hirshleifer (1985: 53, italics in the original) clearly describes its *ethos*:

> *There is only one social science.* What gives economics its imperialist invasive power is that our analytical categories – scarcity, cost, preferences, opportunities, etc. – are truly universal in applicability. Thus economics really does constitute the universal grammar of social science.

Lindley Darden and Nancy Maull (1977) criticize the reductionist picture of the unity of science and suggest focusing attention on 'interfield theories', which they actually identify within biological sciences. Defined as theories which bridge two fields of science, interfield theories are likely to be generated when two fields share an interest in explaining different aspects of the same phenomenon. Furthermore, one field does not reduce another field. It is a notion very close to the concept of interdisciplinarity. According to them, 'fields' use particular methods to solve a central problem.

Sandra Mitchell (2009) proposes to adopt an 'integrative pluralist' approach to address the contingency of complex systems. She defines it as 'an expanded epistemology of science that embraces both traditional reductive and new, multilevel, context-dependent approaches to scientific explanation and prediction' (2009: 2). She holds that 'complexity is everywhere' (2009: 1). She mainly draws upon examples from the biological sciences, but she also believes that her proposal has a 'clear application to the social sciences whose complexity includes what is true of the biological and goes beyond' (2009: 20). Throughout her book, she highlights the relevance of her approach for the crafting of policies and, while proposing some strategies, she recognizes that there is no 'algorithmic' method for combining the different kind of causes of complex phenomena approached from integrated multilevel explanations (2009: 114).

The literature about different forms of interaction between disciplines – multi-, inter-, cross-, and trans-disciplinarity – is huge and evolving. The very concept of 'discipline' is evolving. The term 'discipline' does not appear in philosophical dictionaries as the *Stanford Encyclopedia of Philosophy* (https:// plato.stanford.edu/contents.html#s), the *Concise Routledge Encyclopedia of Philosophy* (Routledge, 2000), and Mario Bunge's *Philosophical Dictionary* (Prometheus Books, New York, 2003).

Stephen Toulmin (1972) conceives 'discipline' in much the same sense as Darden and Maull's fields. Seongsook Choi and Keith Richards (2017) devote a chapter to the 'Disciplinary Landscape', collecting the relevant previous bibliography on the concept of 'discipline'. Their conclusion is discouraging: 'disciplines cannot be neatly characterized in ways that will allow them to be used as building blocks in the construction of new academic entities' (2017: 9). Different characterizations place emphasis on organizational, epistemological, conceptual, cultural or social, moral, and political aspects.[8]

For Robert Frodeman (2017: 4), the meanings of interdisciplinarity (used as an umbrella term that covers all its forms) are 'varied and even contradictory'. Julie Thompson Klein presents a complete and updated typology of interdisciplinary relations, and she warns: 'typologies are neither neutral nor static' (2017: 21). Choi and Richards (2017: 42) also remark that interdisciplinarity is an elusive, indeterminate, flexible, and ambiguous concept. Frodeman holds that interdisciplinarity emerges as a demand of society, as a bridge between 'sophists' (in a non-pejorative sense) and society (2017: 7), and that it is consequently dynamic.

Jordi Cat (2017) synthesizes much previous work and offers these definitions:

> *Interdisciplinary* research or collaboration creates a new discipline or project, such as interfield research, often leaving the existence of the original ones intact. *Multidisciplinary* work involves the juxtaposition of the treatments and aims of the different disciplines involved in addressing a common problem. *Crossdisciplinary* work involves borrowing resources from one discipline to serve the aims of a project in another. *Transdisciplinary* work is a synthetic creation that encompasses work from different disciplines.

Multidisciplinarity is often needed in order to study deeply complex topics incorporating multiple disciplines. It is a juxtaposition of disciplines, which remain separate (Klein 2017: 23, see also Choi and Richards 2017: 51). For Klein (2017: 24ff.), interdisciplinarity is more than collaboration, it supposes integration.

Cross-disciplinarity must be practiced with caution to avoid a spirit of 'slavish imitation' or 'scientism', usually using concepts or methods of the natural sciences in other sciences (expressions used by Herbert Simon and Friedrich Hayek respectively; see Kellert 2008: Chapter 2). Davis (2008: 365) has also warned that 'economics, as other sciences, has regularly imported other science contents in the past, and having subsequently "domesticated" them, remade itself still as economics'. Cross-disciplinary practices may produce this kind of domestication, as Davis (2018) also shows. He cites the example of behavioural economics. In my previous book, I explain the link between this 'domestication' and the physicalist orientation of 'imported' disciplines. This is the case not only of behavioural economics but also – albeit with 'tensions' between accepting physical determinism and human freedom – of neuroeconomics and evolutionary economics, while happiness economics, institutionalism, the capability approach, and civil economy 'avoid' this tendency.

Transdisciplinarity suggests a 'transgression' or 'transcendence' of disciplines that considers the growing importance of the 'context of application' (see Barry et al. 2008: 21). It tends to 'think laterally, imaginatively, and creatively not only about solutions to problems but to the combination of factors that need to be considered' (Bernstein 2015: 8). Jay H. Bernstein (2015) cites hunger, poverty, global climate change, extinction of species, depletion of natural resources, and the destruction of ecosystems as topics that have to be dealt with in a transdisciplinary way. We might add well-being and economic crises. In fact, Anna Alexandrova (2017) speaks about 'the science of well-being', which combines insights from different sciences, producing a new science which is not only theoretical but also 'performative'. Frodeman (2017: 4) relates transdisciplinarity to 'Mode 2 knowledge', a knowledge co-produced by academics and non-academic actors working together ab initio (see Michael Gibbons et al. 1994). It is a very dynamic concept.

This broad scenario features its pros and cons. While it offers a comprehensive panoply of possibilities to describe the links between sciences or disciplines, this must be done cautiously, moving towards precise concept definitions. I have used the term economic sciences, not disciplines. If I were to consider economic science in its wide sense, the different branches that I have listed following Mill, Menger, and Keynes would be termed disciplines, and economic science would be a multidisciplinary science. However, there are various reasons for my word choice. First, as shown, the concept of disciplinarity and its literature still remain open to discussion. Second, I think those branches can be separately considered as sciences.

I have postulated an analogical concept of the economy and a consequently analogical concept of science that may embrace all economic sciences. Science is another fluctuating concept. The word, too, does not appear in the *Stanford Encyclopedia of Philosophy* nor in the *Concise Routledge Encyclopedia of Philosophy*. Mario Bunge defines it in his *Philosophical Dictionary* (2003: 259) as 'the critical search for or utilization of patterns in ideas, nature, or society', which I find lacking. Sara Mitchell (2009: 115) states that 'scientific knowledge consists of *claims* about the causal structure of the world'. Karl Popper affirms that 'the aim of science is to find satisfactory explanations of whatever strike us as being in need of explanation' (1969: 128).

These last definitions come closer to the classical analogical concept of science that goes back to Plato and Aristotle. Terence Irwin, in his Glossary at the end of his translation of Aristotle's *Nicomachean Ethics*, describes the Greek philosopher's concept of science as 'any systematically organized, rationally jus- tifiable and teachable, body of doctrine or instructions' (Aristotle 1999: 347). *Epistemai* [sciences], therefore, include crafts such as medicine, and practical sciences such as political and legislative sciences and ethics (1999: 347 and 241). I will address Aristotle's classification of sciences into theoretical, practical, and technical sciences in Chapter 3. In addition, for Aristotle, science is explained in terms of its causes (I will come back to this in Chapter 5).

Another classical contribution involves the criteria for scientific demar- cation. According to classical philosophy, sciences have a *material* object, or a subject matter, the 'about what' the science deals with, and a *formal object*, the specific perspective from which the subject matter is approached.[9] For example, the human being (a material object) can be studied from different perspectives (a formal object) such as medicine, psychology, or sociology.

All economic sciences deal with the same material object: economic phe- nomena, as will be conceptualized in Chapter 2, distinguishing their different analogical meanings. Statistics and economic history study economic phe- nomena and relate the facts of economic life. Economic theory seeks to explain and understand the causes of economic phenomena. Normative economics concentrates on defining the ends of economic activities, and the art of eco- nomics on designing and implementing economic policies.

Statistics and economic history need economic theory and vice versa: there is a *cross-disciplinary* relationship between them. I will focus on these particular sciences in Chapter 4, additionally revealing how they are also related to nor- mative, ethically relevant concepts. The history of economic thought also sheds light on all economic sciences.

If *conceptually* integrating the tasks of explaining causes and understanding reasons or ends were to be defined as an interdisciplinary development, eco- nomic theory should then be labelled an 'interdisciplinary' enterprise. I use the potential mood because, at present, economic theory is positive economics. Therefore, while aiming to explain economic phenomena as well as looking for efficiency, it should also perform an interpretive role to understand the ends people pursue: to discover and take into account the different ends that influence economic phenomena, as some reverse imperialist currents do. These two dimensions of economic theory have different approaches to the same subject, economic reality or phenomena, or simply, the economy. They should work together to become a new project, a more comprehensive economic theory, keeping themselves apart but enriching each other. There is no conflict between a 'positive' and an 'interpretivist' approach: they can coexist and work together. I will come back to this relation in Chapter 7. Furthermore, it should also be borne in mind that reverse imperialist currents import insights from other sciences in a cross-disciplinary way.

Normative economics has a strong relation with ethics. Davis (2018 and forthcoming), commenting on Mark White (2018), proposes treating economics and ethics as a transdisciplinary field. Davis draws from Herbert Simon's (1962) vision of complex systems, in which the different disciplines – independent subsystems – contribute to an emergent discipline and mutually interact and influence each other.[10] In my opinion, Mary Hirschfeld's 'Thomistic economics' proposal (2018) should be regarded as an example of a transdisciplinary project that takes elements from standard economics (Rational Choice Theory), Thomistic theology and philosophy, and insights from other social sciences to produce one form of normative economics.

The most *transdisciplinary* discipline is the art of economics: it needs inputs from all the other sciences and from interactions with non-academic actors to shape a new discipline. If we want not only to explain and predict economic behaviour, but also to adequately implement economic policies, we need to consider all the evidence and causes that influence or have an impact on them, thus going beyond the evidence and causes taken into account by positive economics. As Arnold Harberger stated in his Richard T. Ely Lecture at the 1993 Annual Meeting of the American Economic Association, 'the real world is different in that policy is usually subject to many constraints, most of them very hard to specify in clear analytical terms' (1993: 4). The real world has many 'non-economic' causes of economic phenomena.

The influence of non-economic causes on positive economics depends on the nature of the economic behaviour that we want to explain or predict, on the context and on its specificity. It is one thing to explain or predict the evolution of soybeans price on the Chicago commodities market taking into account crop yields obtained by major producers (where perfect competition reasonably applies), and another thing to foresee the success or failure of a new disruptive product (which depends on a lot of variables). It is one thing to predict the effect of an interest rate rise on the demand for money in a country with a stable monetary policy, and it is a very different thing to attempt to do so in a country with an erratic monetary policy. It is one thing to foresee the behaviour of a financial agent expecting a rise in the price of an asset, and it is quite another thing to predict the reactions of a trade unionist negotiating a wage increase. An experienced economist acquainted with different economic phenomena will be familiar with major influencing factors, so he/she will collect the information necessary to determine the important variables and their weight and will then proceed to approximately explain or predict the matter at hand. Next, he/she will be able to implement adequate policies – albeit not always successfully.

Harberger compares the economist with a hunter seeking an elusive prey or a detective trying to solve a very difficult task (1993: 5). It is a task that requires, in his own words, 'sharp eyes, subtle perceptions and artfully molded prescriptions, possibly as much as the life of the medical practitioner' (1993: 3). The metaphor of the medical practice is suggestive.

All practical economists know that social psychology, the idiosyncrasy of people or of a particular group in society, may 'irrationally' impact their economic behaviour. Therefore, they must try to understand and consider these 'irregular' factors. This plurality of motives or causes for action calls for a plurality of sources of evidence, a plurality of methods for recollecting data and detecting causes, and a plurality of tools to design and implement policies.

This is no walk in the park. As Joseph Schumpeter wrote in his personal diary (December 21, 1943, quoted by McCraw (2007: 405): 'Two kinds of people I distrust: architects who profess to build cheaply and economists who profess to give simple answers'. Coming back to Harberger (1993: 5), he insists on the idea that the economist has to perceive and deal with all the previous 'constraints' while '*still* finding ways to improve overall economic efficiency', which is an art, the kind of art already formulated by John Neville Keynes ([1891] 1955: 36, 55–60, 74–83; my italics) and stressed by David Colander in his 'lost art of economics' (1992).

The effort to cover all the topics described above yielded this extremely ambitious – perhaps too ambitious – book. The following overview of the chapters speaks for itself. Chapter 2 will try to ascertain what 'the economic' is, that is what is the essence of the economic stuff. As mentioned, I will distinguish two main notions of it. A description of 'the economic stuff' will show its contextual, indeterminate, and social character. Chapter 3 will expand on the definition and typology of economic sciences. The next chapters will address these sciences one by one. Chapter 4 will deal with statistics as a source of economic research. Prior to focusing on economic theory, Chapter 5 will provide some philosophical concepts – the meaning of explanation and causality – and will introduce the 'abductive reasoning' mode of postulating hypotheses. Chapter 6 will focus on positive economics, that part of economic theory that considers only 'economic' motivations. Chapter 7 will enlarge the scope of economic theory and analyse the impact of considering other ends. Before turning to normative economics in Chapter 9, Chapter 8 will clarify – as a prior necessary step – the role of values in the social sciences. Values are present in all economic sciences. As Julian Reiss asserts, 'economics is an enormously value-laden endeavour' (2008: 13). Even statistics and positive economics are permeated by values. Finally, Chapter 10 will deal with the 'art of economics', the most difficult and synthesizing economic discipline. Each chapter deserves an entire book of its own. Consequently, they cannot but be partial.

And so we have come to the end of this introduction. The first step will now be to expand on the nature of economic reality and 'economic sciences', and then I will delve into the method and roles of the latter.

Notes

1 The expression 'focal meaning' was coined by G. E. L. Owen (1960). There are different classifications of analogy. Ralph McInerny's (1961) book proves enlightening on this topic. See also E. Jennifer Ashworth (2017). However, I will not delve further into this.
2 *Metaphysics* IV, 2, 1003a33–35:

> There are many senses in which a thing can be said to be, but all that is related to one central point, one definite kind of thing, and is not said to be by a mere ambiguity. Everything which is healthy is related to health
>
> (Aristotle 1952).

3 I use the term 'phenomena' in the sense used by Bogen and Woodward. In their view (see Bogen and Woodward 1988 and Woodward 1989: 393), phenomena are stable and general features of the world that are beyond data, and that can be explained and predicted by general theories. Phenomena, explains Bogen (2009), are processes, causal factors, effects, facts, regularities, and other pieces of ontological furniture. I include decisions and actions.

4 I do not discard the role of emotions, desires or even instincts in economic phenomena. However, given that the human being is a unity, reason is always somewhat present.

5 An optimum is at best a qualitative characteristic, while a maximum is a quantitative characteristic.

6 This question was posed by Ewald Engelen while I was defending my PhD thesis at Amsterdam University (7 September 2011). If I interpreted him correctly, he was worried about economics imposing its logic on all reality.

7 See, for example, the survey article by Toke S. Aidt (2003).

8 See also Stephen Turner (2017) for a history of the concept of 'discipline'.

9 Though defined as such – formal and material objects – during scholasticism, these notions had their origin in Aristotle: see, e.g., Ryan Douglas Madison (2011: 400–401). For an explanation of these notions, see Henry van Laer (1956: 43–49).

10 Davis (2019) also argues for conceiving economic pluralism as a complex system.

References

Aidt, T. S. (2003). 'Economic Analysis of Corruption: A Survey', *Economic Journal*, 113/491: F632–F652.

Alexandrova, A. (2017). *A Philosophy for the Science of Well-Being*. Oxford: Oxford University Press.

Anderson, E. (2005). Dewey's Moral Philosophy. In: E. N. Zalta (ed.), *The Stanford Encyclopedia of Philosophy*, http://plato.Stanford.edu/entries/dewey-moral/. Accessed 23 March 2017.

Aristotle (1952). *Metaphysics*. Translated by David Ross. Oxford: Oxford University Press.

Aristotle (1999). *Nicomachean Ethics*. Second edition, translated with Introduction, Notes and Glossary, by Terence Irwin. Indianapolis/Cambridge: Hackett Publishing.

Ashworth, E. J. (2017). 'Medieval Theories of Analogy'. In: E. N. Zalta (ed.), *The Stanford Encyclopedia of Philosophy*. https://plato.stanford.edu/cgi-bin/encyclopedia/archinfo.cgi?entry=analogy-medieval. Accessed 23 August 2019.

Barry, A., G. Born and G. Weszkalnys (2008). 'Logics of Interdisciplinarity', *Economy and Society*, 37/1: 20–49.

Bernstein, J. H. (2015). 'Transdisciplinarity: A Review of Its Origins, Development, and Current Issues', *Journal of Research Practice*, 11/1: 1–16.

Bogen, J. (2009). '"Saving the Phenomena" and Saving the Phenomena', http://philsci-archive.pitt.edu/archive/00004554/01/Sumitted_'Saving'-Saving.doc. Accessed 19 January 2010.

Bogen, J. and J. Woodward (1988). 'Saving the Phenomena', *Philosophical Review*, 97/3: 303–352.

Boudon, R. (2004). Théorie du choix rationnel, théorie de la rationalité limitée ou individualisme méthodologique: que choisir?' *Journal des Economistes et des Etudes Humaines*, 14/1: 45–62.

Cat, J. (2017). 'The Unity of Science'. In: E. N. Zalta (ed.), *The Stanford Encyclopedia of Philosophy*, https://plato.stanford.edu/archives/fall2017/entries/scientific-unity/. Accessed 12 September 2018.

Choi, S. and K. Richards (2017). *Interdisciplinary Discourse. Communicating Across Disciplines*. London: Palgrave Macmillan.

Colander, D. (1992). 'Retrospectives: The Lost Art of Economics', *Journal of Economic Perspectives*, 6/3: 191–198.

Crespo, R. F. (2013). *Philosophy of the Economy. An Aristotelian Approach*. Dordrecht: Springer.

Darden, L. and N. Maull (1977). 'Interfield Theories', *Philosophy of Science* 44/1: 43–64.

Davis, J. B. (2008). 'The Turn in Recent Economics and the Return of Orthodoxy', *Cambridge Journal of Economics*, 32: 349–366.

Davis, J. B. (2011). *Individuals and Identity in Economics*. Cambridge and New York: Cambridge University Press.

Davis, J. B. (2018). 'Comment on White on the Relationship between Economics and Ethics', *Annals of Fondazione Luigi Einaudi* 52/2: 45–55.

Davis, J. B. (2019). 'Specialization, Fragmentation, and Pluralism in Economics', *European Journal of the History of Economic Thought*, https://doi.org/10.1080/09672567.2018.1555604.

Davis, J. B. (forthcoming). 'Ethics and Economics: A Complex Systems Approach' (3 May 2018). In: M. D. White (ed.), *Oxford Handbook of Ethics and Economics*. Oxford: Oxford University Press. Available at SSRN: https://ssrn.com/abstract=3172990.

Frey, B. and M. Benz (2004). 'From Imperialism to Inspiration: a Survey of Economics and Psychology'. In: J. B. Davis, A. Marciano and J. Runde (eds.), *The Elgar Companion to Economics and Philosophy*. Cheltenham and Northampton: Edward Elgar, pp. 61–83.

Frodeman, R. (2017). 'The Future of Interdisciplinarity'. In: R. Frodeman, J. T. Klein and R. C. S. Pacheco (eds.), *Oxford Handbook of Interdisciplinarity*. Second Edition. Oxford: Oxford University Press, pp. 1–8.

Gibbons, M., C. Limoges, H. Nowotny, S. Schwartzman, P. Scott and M. Trow (1994). *The New Production of Knowledge: the Dynamics of Science and Research in Contemporary Societies*. London: Sage.

Harberger, A. C. (1993). 'The Search for Relevance in Economics', *American Economic Review*, 83/2: 1–16.

Hirschfeld, M. (2018). *Aquinas and the Market. Toward a Humane Economy*. Cambridge (MA): Harvard University Press.

Hirshleifer, J. (1985) 'The Expanding Domain of Economics', *American Economic Review*, 75/6: 53–68.

Kellert, S. H. (2008). *Borrowed Knowledge: Chaos Theory and the Challenge of Learning across Disciplines*. Chicago and London: University of Chicago Press.

Keynes, J. N. ([1891] 1955). *The Scope and Method of Political Economy*. New York: Kelley and Millman.

Klein, J. T. (2017). 'Typologies of Interdisciplinarity'. In: R. Frodeman, J. T. Klein and R. C. S. Pacheco (eds.), *Oxford Handbook of Interdisciplinarity*, Second Edition. Oxford: Oxford University Press, pp. 21–40.

Madison, R. D. (2011). First Philosophy: Aristotle's Concept of Metaphysics, ProQuest, UMI Dissertation Publishing (3 September 2011).

McCraw, T. K. (2007). *Prophet of Innovation. Joseph Schumpeter and Creative Destruction.* Cambridge (MA) and London: Belknap Press of Harvard University Press.

McInerny, R. (1961). *The Logic of Analogy.* The Hague: Martinus Nijhoff.

Mitchell, S. D. (2009). *Unsimple Truths. Science, Complexity, and Policy.* Chicago and London: University of Chicago Press.

Nel, P. (2019). 'When Bribery Helps the Poor', *Review of Social Economy,* DOI: 10.1080/00346764.2019.1618482.

Owen, G. E. L. (1960). 'Logic and Metaphysics in Some Earlier Works of Aristotle'. In: I. Düring and G. E. L. Owen (eds.), *Aristotle and Plato in the Mid-Fourth Century,* Papers of the Symposium Aristotelicum held at Oxford in August 1957, Studia Graeca et Latina Gothoburgensia, XI, 1960, Göteborg: Elanders Boktryckeri Aktiebolag, pp. 163–190.

Popper, K. R. (1969). 'The Aim of Science'. In: R. Klibausky (ed.), *Contemporary Philosophy III.* Firenze: La Nuova Italia Editrice, pp. 128–142.

Reiss, J. (2008). *Error in Economics.* New York and London: Routledge.

Robbins, L. C. (1935). *Essay on the Nature and Significance of Economic Science.* Second Edition. London: Macmillan.

Sen, A. (1987). *On Ethics and Economics.* Oxford: Basil Blackwell.

Sen, A. (2002). *Rationality and Freedom.* Cambridge (MA) and London: Belknap Press of Harvard University Press.

Simon, H. A. (1962). 'The Architecture of Complexity', *Proceedings of the American Philosophical Society,* 106/6: 467–482.

Simon, H. A. (1992). 'Methodological Foundations of Economics'. In: J. L. Auspitz, W. W. Gasparski, M. K. Mlicki and K. Szaniawsk (eds.), *Praxiologies and the Philosophy of Economics.* New Brunswick (NJ): Transactions Publishers, pp. 25–42.

Toulmin, S. (1972). *Human Understanding,* vol. 1. Princeton (NJ): Princeton University Press.

Turner, S. (2017). 'Knowledge Formations. An Analytic Framework'. In: R. Frodeman, J. T. Klein and R. C. S. Pacheco (eds.), *The Oxford Handbook of Interdisciplinarity.* Second Edition. Oxford: Oxford University Press, pp. 9–20.

Van Laer, H. (1956). *The Philosophy of Science.* Pittsburgh: Duquesne University and Louvain: Editions E. Nauwelaerts.

Ward, B. (1972). *What's Wrong with Economics?* New York: Basic Books.

White, M. D. (2018). 'On the Relation between Ethics and Economics', *Annals of Fondazione Luigi Einaudi,* 52/2: 45–56.

Woodward, J. (1989). 'Data and Phenomena', *Synthese,* 79/3: 393–472.

2 Two notions of economy

In this chapter, I will work on discerning the deep meaning – the nature or essence – of the economy or, more broadly, of that which is 'economic' – what Uskali Mäki calls 'the economic realm' (2001: 4). This investigation logically precedes the inquiry about the nature, roles and methodology of economic sciences, which will be the topic of the next chapters.

Margaret Schabas has stated: 'Economists study "The Economy", or so one might suppose. Yet this overarching entity is strikingly absent from mainstream economics' (2009: 3). She also notes that the entry 'economy, the' is absent in dictionaries of economics. When speaking about 'the economy', she refers to it as the whole economic system. As such, for her, 'the economy' is a theoretical construct. However, 'the economy' is not only the economic system. There are a lot of other things that are also 'economic': actions, decisions, goods, ideas, policies, strategies, news, ministers, sources of energy, houses and cars, and so on.

Uskali Mäki has always been worried about capturing the meaning of the economy, because, he states, 'I believe the study of economic ontology [that is, the nature or essence of the economy] is a prerequisite for understanding economics as a scientific discipline' (2001: xv). On 5 October 2010, I had dinner with Uskali at a restaurant in Buenos Aires. I remember that I asked him about the meaning of the economy and he answered that this was the most difficult question of the philosophy of economics and that he was still thinking about it. Like me. A few months ago I was reading the schedule of a seminar to be held at Madrid (7 May 2018) and discovered that Uskali was delivering a presentation titled 'Still Chasing the Essence of Economics'. When I asked him about the paper he answered: 'it won't be about the essence of the economy, but rather of economics as a scientific discipline (and I am not sure how far I'm prepared to admit it has an "essence" after all…). But I promise that once I have a paper on the economy, I'll share it with you!' (email message from 5 May 2018). Thus, he is still thinking about it. However, he has already relevantly contributed to exploring the meaning of the economy. He maintains that 'the economic realm', which is the subject matter of economics, connects with other realms; it presupposes the existence of the physical, the biotic, and the psychic realms. In effect, I think that the economy is a typical human reality, such as language or sociality, in which all these realms intersect. Mäki adds that the realms of morality and politics shape the functioning of the economic realm (2001: 4).

Coming back to Schabas, she also notes that 'whatever is meant by "The Economy" in folk economics appears to be significantly divergent from what is posited in scientific economics' (2009: 3). This difference has been intentionally established by the author of the most used definition of economics. Robbins asserted (1935: 5, nt.; italics in the original):

> It is often urged that scientific definitions of words used both in ordinary language and in scientific analysis should not depart from the usages of everyday speech. No doubt this is a counsel of perfection, but in principle the main contention may be accepted. Great confusion is certainly created when a word which is used in one sense in business practice is used in another sense in the analysis of such practice [...] But it is one thing to follow everyday usage when appropriating a term. It is another thing to contend that everyday speech is the final court of appeal when defining a science. For in this case the significant implication of the word *is* the subject-matter of the generalizations of the science.

This is not the position upheld by, for example, Alfred Marshall about economic terms ([1920] 1962: 43):

> Our task is difficult. In physical sciences indeed, whenever it is seen that a group of things have a certain set of qualities in common, and will often be spoken of together, they are formed into a class with a special name; and as soon as a new notion emerges, a new technical term is invented to represent it. But economics cannot venture to follow this example. Its reasonings must be expressed in language that is intelligible to the general public; it must therefore endeavour to conform itself to the familiar terms of everyday life, and so far as possible must use them as they are commonly used.[1]

Marshall's position accords with the philosophical tradition. According to Aristotle's criterion, 'we ought to use our terms to mean the same things as most people mean by them' (*Topics* II, 2, 110a 16–17). Ludwig Wittgenstein states, thus relating semantics and pragmatics, that 'the meaning of a word is its use in the language' (& 43, 1958, p. 20e). Although ordinary language may be supplemented, improved and/or superseded by technical language, it is the *first* word, as J. L. Austin affirmed (1970: 185). It is legitimate and useful that science has its technical terminology, but its subject matter at least should conform to its ordinary meaning.[2] Hence, it has been natural that sociology has dealt with society, psychology with psyche and economics with the economy, meaning the things that people consider to be society, psyche and the economy.

Aristotle, one of the first thinkers who wrote about the economy, did not speak of the economy or economics but rather about 'all things economic' (*oikonomikè*), taking an adjective that describes a characteristic of reality and turning it into a noun: 'the economic'. In this chapter, as already indicated, I will try to establish the meaning of 'the economic'. I believe this expression encompasses all possible meanings of the economy. One reason already mentioned for the relevance of this task is that the subject matter of a science is prior to the science itself and determines its content, and not the other way around. Sciences must be adapted to their subjects. If, on the contrary, science determines the subject, it risks becoming a science about a fiction and not about something real. This has been a regular occurrence. As Sheila Dow (2002: 61) has indicated, the concept of economics is often bound up with the methodology of economics, in the sense that economic reality has been shaped at the 'convenience' of the science which seeks to study it. This is one of the arguments developed by Till Düppe (2011). Some historical circumstances and the sociology of the profession, Düppe convincingly maintains, have driven economics to create its own subject matter.

Menger, instead, in his *Investigations into the Method of the Social Sciences* ([1883] 1985), maintains that the right way to proceed is 'first taking account of the object by a separate investigation and going on to the definition of economics after the solution of the pertinent preliminary question' ([1883] 1985: 198, Appendix II, note 131). This is also John Neville Keynes' indication ([1890] 1955: 2–4).[3] James Buchanan also complains about the mechanistic vision of economics and claims that economists 'should at least try to know their subject matter' (1987: 22). Raymond Bye, in an older paper, clarifies that 'the question of definition is one of subject matter, rather than of method' (1939: 623). Walter Eucken ([1939] 1947: 9) has warned of the dangers of defining the subject matter by its science.

To adapt economics to the nature of the economy is not an easy task because the real economy is far more complex than the subject shaped by standard economics. Consequently, if economics has to deal with the real economy, it will become an extremely difficult discipline: the real economy is a rather unmanageable subject matter, often, as Phyllis Deane states 'for reasons that may lie outside the traditional boundaries of the discipline' (1983: 11–12). Sciences simplify their subjects to deal with them and this is legitimate. However, sometimes this simplification falls into reductionism, departing from the real essence of the phenomena studied. As again Schabas states, 'given the strong emphasis placed on reductionism in science, any efforts to restore "the economy" to the forefront of mainstream economics must swim against this strong current' (2009: 13).

As the title to this chapter reads, the analysis of the notion of economy will conclude that there are two main notions: a broad notion and a restricted one. This chapter aims to, in the first place, explore the meaning of 'the economic' through some unusual, let us say 'metaphorical', notions that I consider interesting because they help identify some of its central characteristics. I will follow the ideas of my fellow countryman, sociologist Julio Soler Miralles. He states that a reflection on the philosophy of the economy 'begins with the economy-reality or sector of the real universe that is generically called "the economic", which is to be subsequently a consideration of the conceptual system constituted by the human mind by cognitively penetrating the economic reality' (1952: 129–139, 133, my translation).

Second, I will consider dictionary definitions of 'the economy', 'economic' and 'economical'. The aim of this exploration is to detect the everyday language meaning of these terms for the purpose of reversing the order of the process: instead of creating a subject matter adapted to economic science, I will try to determine what is the subject matter to which the economic science will have to be adapted. Both the broad notion and the restricted one will stem from this exploration.

In the third section, I will introduce Menger's classification of the economy in the second edition of his *Principles of Economics* (*Grundsätze der Volkswirtschaftslehre*, 1923), posthumously prepared by his son Karl, and I will show that it fits with the conclusions of the dictionary exploration.[4]

Then, I will consider definitions or characterizations of the economy proposed by some economists or social scientists that I believe may complement the ideas presented in this chapter. Finally, I will provide a conclusion. This exploration is the first logical step of the investigation of the present book. Neville Keynes starts his book *The Scope and Method of Political Economy* ([1890] 1955: 1) noticing the ambiguity of the terms *economy* and *economic*. The aim of this chapter is to disambiguate these terms.

Some unusual but interesting meanings of the economic[5]

As mentioned, I think that it will be useful to take into account some unusual meanings of the 'the economic'. They refer to the 'economic anthropological condition' of the human being.[6] I come back to Soler Miralles. He asserts (1952: 134):

> Economic reality is a primarily spiritual activity of man; it is part of his interior nature as a free and rational entity submitted to the physical condition of a body that must be sustained and protected, and a soul that can only express itself through this physical and corporal condition.

Today, when it seems that neurological reactions can explain all human feelings, actions and so on, Soler's references to the spiritual and the soul may sound outdated (replace them by 'psychological' and 'psyche' if you want). However, this is not relevant to the argument that I am developing here. The fact is that materiality places limitations on the human person: first, people need goods to survive and to develop and, second, they cannot do everything; given that their time and capabilities are limited, they must choose and work in order to satisfy their needs according to certain priorities. We could speak then of *a 'basic economic condition' of the human person at the anthropological level*. In this sense, the human person is an 'economic animal', as even Aristotle characterizes it (*Eudemian Ethics* VII, 10, 1242a 22–23), referring to his insertion into a home because, for Aristotle, the home is the place to satisfy the basic needs.

Soler Miralles (1952: 134–135) distinguishes three strata of the 'economy-reality': the first stratum has to do with the limited nature of the human person – he/she has necessities; the second stratum involves intentional actions; and the third is a social stratum (by virtue of the human person's social nature). The first 'anthropological' meaning concerns the first stratum in the sense *that the human person is economic to the extent that he/she is in need.*

Let us move now to the second stratum of 'the economic': an intentional human action. The human person should know how to use the means available to satisfy his/her needs. And since humans must accomplish this in the most reasonable way possible, according to the availability of resources and their defined priorities, a person's reason must be adjusted to his/her particular way of making choices. As philosopher Nicholas Rescher (1988: 2) asserts, human rationality has an economic dimension. In Rescher's words, 'rationality consists in the appropriate use of reason to resolve choices in the best possible way'. Having deliberated with reason, the human person can choose and act 'economically', trying to use his/her resources in the best way possible: what economics calls maximization. This deliberation assumes that the human person is free, within the limits imposed by his/her limitations. Hence, *human persons are economic to the extent they can make choices and do the best they can through these choices.*[7]

Finally, according to the third stratum of 'the economic' proposed by Soler Miralles, the human person's social condition is connected to his/her material limits. This is also the sense of Aristotle's connection of the economic condition of the human being to the home. Actions leading to the use of goods are usually interactions between individuals. Extracting something from nature is not in itself an economic action. The thing extracted – gold, petroleum or corn – must have a value recognized by other people making it interchangeable to become economic. Economic actions entail social interactions. On the one hand, we can assume that the necessary division of labour imposed by human limitations gives rise to social relations. On the other hand, we can infer the opposite: the human person's social condition comes to his/her rescue as a solution to these limitations. Besides, economic institutions in which the social and 'the economic' are inevitably intertwined, such as money and the market, consolidate economic relations (see Searle 2005). These institutions are not isolated but are part of a broader social whole: civil society. The human person's sociability implies that his/her individual economic actions have social outcomes. Thus, *the economic is social just like the human person.*

The economy, the economic, and the economical: customary use of the terms

The above paragraphs already tell us something about the meanings of 'the economic'. The three mentioned meanings corresponding to the three strata proposed by Soler Miralles suggest that 'the economic' is a characteristic of the human person, who is a limited and social animal with an 'economic reason'. However, 'the economic' is not often used in this very general sense in ordinary language. Of course, we can discuss human economic nature and human economic reason. However, we recognize that such a high level of generality can only yield an unusual notion of 'the economic'. When we speak of 'the economic', we refer to something more specific. As Soler Miralles (1952: 135) himself also states,

> economics is not the science of the spiritual attitudes of the human person in general; nor is it a generic science of the ends of free conduct; nor the science of the social reality in which this free conduct takes place.

However, albeit not the most common, these meanings are important because they point at the very root of 'the economic': human limitations due to materiality (linked, consequently, to temporality), and man's capacity to efficiently overcome these limitations by his reason in a social context. However, these meanings, though enlightening, are 'metaphorical' when compared to that which is properly economic. 'Metaphorical', as used here, is not equivalent to illegitimate. It is an analogical use of the term 'economic', as explained in Chapter 1, but not its 'focal meaning'.

To look for the non-metaphorical or focal meaning (that I will also call 'literal'[8]) of the economy, according to the mentioned philosophical maxim of defining things by their meaning in the ordinary language use of them, I will analyse what people think 'the economy', 'the economic' and 'economical' are and use these folk notions as initial criteria for defining them. Therefore, the first thing we need to ask ourselves is: what is usually understood by these words? To this purpose, I have checked the Merriam-Webster dictionary (www.merriam-webster.com) definitions. For this dictionary, among other less related definitions, 'economy' refers to the structure of economic life, or an economic system. It also means efficient use of material resources. 'Economic' means 'related to production, distribution, and consumption of goods and services'. Finally, 'economical' is a careful, efficient use of resources.

I also consulted the *Webster's Dictionary*. It (1996: 618) defines economy as

> thrifty management; frugality in the expenditure or consumption of money, materials, etc.; the management of the resources of a community, country, etc., with a view to its productivity; the disposition or regulation of parts or functions of any organic whole; the efficient, sparing or concise use of something; the management of household affairs.

Although some of these meanings do not serve our specific purpose, they provide a clear indication of the broad meaning of this term.

In sum, based on the previous definitions, we can differentiate two main groups of meanings: first, economy and 'the economic' refer to the management of resources in order to satisfy human needs and, second, they point to an efficient, concise, careful or prudent way of doing it.

The meanings of 'the economic'

Hence, what is the meaning of the economic? I propose two 'literal' or non-metaphorical meanings following the thread of the conclusion stemming from the dictionaries. The first and broadest refers to human need. We can affirm that acts aimed at the acquisition, possession and use of goods for the satisfaction of human needs are economic. For the French anthropologist Maurice Godelier (1966: 23), the 'economic' includes all decisions and actions aimed at the satisfaction of human, material or spiritual needs, measured in material terms. I believe that this definition, though still broad, is more specific and allows us to speak of a literal concept.

The second literal meaning is even more specific or restricted. It introduces a particular way of undertaking economic actions: the 'efficient', 'maximizing' or 'economic principle', as economists call it. In fact, returning to the dictionary definition, we notice that everything related to the satisfaction of the human person's material needs or measured in material terms can be called economic. However, it is also economic to perform an action attempting to get the most possible out of available resources. This is to act 'economically', 'as regards the efficient use of income and wealth' (Webster 1996: 618).

Thus far, we have distinguished between a metaphorical meaning – which refers to the anthropological roots of 'the economic' – and two literal meanings that define the subject matter of economics. The first is broad and the second is more specific or 'restricted' (see Figure 2.1).

1   Metaphorical meaning of economy: the anthropological character of 'the economic'.
2   The literal meaning of economy.
    2.1   The literal meaning of economy in its broad sense: economic phenomena: decisions and actions related to goods for the satisfaction of needs and determination of these needs.
    2.2   The literal meaning of economy in its restricted sense: the 'economic principle' applied to economic phenomena.

The broad literal notion of 'the economic' roughly coincides with the subject matter of Karl Polanyi's notion of 'substantive economics'. He defines it in relation to the 'formal' meaning of economics (1971b: 139–140):

> The substantive meaning of economics derives from man's dependence for his living upon nature and his fellows. It refers to the interchange with his natural and social environment, insofar as this results in supplying him

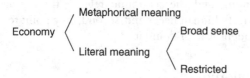

Figure 2.1 The meaning of the economy.

with the means of material want-satisfaction. The formal meaning of economics derives from the logical character of the means-ends relationship, as
apparent in such words as 'economical' or 'economizing'. It refers to a definite situation of choice, namely, that between the different uses of means
induced by an insufficiency of those means [...] The latter derives from
logic, the former from fact.

He points out the elemental fact that human beings, as all living beings, cannot
subsist without a natural and human environment to sustain them. The economic process provides them with the means to satisfy their needs. It is an
instituted process of interaction; it 'is embedded and enmeshed in institutions,
economic and non-economic' (1971b: 148). The economy in the restricted
literal sense would be similar to the subject matter of Polanyi's 'formal economics' – economizing in situations of scarcity, as described in the quoted
definition.

Carl Menger on the economy

Polanyi has based his classification on Menger's classification of the economy in
Chapter 4 of the second edition of his *Principles of Economics* (1923), prepared by
his son Karl.[9] On the occasion of the re-edition of the original German version
of Menger's works, Hayek (1934), who was in charge of it, neglected this second
edition of the *Principles*. Hayek was fully conscious that Menger did not want
to reprint the first edition of his book because he wanted to revise it (Hayek
1934: 415).[10] Later, Frank Knight decided to publish the English translation of
the first edition of the *Principles* ([1871] 1950), thus implicitly discarding the
second edition.[11] Thanks to Italian economist Maffeo Pantaleoni, there is an
Italian translation of the second edition, and thanks to economist Francisco
Navarro Vilches, a disciple of Carlos Becker (a German economist involved in
the Austrian economics tradition who emigrated to Argentina),[12] there is also a
Spanish mimeographed edition (Universidad Nacional de Cuyo, 1960).

What are Menger's new ideas about the topic here concerned? He distinguishes
two orientations of the economy: a 'technical-economic' ('die technisch-
ökonomische Disposition' 1923: 73) and an 'economizing' ('die spandere'
1923: 74; 'die ökonomisierende' 1923: 76). The first orientation aims at providing
the goods that we need, and the second, when insufficiency of means prevails, aims
at doing so by 'economizing' in the best possible way. We cannot identify, Menger
states, the concept of 'economy' (*Wirtschaft*) with the concept of 'economical'
(*Wirtschaftlichkeit*, 1923: 61). Thus, he affirms, it is not paradoxical to speak of an
'economic economy' ('einer wirtschaflichen (ökonomischen) [...] Wirtschaft')
and of a 'non-economic economy' ('unwirtschaftlichen (unökonomischen)
Wirtschaft', 1923: 61). He characterizes both directions in this way:

(1) On the one hand, an economy would be fully determined by the
technical direction (the objective aspect) if the resources at hand, suitably

arranged, would suffice for completely satisfying all human needs. In such a situation of affluence the economy would be characterized only by its technical aspect, the task would consist in putting the existing resources to alternative uses in such a way that affluence can indeed be accomplished. (2) On the other hand, if the resources of an economy were rigidly given (and neither production nor the transfer of resources to alternative uses possible), then only the economizing direction (the subjective aspect) would be relevant for this economy. In this sense, economizing is the response to scarcity.

(Menger 1923: 78; translation Becchio 2014 nt 19)

Menger understands both orientations as independent:

I shall designate the two directions in which the human economy may point – the technical and the economizing – as elemental, for this reason. Although in the actual economy these two directions as presented in the two previous sections occur as a rule together, and indeed almost never found separately, they nevertheless spring from *essentially different and mutually independent sources* [Menger's italics in all his quotations]. In some fields of economic activity the two occur, in fact, separately, and in some not inconceivable types of economies either of them may in fact regularly appear without the other [...] The two directions in which the human economy may point are not mutually dependent upon one another; both are primary and elemental. Their regular joint occurrence in the actual economy results merely from the circumstance that the causative factors that give rise to each of them without exception happen to coincide.

(1923: 77; Polanyi's translation 1977: 23)

Though independent, one may interpret Menger's economic directions as complementary, as Becchio considers them. She states that

Menger clarified that these two basic directions of human economy 'spring from *causes that are different and independent from one another*' and they are actually independent of one other, but they are connected and their connection determines the most complete meaning of the nature of the human economy.

(2010: 17)

Instead, Polanyi (1971a and 1977), though recognizing the comprehensive character of Menger's conception of the economic, stresses the differences emphasizing the existence of non-market economies, and the possibility of non-utilitarian motivations for economic actions (1971a: 18). My proposal – closer to Becchio's – is illustrated in Figure 2.2.

The larger circle represents the broad literal notion of the economy, decisions, and actions in order to satisfy human needs through material means or services.

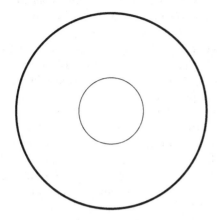

Figure 2.2 Menger's concept of the economy.

It includes the small circle representing the restricted literal notion, a specific way of performing the economic task: optimizing the use of means given their scarcity. Their logics are different but – except in some 'not unconceivable situations' (Menger 1923: 77) – they actually coincide in real life. The motivations implied in the large circle are of all types: psychological, sociological, ethical and aesthetical, and can additionally be looking for an efficient use of means (the small circle). In the small circle, the maximizing motivation is always present. However, there may be other additional motivations. I do not always make my decisions related to the use of resources trying to get the most possible out of them, but also for other reasons: taste, whim, habit, and so on, especially in certain sociological settings. The standard economist would reply that all these reasons are preferences that can be put into a utility function. In the next chapter, I will explain the mistake involved in this common line of economic reasoning.

In his 1883 *Investigations into the Method of the Social Science*, Menger defined the economy as 'the precautionary activity of humans directed toward covering their material needs' ([1883] 1985: 63) or as 'the premeditative activity of humans aimed at the direct or indirect satisfaction of their material needs' ([1883] 1985: 193, Appendix 1, nt128). This definition, established at the time when Menger was considering a revised edition of his 1871 *Principles*, supports my interpretation. He additionally states that in real life not only the predominance of egoism ([1883] 1985: 64) or 'individual interest' ([1883] 1985: 64) but also 'error, ignorance and external compulsion' ([1883] 1985: 64); 'good will toward others' ([1883] 1985: 71); and 'the freedom of the human will' ([1883] 1985: 214) influence economic actions.

However, Menger would have probably drawn the external circle closer to the internal one in my figure. But this depends on the specific culture or situation considered. Actually, Menger believes that the external circle is broader for more complicated phenomena ([1883] 1985: 68–69). In his previous book,

Investigations into the Method, the words *Wirtschaftlichkeit* and *Unwirtschaftlichkeit* also appear, respectively referring to the abstract consideration of the economic world and to 'the *real* phenomena of human economy (which, indeed, in their "full empirical reality" also contain numerous elements *not emergent from an abstract economic world!*)' ([1883] 1985: 73). Combining both sources – the *Untersuchungen* (*Investigations into the Method*) and the second edition of the Grundsätze (*Principles*) – two elements characterize both notions of economy: scarcity and individual interest ('specifically economic propensities', [1883] 1985: 80; 'human self-interest', [1883] 1985: 87–88) are characteristics of the 'economic economy'. Non-consideration of scarcity and a plurality of motives (including 'non-economic factors of human economy', [1883] 1985: 80) constitute features of the 'non-economic economy'. For Menger, there is 'only *one* road' that is the 'most suitable', 'determined economically', 'strictly determined *economic*' ([1883] 1985: 218). At the same time,

> the *real* phenomena of human economy, as paradoxical as it may sound at first, are to no small extent of an uneconomic nature, and as a result of the fact are by no means strictly determined phenomena, viewed from the standpoint of economic reality.
>
> ([1883] 1985: 218)[13]

That is, he considers both economic notions.

Neville Keynes also adopts both visions of the economy. On the one hand, he broadly defines 'economic activity' as a human *activity* directed to the production and appropriation of exchangeable means satisfying human needs ([1890] 1955: 99–100) and, on the other hand, economic *action* 'when it attains its end with the least possible expenditure of money, time and effort' ([1890] 1955: 1).

Herbert Simon's vision of human behaviour as a satisfying rather than a maximizing behaviour, and of the latter as a subset of the former, implicitly recognizes, if applied to the economy, two conceptions of it. In fact, he starts his 1978 Richard Ely Lecture quoting his definition of economics as concerned 'with a particular subset of man's behavior' – the first meaning – and then he critically refers to today's vision of the economy reduced to the second meaning (1978: 1).

This double conception of the economy has an effect on the concept of economic science, as will be developed in the next chapter. Now, I will complete the characterization of the economy drawing from other economists' ideas.

A characterization of the 'economic'

As defined earlier, the first literal notion – the broader of the two – includes 'actions related to the acquisition, possession, and use of goods for the satisfaction of human *needs*', and the second literal notion refers to the efficient way of doing so. Some authors have dwelled on related concepts in different ways and it may prove useful to pay attention to their ideas in order to refine these notions.

First, *a contrario sensu* to the first literal notion of 'the economic' oriented to the satisfaction of *needs*, we may *desire* things that we do not *need*, and we sometimes do not *desire* things that we actually *need*. Possession of goods for satisfying preferred desires is called 'utility' by economists. However, Eduard Spranger ([1914] 1928: 130) defines utility as 'the quality of the material goods in virtue of their aptitude for the satisfaction of *necessities* within the framework of the maintenance and promotion of physical life' (my italics). In his view, utility entails rationality at a 'higher mental level'. In his view, utility is related to needs, not desires, and it is rational. In contrast, for Max Weber ([1923] 1956: 3), an activity is economic when it is oriented towards the probability of obtaining or to obtaining *desirable* 'utilities' (my italics).

The term 'utilities' is also used by Menger in the first pages of his *Principles* ([1871] 1950: 152). Still, for something to be truly economic, Menger claims, it must have a known causal relationship with the satisfaction of a human need. Menger ([1871] 1950: 53) distinguishes between real (or 'objective') and imaginary needs, which are inexistent needs.

Vilfredo Pareto ([1906] 1971: 122) distinguishes utility (referring to an objective characteristic of goods) from *ophelimity* (valuation or subjective aspect). Consequently, Pareto draws a distinction between objective needs and subjective desires. This vision differs from that of subsequent economists who only consider subjective preferences. A broad notion of 'the economic', as understood by ordinary people, includes both elements: objective needs and subjective preferences. However, this distinction is still relevant, especially for normative economics.

Second, the kind of acts included in 'the economic' implies decision-making. Many economists speak of economics as the science of choice, which would make of 'the economic' a human choice. According to Röpke (1955: 29), economics is a 'theory of alternatives'. Economist George Shackle (1979: 37) argues that 'economics is the study of the business of choice'. This is also the case of Robbins, whose definition of economic science is 'the science which studies human behavior as a relationship between [given] ends and scarce means which have alternative uses' (1935: 16). This conduct implies choice. But this is still too general when related to the colloquial use of the term 'economy'; it 'is too abstract, general and lacking in empirical content', as A. W. Coats remarks (1983: 93). Choices come in many varieties; they are not just economic. John Searle, referring to Robbins' definition, ironizes, 'Two dogs fighting over a bone or two schoolboys fighting over a ball are also engaged in the "disposal of scarce commodities", but they are not central to the subject matter of economics' (2005: 1). Economists that remain at this level of generality are confusing the literal notion of 'the economic' with its metaphorical sense. Buchanan (1987: 22ff.) is highly critical of this position and he prefers to concentrate on exchange rather than on choice.

I think that the late Pietro Pavan (who had studied economics, philosophy and theology) will also contribute to this characterization of the economy. He describes economic activity as *conscious, free, responsible, social, and directed at the production of wealth* (1956: 9, my italics). First, conscious. Pavan's description characterizes an action with strong interior content. In this line of thought, Ludwig von Mises ([1949] 1998: 92; italics in the original) writes:

> Economics is not about things and tangible material objects; it is about men, their meanings and actions. Goods, *commodities*, and wealth and all the other notions of conduct are not elements of nature; they are elements of human meaning and conduct.

Weber ([1922] 1978: 64) claimed that 'the economic' and economic processes become such because of the meaning instilled in them by human action. Soler Miralles spoke of the human person's spiritual outlook, innate to his/her interior nature as a free and reasoning entity. It is the human person who impresses an economic character on material elements (and services) to the extent to which he/she values them because they are useful for the satisfaction of current or future necessities or desires. Scarcity alone, without (human) demand, does not generate the economic nature of a good. Intentionality is needed.

Second, free. Freedom as a characteristic of 'the economic' is another attribute that makes this type of activity particularly human. Freedom enters into the realm of 'the economic' at various levels. On the one hand, it is a choice or a free action. And by 'free action' I mean, similar to Aurel Kolnai, 'not uncaused action but action caused, in any direct sense of the word, by the agent's choice or decision alone, not by a machinery of psychic "determinants"' (1968: 27), which may condition but not determine action. That is, I am referring to free will.

The human person's economic practices are free in the sense that needs are not necessarily univocally determined. If needs were fixed, economics could be 'solved' through technique alone. This is why it is improper to set the ends of economics as a science, as if they were simply given data. Part of economics is the choice of ends. The indeterminate nature of needs or ends is a condition of 'the economic'. Even when needs are determined because they are basic, the act remains free. What is free is sometimes not what is needed – we are obliged to eat –, but rather the specification of some choice: to eat from one menu or another. Pavan mentions also 'responsible' as another characteristic of the economic. Responsibility, in effect, stems from freedom.

The freedom at play in 'the economic', the particular characteristics of each economic agent or society, and the fact that a good part of 'the economic' occurs in the future account for another of its characteristics: *uncertainty* (Spranger [1914] 1928). It could not be any other way, given that it deals with future freely made actions of particular individuals. One implication of this is that, as John Hicks expresses it, 'the facts which we study are not permanent, or repeatable, like facts of the natural sciences; they change incessantly, and change without repetition' (1976: 207). Joseph Schumpeter, among others, stresses the complexity of economic facts: 'very complicated phenomena' ([1912]

2002: 94). For him, 'freedom of the will' is obvious, implying that 'economic life' is a 'peculiar jumble of conditioning and freedom' ([1912] 2002: 122). In Jack Wiseman's words, 'the world we are trying to explain is confusing and unmanageable' (1983: 2). Consequently, uncertainty is not only an epistemic limitation but also an ontological condition of the human realm and thus of economic matters, which makes it difficult to know the future. This topic has been keenly explored by such economists as Frank Knight (in his 1921 work *Risk, Uncertainty and Profit*), John Maynard Keynes (in his 1936 *General Theory*, among other writings), George Shackle and Brian Loasby, among others.

Third, 'the economic' is also social. Economics, in fact, is the field or area of social life defined by the exchange of goods and services, market exchange, as well as other forms such as reciprocity within a community or between different communities. This is why one condition of economic goods is that they be exchangeable. I am not claiming, however, that they are in fact so. Not every economy is a market economy. But a good that is only useful to one individual alone is not an economic good. As anthropologist-economist Stephen Gudeman (2001: 147) asserts, 'the relationship between people as mediated by things – whether in the market or in the community, whether via capital or the base – is the stuff of economy'. For Buchanan (1987: 27), Robinson Crusoe's problem was not economic but computational, before Friday arrived at the island. Only then the economic problem may emerge.

Another implication of the social character of 'the economic' is that it is more than the sum of its parts. The economy as a whole is not the mere aggregate of individual actions, because these actions are not exclusively individual but have an intrinsic relation with other individual actions, given their social condition. Social relations are real relations providing individuals – unique substantial components of society – with actual guidance towards a shared end (Lachance 2001). Social relations add something real: for example, it is not the same for two people to be father and son and/or friends. The social realm is thus a relational whole composed of substantive individuals and real relations between them. This relation adds an 'order towards', without which individual action cannot be explained. This 'unit of order' is dynamic, behavioural. The economy and the market are one dimension of society, one form of social relationship. Society is prior. The idea of the economy as a whole more than the sum of its parts could also be conceived in terms of Searle's (1995, 2005, 2015) theory of social intentionality and institutions (see also Schabas 2009: 13–15). This does not mean that individual economic actions do not exist. However, first, these individual actions have an intrinsic relation with others and, second, the economic system as a whole, as put by Schabas, 'is an emergent property of our world, it resists reduction down to individual agency' (2009: 16).

Pavan finally asserts, 'directed at the production of wealth'. This, beyond the arguable specificity of wealth, points at defining a determinate portion of reality, not every human reality.

On a final note, violent decisions and actions are not economic; in fact, robbery is not an economic action. Fraud is not in itself an economic action, but the latter might contain the former. Thus far, we have already established a broad literal notion of 'the economic': *free actions related to the acquisition, possession or use of goods for the satisfaction of human needs and desires in a social context.* This broad literal meaning of 'the economic' determines a portion of human reality, a specific field that is broadly approached.

The restricted literal meaning provides a specific perspective to approach that field. In this restricted sense, something is 'economic' when it is a specific way of satisfying human needs (both basic and non-basic) and/or desires: done in the best way possible, getting the best performance possible. That is to say, when the relationship between inputs, means or resources, and the results or objectives achieved reaches its maximum, the 'economic principle' is applied. From an economically restricted perspective, behavioural acts that do not maximize are considered 'bad behaviour'. Bye (1939: 625), for his part, explains that 'economizing is a process of so managing one's resources as to make them go as far as possible'. The idea is to get the most possible out of given resources.

Nevertheless, a purchase or a sale is an economic action regardless of whether it is or is not economically performed. Robert Scoon distinguishes between the adjectives 'economic' and 'economical' in the same sense; he claims that they should not be confused, and that economics should not reduce the 'economic' to the 'economical' (1943: 311).

The 'economic principle' can be applied to non-economic realities: for example, the use of one's time on the weekend or the optimal distribution of classrooms, schedules and courses in an educational institution. Some applications, such as those mentioned, are legitimate. Other cases, such as those involving family, crime, education, politics, religion, and so on, may raise doubts about their legitimacy as predominant criteria, because they do not seem to point to maximization-seeking, but rather love, justice or the common good.

How did this second – the restricted – meaning come to be? It is the result of what economists regard as a key component in defining 'the economic': scarcity. According to this view, human actions are economic to the extent to which they are motivated by or faced with the problem of scarcity of the necessary means for reaching desired ends. Economic deliberations and actions deal with the allocation of limited useful goods. Weber wrote in 1904 (1949: 65; italics in the original):

> Specifically economic motives, – i.e., motives which, in their aspect most significant to us, are rooted in the above mentioned fundamental fact – operate wherever the satisfaction of even the most immaterial need or desire is bound up with the application of *scarce* material means.

The reality of scarcity implies opportunity cost: if I use something with one end in mind, I cannot use it simultaneously for another end.

The reality of limitations is an evident anthropological feature. The issue of scarcity has also been a matter of reflection for many thinkers. It was excellently expressed by Robert Malthus. Malthus' theodicy (understood as an explanation of scarcity) considers need and scarcity as instruments that shape the human mind. Albino Barrera (2005, passim), commenting on Malthus, argued in both philosophical and theological terms, that God created the world with sufficient matter to cover the needs of all of humanity; but that this sufficiency is conditional on the human person's work to avoid various types of limitations. Thus, in seeking human fulfilment, the economic dimension cannot be ignored. The material sufficiency provided by God is conditional. Human action, therefore, is a secondary cause of fulfilment. God desires a state of material sufficiency for the human person, not of scarcity (as in Malthus). However, reaching this state depends on human conduct. The human person is obliged to undertake economic activity, to the extent that it is necessary to obtain what he/she needs (Pavan 1956: 19). Within this conception of 'conditional sufficiency', the intersection of both notions of the economy becomes clear. The economy looks for the satisfaction of our needs and desires but, first, it has to efficiently use the disposable means to achieve this aim and, second, desires have to be limited, thus implying the need of a mutually dynamic interaction between means and ends.

If wants were unlimited, scarcity would exist in every conceivable situation. In the face of such limitlessness, optimal performance or maximizing would be insufficient because desires would never be fulfilled. This occurs when the human person allows himself/herself to be ruled exclusively by desires, which can be unlimited, instead of covering his/her necessities, which are always limited. Aristotle had already noted this through his notion of an unlimited chrematistics (*Politics* I 9 1258a). Polanyi develops the above idea of Aristotle:

> Man, like any other animal, was presented by him as naturally self-sufficient. The human economy did not, therefore, stem from the boundlessness of man's wants and needs, or, as it is phrased today, from the fact of scarcity (1957: 66). […] Therefore, if scarcity springs 'from the demand side', as we would say, Aristotle attributes it to a misconceived notion of the good life as a desire for a greater abundance of physical goods and enjoyments' [than needed].
>
> (1957: 81)

The 'ethos of the unlimited' transforms means into ends. Thinkers such as Weber and Karl Marx support this view. Both interpret the capitalist phenomenon in this way. According to Weber's diagnosis, modern rationalization brought along with it the domination of ends by their means; while Marx believed that alienation had brought about the human person's domination by merchandise (see Löwith 1982, pp. 48 and 76). However, the economic law of marginal decreasing utility implicitly recognizes the limited character of desires. But in fact, economists often implicitly think as if desires were unbounded (see Mary Hirschfeld 2018: Chapter 2).

Having presented different but related meanings of 'the economic', let us summarize our findings.

Conclusion

A philosophy of the economy must begin by determining what 'the economic' means. I have distinguished between various meanings of this term. First of all, we may identify a metaphorical meaning that refers to the root of 'the economic': the fact that the human person is limited implies that he/she requires resources that are also limited, and that he/she uses his/her reason to distribute them in the best way possible. This situation relates also to realities that go beyond 'the economic'. That is why both the human person and human reason are only economic in a metaphorical sense.

The non-metaphorical or literal meaning of 'the economic' could have two sub-meanings: in the broad sense and in the restricted sense. 'The economic' in its broad sense is the subject matter of, in Polanyi's words, substantive economics, all that which is related to the use of resources for the satisfaction of human needs.

In the restricted sense, 'the economic' is the best way of using this matter, an efficient allocation of the resources for human necessities. It is not necessary for all of 'the economic' to adjust to this precise definition. Economics can simply be action, often not maximizing, for the satisfaction of needs. The broad meaning deals with 'the economic', and the restricted meaning, in addition, does so 'economically'. I have also shown the presence of these two meanings in Menger, Neville Keynes, and Simon.

Frank Knight provides very interesting reflections on these issues. He notices that, from a 'scientific' point of view, all practical problems, 'the problem of life', boil down to using resources 'economically'. However, he goes on, the scientific view of life is limited and partial, and he assigns priority to finding out 'our real wants', our ends or values (1935: 105; and see also 1956. 128–129). The economic problem in its broad sense comes first, and only then the restricted sense.

Let us go back to the notion of analogy introduced at the beginning of the chapter. I conclude that the economy is an analogical concept. Therefore, its 'focal meaning' will be the broad non-metaphorical sense of the word, that is, a human action aimed at using material resources for satisfying needs. It is, in Buchanan's words, 'a characteristic form of human activity' (1979: 20). The restricted sense of 'the economic' is a particular way of performing this action, a secondary or derived (but not less important) meaning of the economic.

Having analysed the meaning of 'the economic', the next step is to determine what type of human rationality is adequate for its study and, consequently, what kind of science is adequate for the task. John Stuart Mill starts his essay 'On the Definition of Political Economy' complaining that it has remained deprived of 'a definition exactly co-extensive with the thing defined' ([1874] 1974: 123). Now that we have defined the object of study, I hope to identify its corresponding science in the next chapter. Mill himself, Menger, and Neville Keynes will contribute to it.

Notes

1 Friedrich A. von Hayek also notes this contrast and holds that social science has to take into account the concepts and ideas of the people ([1952] 1979: 27–28, 57–58, 61).

2 As the German philosopher Josef Pieper (1998: 73) has suggested, although it is possible and legitimate to use technical terms with specific meanings, we should mistrust all conceptual determination departing with originality from the common language of learned people.

3 From now on 'Neville Keynes', to make clear the distinction with his son John Maynard.

4 A classification somewhat anticipated in his 1883 *Untersuchungen über die Methode der Sozialwissenschaften* ([1883] 1985).

5 This and the following sections partially draw on Crespo 2013a and 2013b.

6 I use the term 'anthropological' in its philosophical sense, not referring to cultural anthropology.

7 The idea of freedom appears occasionally throughout this book. In spite of the impact of current reductive physicalist tendencies on the contemporary world vision, I will consider freedom as one characteristic of the human being. In my previous book (2017) on new economic currents, I showed that, despite strong influences of this reductive wave on new economic currents such as behavioural economics, neuroeconomics or evolutionary economics, they still strive to defend freedom. So, in the free will versus determinism debate, I take the side of free will. This is, of course, a metaphysical position that, though suggested as a result of inner experience and even some empirical experiments, cannot be definitively proved. As Robert Northcott (2019) argues, free will is neither verifiable nor falsifiable by empirical evidence. However, there is a long-standing tradition of free-will supporters starting with Aristotle and including Augustine, most medieval scholastics, Immanuel Kant, William James, Henri Bergson, Elizabeth Anscombe and many others, up until the present.

8 One antonym of 'metaphorical' according to the Merriam-Webster dictionary.

9 To avoid any suspicion of unfaithful changes, Giandomenica Becchio clarifies that 'draft materials [written by Menger's father] of the second edition of Menger's *Principles* actually match the published second edition'; 2014: footnote 3. On the history of this publication, see Campagnolo 2008 and 2011, who has some doubts about the faithfulness of Karl's version; Becchio 2010, 2011 and 2014. Scott Scheall and Reinhard Schumacher (2018), based on Karl's diaries, deal with the relation between Carl and Karl. They show that Karl did a great part of his work of revising the text during Carl's last years of life, from 1918 (Carl died in February 1921), and 'he [Karl] noted that organizing the chapter on the economy was his greatest accomplishment as editor of the second edition' (Scheall and Schumacher 2018: 666).

10 Becchio (2014) explores the reasons why he did not want to take into account the second edition. Hayek explains:

> an inspection of his manuscript has shown that, at one time, considerable parts of the work must have been ready for publication. But even after his powers

had begun to fail he continued to revise and rearrange the manuscripts to such an extent that any attempt to reconstruct this would be a very difficult, if not an impossible task. Some of the material dealing with the subject-matter of the *Grundsätze* and partly intended for a new edition of this work, has been incorporated by his son into a second edition of this work, published in 1923. Much more, however, remains in the form of voluminous but fragmentary and disordered manuscripts, which only the prolonged and patient efforts of a very skillful editor could make accessible. For the present, at any rate, the results of the work of Menger's later years must be regarded as lost.

(Hayek 1934: 416)

In fact, this is an easy way of putting away a work containing Menger's new visions probably opposing some of Hayek's ideas. I will not delve into this issue (see Becchio 2010 and 2014 on this). Hayek did not mention the second edition in his paper on the relevance of the *Principles* for the History of Economic Thought (1973).

11 Concerning Frank Knight, even he did not mention the second edition of the *Principles* in his Introduction to the English translation of the first edition (1950). James Dingwall and Bert F. Hoselitz, who translated the book, explain (Dingwall and Hoselitz 1950: 39):

The translation presented here is a complete rendering of the first edition of the *Grundsätze* which was published in Vienna in 1871. A second German edition was published in Vienna in 1923, two years after Menger's death. We rejected the possibility of a *variorum* translation because it was the first edition only that influenced the development of economic doctrine, because of the posthumous character of the second edition, and because the numerous differences between the two editions make a *variorum* translation impractical.

12 On Carlos (Charles) Becker Mechow and Francisco Navarro Vilches, see Luis Alberto Coria (2011).

13 Weber also distinguishes different economic phenomena (1949: 64–65). 'Specifically economic' phenomena are related with scarcity. But he thinks that the *Archiv für Sozialwissenschaft und Sozialpolitik* should also deal with 'economically relevant' and 'economically conditioned' phenomena that either have consequences of interest from an economic perspective or are influenced by economic factors. He mentions religious phenomena and artistic tastes as examples, respectively.

References

Aristotle (1984). *The Complete Works of Aristotle.* Edited by Jonathan Barnes. Princeton: Princeton University Press.

Austin, J. L. (1970). *Philosophical Papers.* Second Edition, edited by J. O. Urmson and G. J. Warnock. Oxford: Oxford University Press.

Barrera, A. (2005). *God and the Evil of Scarcity.* Notre Dame (IN): University of Notre Dame Press.

Becchio, G. (2010). 'Carl Menger and the Second Edition of his Principles', presentation delivered at the 11th Summer Institute for the History of Economic Thought. University of Richmond, Jepson School of Leadership Studies, 22 June

2010.   www.academia.edu/575563/Carl_Menger_and_the_Second_Edition_of_ His_Principles. See also the presentation at www.youtube.com/watch?v=ISh- vRJ1wuE. Accessed 20 June 2018.

Becchio G. (2011). 'Existe-t-il une "doctrine-Menger" qui soit "hétérodoxe"? Sur la lecture et l'interprétation des Grundsätze der Volkwirtschaftslehre (seconde version- 1923) par Karl Polanyi'. In: G. Campagnolo (ed.), *Existe-t-il une doctrine Menger?*, Aix-en-Provence: Presses Universitaires de Provence, pp. 167–186.

Becchio, G. (2014). 'Social Needs, Social Goods, and Human Associations in the Second Edition of Carl Menger's Principles', *History of Political Economy*, 46/2: 265–280.

Buchanan, J. M. (1979). *What Should Economists Do?* Indianapolis: Liberty Fund.

Buchanan, J. M. (1987). *Economics. Between Predictive Science and Moral Philosophy*. College Station: Texas A&M University Press.

Bye, R. (1939). 'The Scope and Definition of Economics'. *Journal of Political Economy*, 47/5: 623–647.

Campagnolo, G. (2008). 'Carl Menger: From the Works Published in Vienna to His *Nachlass*'. In: G. Campagnolo (ed.), *Carl Menger. Discussed on the Basis of New Findings*. Frankfurt: Peter Lang, pp. 31–58.

Campagnolo, G. (ed.) (2011). 'Note editorial'. In: G. Campagmolo (ed.), *Existe-t- il une doctrine Menger? Aux origines de la pensée économique autrichienne.* Aix-en- Provence: Presses Universitaires de Provence, pp. 1–12.

Coats, A. W. (1983). 'The Revival of Subjectivism in Economics'. In: J. Wiseman (ed.) *Beyond Positive Economics?* London: Macmillan, pp. 87–103.

Coria, L. A. (2011). 'Evolución y contradicciones de la escuela austriaca', *Proceedings of the Forty-Sixth Annual Meeting of the Argentine Association of Political Economy*, www. aaep.org.ar/anales/works/works2011/Coria.pdf. Accessed 20 June 2016.

Crespo, R. F. (2013a). *Philosophy of the Economy. An Aristotelian Approach*. Dordrecht: Springer.

Crespo, R. F. (2013b). 'Two Conceptions of Economics and Maximisation', *Cambridge Journal of Economics*, 37/4: 759–774.

Crespo, R. F. (2017). *Economics and Other Disciplines. Assessing New Economic Currents.* Abingdon: Routledge.

Deane, P. (1983). 'The Scope and Method of Economic Science', *Economic Journal*, 93/ 369: 1–12.

Dingwall J. and B. Hoselitz (1950). 'Translator's Preface'. In: Carl Menger (ed.), *Principles of Economics*. Glencoe (IL): Free Press, pp. 37–40.

Dow, S. (2002). *Economic Methodology: An Inquiry*. Oxford: Oxford University Press.

Düppe, T. (2011). *The Making of the Economy: A Phenomenology of Economic Science.* Lanham (MD): Lexington Books.

Eucken, W. ([1939] 1947). *Cuestiones fundamentales de la economía política*, Revista de Occidente, Madrid: Alianza (*Die Grundlagen der Nationalökonomie*).

Godelier, M. (1966). *Rationalité et irrationalité en économie*. Paris: Francois Maspero.

Gudeman, S. (2001). *The Anthropology of Economy*. Malden and Oxford: Blackwell.

Hayek, F. A. v. (1934). 'Carl Menger', *Economica*, 1: 393–420.

Hayek, F. A. v. ([1952] 1979). *The Counter-Revolution of Science.* Indianapolis: Liberty Fund.

Hayek, F. A. v. (1973). 'The Place of Menger's *Grundsätze* in the History of Economic Thought'. In: J. R. Hicks and W. Weber (eds.), *Carl Menger and the Austrian School of Economics*. Oxford: Clarendon Press, pp. 1–15.

Hicks, J. (1976). '"Revolutions" in Economics'. In: S. J. Latsis (ed.), *Method and Appraisal in Economics*. London: Cambridge University Press, pp. 207–218.

Hirschfeld, M. (2018). *Aquinas and the Market. Toward a Humane Economy*. Cambridge (MA): Harvard University Press.

Keynes, J. N. ([1890] 1955). *The Scope and Method of Political Economy*. Fourth Edition. New York: Kelley and Millman.

Keynes, J. M. (1936). *The General Theory of Employment, Interest and Money*. London: Macmillan.

Knight, F. H. (1921). *Risk, Uncertainty and Profit*. Boston: Houghton Mifflin.

Knight, F. H. (1935). *The Ethics of Competition and Other Essays*. London: George Allen & Unwin.

Knight, F. H. (1950). 'Introduction'. In: Carl Menger's *Principles of Economics*. Glencoe (IL): Free Press, pp. 9–35.

Knight, F. H. (1956). *On the History and Method of Economics*. Chicago: University of Chicago Press.

Kolnai, A. (1968). 'Agency and Freedom'. In: *The Human Agent*, Royal Institute of Philosophy Lectures, vol. 1: 1966–1967. London: Macmillan, pp. 20–46.

Lachance, L. (2001). *Humanismo político*. Eunsa: Pamplona (Montréal 1964).

Löwith, K. (1982). *Max Weber and Karl Marx*. London: George Allen & Unwin.

Mäki, U. (2001). 'Economic Ontology: What? Why? How?'. In: U. Mäki (ed.), *The Economic World View. Studies in the Ontology of Economics*. Cambridge: Cambridge University Press, pp. 3–14.

Marshall, A. ([1920] 1962). *Principles of Economics*. London: Macmillan.

Menger, C. ([1871] 1950). *Principles of Economics*. Glencoe (IL): Free Press (*Grundzätze der Volkswirtchaftslehre*, First Edition), translated by J. Dingwall and B. Hoselitz.

Menger, C. (1871). *Grundsätze der Volkswirtschaftslehre*. Wien: Wilhelm Braumüller.

Menger, C. ([1883] 1985). *Investigations into the Method of the Social Sciences with Special Reference to Economics*, edited by Louis Schneider and translated by Francis Nock. New York: New York University Press.

Menger, C. (1923). *Grundsätze der Volkswirtschaftslehre*. Mit einem Geleitwort von Richard Schüller, aus dem Nachlass herausgegeben von Karl Menger. Wien: Hölder-Pichler-Tempsky/Leipzig: G. Freytag.

Mill, J. S. ([1874] 1974). 'On the Definition of Political Economy', in *Essays on Some Unsettled Questions of Political Economy*. Second Edition. London: Longmans, Green, Reader and Dyer; Reprinted, Clifton: Augustus M. Kelley Publishers.

Mises, L. v. ([1949] 1998). *Human Action. A Treatise on Economics*. Auburn (AL): Ludwig von Mises Institute.

Northcott, R. (2019). 'Free Will Is Not a Testable Hypothesis', *Erkenntnis*, 84: 617–631.

Pareto, W. ([1906] 1971). *Manual of Political Economy*. New York: A. M. Kelley.

Pavan, P. (1956). *El hombre en el mundo económico*. Buenos Aires: Ediciones del Atlántico (*L'uomo nel mondo economico*, Ed. Figlie Della Chiesa, Roma, s/d).

Pieper, J. (1998). 'El filosofar y el lenguaje', *Anuario Filosófico*, 21/1: 1–15.

Polanyi, K. (1957). 'Aristotle Discovers the Economy'. In: Karl Polanyi, C. M. Arenberg and H. W. Pearson (eds.), *Trade and Market in the Early Empires*. Glencoe (IL): Free Press, pp. 64–94.

Polanyi, K. (1971a). 'Carl Menger's Two Meanings of "Economics"'. In: G. Dalton (ed.), *Studies in Economic Anthropology*. Washington, DC: American Anthropological Association, pp. 16–24.

Polanyi, K. (1971b). 'The Economy as Instituted Process'. In: G. Dalton (ed.), *Essays of Karl Polanyi*. Boston: Beacon Press, pp. 139–174.

Polanyi, K. (1977). 'The Two Meanings of *Economics*'. In: K. Polanyi, and H. W. Pearson (eds.), *The Livelihood of Man*. New York: Academic Press, pp. 19–34.

Rescher, N. (1988). *Rationality. A Philosophical Inquiry into the Nature and the Rationale of Reason*. Oxford: Clarendon Press.

Robbins, L. C. (1935). *Essay on the Nature and Significance of Economic Science*. Second Edition. London: Macmillan.

Röpke, W. (1955). *Introducción a la economía política*. Madrid: Revista de Occidente (*Die Lehre von der Wirtschaft*. Zürich: Rentsch).

Schabas, M. (2009). 'Constructing "The Economy"', *Philosophy of the Social Sciences*, 39/1: 3–19.

Scheall, S. and R. Schumacher (2018). 'Karl Menger as Son of Carl Menger', *History of Political Economy*, 50/4: 649–678.

Schumpeter, J. A. ([1912] 2002). 'The Economy as a Whole. Seventh Chapter of the Theory of Economic Development'. Translated by Ursula Backhaus. *Industry and Innovation*, 9/1–2: 93–145.

Scoon, R. (1943). 'Professor Robbins' Definition of Economics'. *Journal of Political Economy*, 51/4: 310–320.

Searle, J. R. (1995). *The Construction of Social Reality*. New York: Free Press.

Searle, J. R. (2005). 'What Is an Institution?' *Journal of Institutional Economics*, 1: 1–22.

Searle, J. R. (2015). 'Status Functions and Institutional Facts: Reply to Hindriks and Guala', *Journal of Institutional Economics*, 11/3: 507–514.

Shackle, G. L. S. (1979). *Imagination and the Nature of the Choice*. Edinburgh: Edinburgh University Press.

Simon, H. (1978). 'Rationality as Process and as a Product of Thought'. *American Economic Review*, 68/2: 1–16.

Soler Miralles, J. E. G. (1952). 'Sobre Filosofía de la Economía', *Revista de la Facultad de Ciencias Económicas*, UNC, No. 12, September–December: 129–139.

Spranger, E. (1928). *Types of Men: The Psychology and Ethics of Personality*. Translated by Paul John William Pigors. Halle (Saale): M. Niemeyer (*Die Lebensformen*, 1914).

Weber, M. ([1922] 1978). *Economy and Society*, edited by G. Roth and C. Wittich. Berkeley and Los Angeles: University of California Press (*Wirtschaft und Gesellschaft*, 1922).

Weber, M. [1923] 1956. *General Economic History, Historia económica general*. México City: FCE.

Weber, M. (1949). *The Methodology of the Social Sciences*. New York: Free Press (*Gesammelte aufsätze zur Wissenschaftslehre*, translated and edited by E. Shils and H. Finch).

Webster's Dictionary (1996). New York: Gramercy Books.

Wiseman, J. (1983). 'Introduction'. In: J. Wiseman (ed.), *Beyond Positive Economics?* London: Macmillan: 1–12.

Wittgenstein, L. (1958). *Philosophical Investigations*. Translated by Elizabeth Anscombe. Second Edition. Oxford: Blackwell.

3   Economic sciences

Throughout history, different concepts of economics as a science have reflected the different notions of the economy that I have analysed in the previous chapter. Economics was originally conceived as the study of 'the economic' in its broad sense. Next, it became the study of 'all things economic' in its restricted sense. Finally, in the twentieth century, it began applying the maximizing logic of its latter meaning to the entire human reality under the title of economics – the so-called economic imperialism, as already mentioned.

Robbins began his work on the definition of economics by stating that this definition still remained unclear (1935: 1): 'We all talk about the same things, but we have not yet agreed what it is we are talking about'. Not knowing what you are talking about is not a good thing. Yet, Robbins wrote at the start of the last century. Things might have changed later. However, in the twenty-first century, Mäki (2002: 8) has argued that the notion of economics still constitutes a dangerous melange of notions: 'there is no one homogeneous economics'. This is one reason why the title of this book and this chapter use the term 'economic science' in the plural – 'economic sciences' – a point that will be progressively made clearer throughout this chapter. Roger Backhouse and Steve Medema claim that 'economists are far from unanimous about the definition of their subject' (2009: 223). After discussing several dissimilar definitions they assert:

> One possible conclusion to draw from this lack of agreement is that the definition of economics does not really matter [...] Another possible conclusion is that the subject of economics is too broad to be usefully pinned down in a short definition [...] Jacob Viner reflected this spirit in his oft-quoted statement: 'Economics is what economists do'.

At present, they claim, 'economists are generally guided by pragmatic considerations of what works [...] not by formal definitions' (2009: 231). This chapter is aimed at sorting out this matter. We cannot avoid reaching for one (or at least a few) definition(s) of economics. This is a fundamental task of any philosophy of the economy that cannot be ignored. The previous chapter has proposed two meanings of the economy. We face two subject matters: a part of human affairs related to the provision of human material necessities or desires, and a specific way of performing this provision – maximizing a material object, economic phenomena – approached from a wide and a narrow formal object, respectively. Given the usual emphasis on scarcity in economics, these two subject matters often coincide. However, this may not be the case because, even when scarcity prevails, other motivations might replace maximization – considering maximization as an empirical principle, as I will explain in the last section of this chapter. This chapter aims to explore what kind of science or sciences are appropriate for the study of these two versions of the economy.

Paradoxical as it may sound, after thorough research, I concluded that the best approaches to the definition and classification of economic sciences were developed in the nineteenth century by Mill, Menger, and Neville Keynes, 'methodological pioneers' of economic science, classically labelled at the time as 'political economy'. Since them, the notion of economic science has usually been reduced to 'economics', a part of it, a discipline focused on the economy in its restricted conception. This leaves aside dimensions of the economy, with negative consequences for the adequacy of the different roles of economic sciences: description, explanation and prediction of economic phenomena, understanding and prescription of ends, and economic policy designed to achieve satisfactory economic results.

The wider view held by these precursors has been progressively reduced during the twentieth century. This process has to do with the concentration on the most 'scientific' of the economic sciences (according to a narrow conception of science). This narrow vision of science is committed to a specific notion of rationality: instrumental maximizing rationality.

This chapter will begin by analysing the thought of these nineteenth century methodological precursors, concluding with a proposal for the classification of the economic sciences based on their combined ideas. Then, it will outline what has happened during the twentieth century. Third, it will show how a combination of different notions of rationality which are wider than the narrow vision already mentioned – instrumental maximizing rationality – leaves room for a plurality of economic sciences converging with the precursors' ideas. Next, the meaning of the maximizing principle will be properly clarified. Finally, this chapter will determine the tasks to be performed by the different economic sciences.

Mill, Menger, and Neville Keynes on the nature and classification of the economic sciences

Mill's ideas on the nature of 'political economy' are probably the best known among economists concerned with this topic. They are specially developed in his essay 'On the Definition of Political Economy; and on the Method of Investigation Proper to It',[1] and in book VI 'On the Logic of Moral Sciences' (particularly, Chapter IX, 3) of his 1843 *System of Logic* (Eighth edition from 1872).[2] Mill states:

> What is now commonly understood by the term 'Political Economy' is not
> the science of speculative politics, but a branch of that science. It does not
> treat of the whole of man's nature as modified by the social state, nor of
> the whole conduct of man in society. It is concerned with him solely as a
> being who desires to possess wealth, and who is capable of judging of the
> comparative efficacy of means for obtaining that end.
>
> ([1844] 2006: 321)

Note first that he considers political economy as a branch of politics in much
the same way as Adam Smith, who considers it as 'a branch of the science of
a statesman or legislator' ([1776] 1828: 189). Second, the last part of Mill's last
sentence anticipates the prevailing current definition of economics: the allocation of scarce means in order to satisfy given ends: 'the scarcity definition'
of economics promoted by Robbins (1935: Chapter 2). This definition fits
with the restricted sense of the economy explained in the previous chapter.
However, Mill is also aware that this description of political economy involves
a simplifying abstraction:

> All these operations, though many of them are really the result of a plurality
> of motives, are considered by Political Economy as flowing solely from the
> desire of wealth [...] Not that any political economist was ever so absurd as
> to suppose that mankind are really thus constituted.
>
> ([1844] 2006: 322)

And consequently, as already quoted in Chapter 1, he also emphasizes the need
to consider additional motives for these 'operations' in order to reach a correct
explanation and prediction – a de-idealization process:[3]

> So far as it is known, or may be presumed, that the conduct of mankind in
> the pursuit of wealth is under the collateral influence of any other of the
> properties of our nature than the desire of obtaining the greatest quantity
> of wealth with the least labor and self-denial, the conclusions of Political
> Economy will so far fail of being applicable to the explanation or predic-
> tion of real events, until they are modified by a correct allowance for the
> degree of influence exercised by the other causes.
>
> ([1844] 2006: 323, see also 326–327)

According to Mill, this is the work of 'practical men' who argue inductively,
'a posteriori', while theorists reason mostly deductively, 'a priori'. Theory and
experience are present in both inquiries, though with a difference in emphasis.
Political economy uses the a priori method and it is an 'abstract' science with
abstract conclusions, only true under certain assumptions (that only specific
economic motives prevail, and that there are no 'disturbing causes'). The a
posteriori method is 'an indispensable supplement to it' (327), a supplemen-
tary chapter or appendix (331), because, according to Mill, it is not a science
but an art. However, he emphasizes the need to combine the two disciplines,

science and art, 'for the guidance of mankind' (333), and complains about their separation (334):

> One of the peculiarities of modern times, the separation of theory from practice − of the studies of the closet from outward business of the world − has given a wrong bias to the ideas and feelings both of the student and of the man of business.

However, for Mill, art has to do not only with the application of theory and the practice of economic affairs but also with the definition of ends. For him, we have to take into account a three-step process when analysing human affairs. He affirms in the *System of Logic* (1882: 653;VI, XXI, 2):

> The relation in which rules of art stand to doctrines of science may be thus characterized. The art proposes to itself an end to be attained, defines the end, and hands it over to the science. The science receives it, considers it as a phenomenon or effect to be studied, and having investigated its causes and conditions, sends it back to art with a theorem of the combination of circumstances by which it could be produced. Art then examines this combination of circumstances, and according as any of them are or are not in human power, pronounces the end attainable or not.

That is, there are two kinds of arts: the art of definition of ends (which concerns morality) and the art of performing the actions directed to these ends, enlightened by science. He states (1882: 657):

> Every art is thus a joint result of laws of nature disclosed by science, and of the general principles of what has been called Teleology, or the Doctrine of Ends; which borrowing the language of the German metaphysicians, may also be termed, not improperly, the principles of Practical Reason [...] There is, then, a *Philosophia prima* peculiar to Art, as there is one which belongs to Science. There are not only first principles of Knowledge, but first principles of Conduct. There must be some standard by which to determine the goodness or badness, absolute or comparative, of ends, of objects of desire.[4]

In conclusion, though for Mill the science of political economy is only an abstract science whose subject matter fits the economy in the restricted sense, there are three branches of knowledge that deal with economic matters:

- the teleological art of defining the ends of economic actions, a normative discipline;
- political economy, an abstract science that uses the a priori method and considers only economic motives: 'the desire of obtaining the greatest quantity of wealth with the least labor and self-denial' ([1844] 2006: 323); it deals with the economy in the restricted sense defined in the previous chapter;

- the art of economic practice, that considers all motives influencing actual economic phenomena; it deals with the economy in the broad sense defined in the previous chapter.

It is interesting to note the sequence – teleological art, political economy, the art of economic practice. As in classical philosophy, the ends are the first step in any process. Let us now turn our attention to Menger.

Menger's ideas on the nature and classification of economic sciences are mainly contained in his methodological book, *Investigation into the Method of the Social Sciences with Special Reference to Economics* (*Untersuchungen über die Methode der Socialwissenschaften und der Politischen Oekonomie insbesondere* [1883] 1985), originally published in English as *Problems of Economics and Sociology* (Urbana: University of Illinois Press, 1963), and in his article 'Toward a Systematic Classification of the Economic Sciences' (1960), English translation of 'Grundzüge einer Klassifikation der Wirtschaftswissenschaften' (*Jahrbücher für Nationalökonomie und Statistik*, ed. J. Conrad, New Series, Jena: Gustav Fisher, 1889, XIX, 465–496). In this last writing – also from a chronological point of view – Menger uses the term 'economic sciences' in the plural. This plural fits with the analogical character of the subject matter – the economy –, proposed in the last chapter. An analogical plurality of subject matters (plural but related) calls for a plurality of sciences (also plural but related). In fact, the aim of his article is to ascertain '*the position of economic theory [Wirtschaftstheorie] within the entire dominion of the economic sciences [Wirtschaftswissenschaften] in general*' (1960: 3; italics in the original), with the former roughly dealing with the economy in the restricted sense and the latter with the economy in the broad sense, as defined in the previous chapter.

I will not discuss here the controversial topic of whether Menger was (or was not) a pure Aristotelian, but it is clear that he had read and incorporated a lot of Aristotle's and classical philosophical teachings.[5] As explained in Chapter 1, for classical philosophy, sciences have a *material* object, or a subject matter, the 'about what' the science deals with, and a *formal object*, the specific perspective from which the material object is approached. This is a criterion clearly adopted by Menger in order to distinguish the different economic sciences.

For example, when referring to two forms of what he calls 'theoretical economics' – the exact and the realistic – he clarifies that both share the same field of research, 'all the economy', while they possess 'formal differences'. He states: 'both the exact and the realistic orientation of theoretical research have the aim of making us understand theoretically *all* the phenomena of the economy, each in *its* way' ([1883] 1985: 68). More generally, in his 1889 article he speaks about two

> essentially distinct principles of classification [of sciences]: on the one hand, according to the nature of the objects of inquiry, i.e., the different *fields* [*Gebieten*] of reality which constitute the subject of scientific cognition; and

on the other hand, according to the different lines of scientific inquiry, i.e., the different *methods of approaching* reality.

(1960: 4, if not explicitly said, all italics are by Menger;
see also [1883] 1985: Appendix II, 198)

As already mentioned in Chapter 1, another classical philosophical notion is the analogy of science. Sciences for Aristotle are theoretical, practical, or poietical (technical). At the beginning of the *Politics* (I, 2), Aristotle describes the human person as a *zoon echon logon* – 'man alone is furnished with the faculty of language [*logos* also means reason and order]'. Here, Aristotle holds the idea that human beings can know what is good and evil, morally just and unjust, technically expedient and inexpedient. He distinguishes between three uses of reason: theoretical, practical and *poietic* (technical or instrumental), paving the way for the three types of corresponding sciences. Each of these distinctions corresponds to a respective subject of study (*Metaphysics* VI, 1, 1025b 20–21 and XI, 7, 1063b 36–1064a):

1   Metaphysics, physics and mathematics comprise the theoretical sciences.
2   Practical sciences study objects stemming from human choices and have a practical end (*Nicomachean Ethics* I, 2, 1095a 6 and II, 2, 1103b 27–28).
3   Technical sciences are concerned with artefacts and rules for their production.

The theoretical use of reason points at understanding the essence and cause underlying anything that can be observed empirically or through experiments. Following in the footsteps of his predecessors, Aristotle asserted, 'Plainly we are seeking the cause. And this is the essence, which in some cases is the end [...], and in some cases is the first mover' (*Metaphysics* VII, 17 1041a 27–30; see also 1041b 10ss). He made a distinction between real causes (efficient, formal, material, and final) (*Metaphysics* I, 3–10; *Physics,* II, 3), leading to four different types of explanations known as 'a doctrine of four "becauses" that answer the following questions: Who made it? Why this object and not another? What is it made of? And to what end was it made?' (Ackrill 1981: 36). Theoretical knowledge is the path to these causes.

According to Aristotle's *Nicomachean Ethics* and *Politics*, on the other hand, the use of practical reason deals with the choice of the ends of human actions. Finally, technical or instrumental reason explores the way to allocate means to achieve a given set of predetermined ends. As already said, though not necessarily, it could also strive for 'maximization'– that is, the best way to achieve this allocation. This shows the difference between pure technical thinking (allocation only) and economic thinking (the best allocation). In sum, practical sciences deal through practical reason with ends and consequently have a strong moral character, and technical sciences deal with means, given ends. The common characteristic of sciences is they are discursive – 'a state or capacity to demonstrate' – and provide certainty (*Nicomachean Ethics* VI, 3).

Human sciences can have theoretical, practical, and technical aspects. Thomas Aquinas completes Aristotle on this point: for him, 'some knowledge is speculative [theoretical] only; some is practical only; and some is partly speculative and partly practical' (*Summa Theologiae* I, q. 14, a. 16). This is the case with social sciences. When Aquinas speaks about the practical, he includes the practical and the technical. He distinguishes three principles to decide whether a science is theoretical or practical. These are the subject matter (*ex parte rerum*), the end (*quantum ad finem*), and the method (*quantum ad modum sciendi*). This threefold classification leaves room for 'mixed' cases, such as the theoretical studies of practical subjects just mentioned above. Aquinas asserts in *De Veritate*:

> Knowledge is said to be practical by its order to act. This can happen in two ways. Sometimes *in actu*, i.e., when it is actually ordered to perform something [...] Other times, when knowledge can be ordered to act but it is not now ordered to act [...]; in this way knowledge is virtually practical, but not *in actu*.
>
> (q. 3, a. 3)

This is an important point because current social sciences, although they may try to be only theoretical, are implicitly ordered towards action. This balance between the relevance of theory and practice seems sensible. Thus, a particular science about a practical subject matter may be theoretical or practical *quantum ad finem*, and consequently *quantum ad modum sciendi*.

These distinctions leave room for plenty of combinations of sciences and corresponding methods of which Menger takes advantage. He explicitly argues against 'epistemologists' (*Erkenntnistheoretiken*) who have a narrow notion of science, and he argues that history and applied economics are sciences because they help us understand (*Verständnis*) human ends. In the mentioned article he presents a 'survey of the system of economic sciences', comprising (1960: 14) the following:

1   The 'historical sciences of economics [*Volkswirtschaft*]': economic statistics and economic history. He had previously said that historical sciences are sciences of the individual. Thus, they investigate concrete economic phenomena. They provide useful information for economic theory.
2   '*The morphology of economic phenomena,* whose function consists in the classification of economic facts in accordance with their general species and subspecies, as well as the demonstration of their generic form' (1960: 14), what probably today we would call 'stylized facts'. He thinks that this science does not have independent significance (1960: 12).
3   '*Economic theory,* which has the task of investigating and establishing the laws of economic phenomena, i.e., the regularities in their coexistence and succession, as well as their intrinsic causation' (1960: 14).
4   *Practical or applied economics,* with its specific method (1960: 16, 21–22).

All these sciences deal with the same material object, that is, economic phenomena, though from different formal perspectives (1960: 5). Though in the rest of the chapter I will come back to these notions, I will here clarify some points. Chapter 4, which deals with statistics, will return to the first group of sciences, the historical sciences, and Chapter 10 will deal with the last, applied economics.

Concerning morphological knowledge, Menger states that, unless it was performed as a systematization of the statistical or historical descriptions, it is an 'integral part of economic theory' (1960: 13) because it assists the understanding (*Verständnis*) of economic phenomena.

Economic theory has the role of demonstrating (*Darstellung*) and understanding (*Verständnis*) (1889: 6; 1960: 7). The German verb and the noun 'to understand' and 'understanding' (*Verstehen* and *Verständnis*), especially at the time Menger was writing, had a specific meaning related to a special way of explaining in the human sciences which has to capture the intentional aspect of human actions: a 'comprehension', or 'appreciation' (from the Langenscheidt Deutsch-English Dictionary, Berlin, 1960). To understand is also a role of applied science (1960: 20). In a note in his article (1889: 18, footnote note 1, 1960: 35, endnote 14), he makes clear that he uses the term 'practical sciences' (*praktische Wissenschaften*) as equivalent to 'applied science', pointing to the meaning of *anthropina philosophia* (an expression of Aristotle, '*all* the sciences of man' [*alle Menschheitswissenschaften*], Menger explains) which *reasonably* (*verständig*, again in italics) apply general principles to specific cases. As mentioned earlier, practical sciences deal with the ends of human action, that is, with their final causes or the teleology of it. Referring to theoretical sciences, Menger also considers both ways of knowledge. He states ([1883] 1985: 43):

> The goal of scholarly research is not only the *cognition* [*Erkenntnis*], but also the *understanding* [*Verständniss* [*sic*]] of phenomena. We have *gained cognition* of a phenomenon when we have attained a mental image of it. We understand it when we have recognized the reason [*Grund*] for its existence and for its characteristic quality (the reason [*Grund*] for its *being* [*Seins*] and for its *being as it is* [*So-Seins*]).

He goes on to differentiate a historical way of understanding a phenomenon – 'investigating its individual process of development' ([1883] 1985: 43) – from the theoretical way – recognizing that it is a case of a generic theoretical law ([1883] 1985: 45). In addition, there are two orientations of theoretical knowledge, the 'realistic-empirical' [*realistisch-empirische*] and the 'exact' [*exacte*]. The former uses the Baconian induction that cannot achieve universal truths or laws, but only general tendencies. It leads to 'real types' and 'empirical laws' ([1883] 1985: 57). The latter uses what would be called, according to Menger's description, 'an essential induction', an abstraction [*abstrahit*] seeking 'to ascertain the simplest elements of everything real' arriving at *qualitatively* [*qualitativ*] strictly typical forms ([1883] 1985: 60). However, as a result of his recognition of the inexact character of the economic stuff, as explained in the previous chapter, Menger acknowledges that these conclusions are not realistic and directly applicable to designing an economic policy. He states that ([1883] 1985: 72–73):

> exact economics by nature has to make us aware of *the laws holding for an analytically or abstractly conceived economic world*, whereas empirical-realistic economics has to make us aware of the regularities in the succession and coexistence of the *real* phenomena of human economy (which, indeed, in their 'full empirical reality' also contain numerous elements *not emergent from an abstract economic world!*).

He thinks, as also already mentioned, that the exact orientation strives for understanding elementary economic phenomena and the empirical-realistic more complex phenomena. Coming back to the notions of material and formal objects of science, both orientations have the same material object, that is economic phenomena, but different formal objects: while the exact orientation analyses these phenomena, taking into account only an abstract economic perspective corresponding to its notion of 'economic economy' (the economic side of human life: [1883] 1985: 87), the realistic-empirical orientation also deals with the 'non-economic economy', abstracting because it concentrates on economic phenomena, while implicitly leaving a place for the non-economic motives of them. For example, real prices of goods already incorporate other motivations than economic, but we are analysing real prices, an economic phenomenon ([1883] 1985: 80). Although they adopt different perspectives (formal objects), both orientations usually work together: 'In scientific *presentation*, however, exact and realistic knowledge are seldom treated separately' ([1883] 1985: 67) – they perform an interdisciplinary task.

Summing up, we have ([1883] 1985: 97):

- the historical sciences of economy, including economic history and statistics;
- the theoretical sciences of economy, with the exact and the empirical-realistic orientations, including the economic morphology. They respectively deal with the economy in the restricted sense and in the broad sense, as defined in the previous chapter;
- the practical sciences of economy, including economic policy and the science of finance.

All of them feature different goals, methods and laws (empirical or normative), but are concerned with the same realm of human life, the economy in its broad sense.

It seems evident that there are similarities between Mill's and Menger's proposals. Menger's exact orientation approximately matches Mill's notion of an a priori economic science, and his empirical-realistic orientation of theoretical economics and economic practical sciences comes close to Mill's a posteriori analysis of the economy.

According to Menger, practical sciences of the economy need to take into account the particular conditions and institutions of each country and age ([1883] 1985: 123–125), a view also espoused by Mill. The difference is that while Mill defined political economy as a science and economic policy as an art, Menger considered both them 'economic sciences' (1889, 1960), or 'political economy in general' ([1883] 1985: 197), or 'economic science' in the 'broadest sense of the word' ([1883] 1985: 208). That is, Menger's notion of science is broader than Mill's. Let us turn now to Neville Keynes.

Neville Keynes published his *The Scope and Method of Political Economy* in 1890. He knew and quoted Mill's and Menger's ideas. He was also familiar with the ideas of his friends Alfred Marshall and Henry Sidgwick. In fact, Marshall's *Principles* also date from 1890. Apart from Mill and Menger, relevant antecedents regarding the classification of economic sciences taken into account by Neville Keynes include elements from Sidgwick's *Principles of Political Economy* (first edition 1883, second edition, 1887), and from the German economist Adolph Wagner (1886). Wagner had published *Grundlegung der politischen Ökonomie* in 1883 and an article in the *Jahrbücher für National-Oekonomie und Statistik* (xlvi/ 3, 1886) under the title 'Systematische Nationalökonomie'. A reduced version of it was translated and published in the first issue of the *Quarterly Journal of Economics* (1/1, 1886) as an Appendix under the title 'Wagner on the Present State of Political Economy'. Marshall, Sidgwick and Neville Keynes knew Wagner's work. Wagner places himself in an intermediate position between Menger and Gustav von Schmoller, who is unjustly blamed for an alleged tendency to reduce economic science to economic history.[6] Marshall took the same position ([1890–1920] 1962: 24; see also 32); he was careful to cite Schmoller on this point.

Wagner's ideas are indeed enlightening. Concerning the motives of economic phenomena, he considers five different possible types, including 1) the typical, economic self-interest, which is 'the basis of the deductive reasoning of the abstract theory' (1886: 118); 2) fear of punishment and hope of approval – this has Smithian resonances –; 3) sense of honour; 4) power; and 5) sense of duty and fear of conscience. However, he thinks that all motives have to be considered in the different steps of the economic work, and that the inductive method is also necessary in all those steps. These steps are 1) the description of phenomena, 2) discovery of the causes upon which they depend, 3) the determination of a standard by which their social merit may be measured, 4) the setting up of an ideal to be attained, and 5) the search of the way for effectively attaining them. For him, 'the first four are too closely connected to permit a separation', and he calls them 'the general or theoretic part of a system of "social economy"', while 'the fifth would belong to the special or practical part' (1886: 128). We can see the parallelism with Menger's proposal. He adds that the two last steps of the theoretical part are the discussion of fundamental principles (*Grundlegung*), and he asserts that he 'would place it at the beginning of the treatise, combining with it the psychological analysis of instincts and motives, some consideration of fundamental concepts, and a history of the literature of the subject'. That is, the part considering the ideals and aims should come first. This part can be compared with Mill's Teleology. Marshall also considers a plurality of motives for economic actions, including 'ethical forces' ([1890–1920] 1962: v, 22). In fact, he assertively quotes the five motives of Wagner ([1890–1920] 1962: Appendix D, 645–646).[7]

Sidgwick (1887: vi) acknowledges 'assistance' from Wagner's work, probably from his *Grundlegung der politischen Ökonomie* (Leipzig: C. F. Winter'sche Verlagshandlung, 1883). On methodological grounds, he maintains two main theses. First, in fact, political economy uses complementary inductive and deductive methods, because the abstract deductive arguments are hypothetical and have to be tested. The utility of these hypothetical arguments 'incontrovertibly' (1887: 41) depends on their closeness to real facts and on our ability – 'insight and skill' (1887: 35) – to modify causes or motives of our economic actions: 'needs, appetites, passions, tastes, aims and ideas' (1887: 36). Second, we must distinguish the abstract science and the art, which are 'different inquiries' (1887: 28) in political economy. Though he states this in passing, I think that it is relevant to his statement that 'we require for the *comprehension* of economic facts some *interpretation* of the *motives* of human agents' (1887: 30–31, my italics). I think that this idea can also be compared with Menger's notion of understanding (*Verständnis*) the intentions or final causes of economic activities.

Neville Keynes keeps following the thread of the previously mentioned economists. He also maintains that the premises of political economy are hypothetical, because a plurality of motives actuate besides the purely economic one and, consequently, it is a science of tendencies ([1890] 1955: 16). To leave room for that plurality of motives he speaks about 'political economy' or 'economic inquiry' 'in the widest sense' ([1890] 1955: 36 and 61). It comprises different 'departments', 'inquiries', or 'subdivisions' ([1890] 1955: 30, 34, 35, 61) with different methods according to the nature of the aspect dealt with. He proposes a threefold distinction between 'positive science', 'normative or regulative science', and 'an art' ([1890] 1955: 34–35), respectively dealing with '*economic uniformities, economic ideals and economic precepts*' ([1890] 1955: 31, 35). He states that

> a *positive science* may be defined as a body of systematized knowledge concerning what is; a *normative or regulative science* as a body of systematized knowledge relating to criteria of what ought to be, and concerned therefore with the ideal as distinguished from the actual; and *art* as a system of rules for the attainment of a given end.
>
> ([1890] 1955: 34–35, all Keynes' italics)

He explains that Adam Smith and his contemporaries use the term 'science' in referring to a systematic body of knowledge of theoretical propositions or practical rules ([1890] 1955: 35, nt 2). For Neville Keynes, Mill's modifications, that is, the art, should have a place within the science ([1890] 1955: 118), not outside it, as Mill maintains. Keynes's position fluctuates with respect to these issues, and I will come back to them in Chapter 8.

Putting together all previous contributions, the following branches of 'political economy in its widest sense' (Neville Keynes) or 'economic sciences in general' (Menger) can be distinguished:

1   The historical sciences of economy, including economic history and statistics: Wagner's description of phenomena.
2   The theoretical sciences of economy (or economic theory), with the empirical-realistic and exact orientations. This means that economic theory would include:

- the exact, abstract investigation of the nature and causes of strict economic phenomena (Mill's a priori, Menger's exact orientation);
- the actual operating causes including economic and non-economic causes (Menger's empirical-realistic orientation, Wagner's discovering the causes); and finally;
- the understanding of the ends (Menger's *Verständnis*, Sidgwick's understanding of motives).

Following Aquinas, it is practical science *ex parte rerum*, but it is theoretical in relation to the end and method. It has to be noted that, while for Menger the conclusions of the exact science are not hypothetical, for Wagner, Sidgwick and Neville Keynes they are hypothetical. Schematically, economic theory comprises:

- pure economic theory: Menger's exact orientation or Mill's political economy;
- menger's empirical-realistic orientation dealing with economic motives and economic stuff, or Neville Keynes' positive economic science;
- menger's empirical-realistic orientation dealing with non-economic motives and economic stuff. Menger's understanding of the ends.

Today, Positive economics embraces the first two.

3   Normative economics, which is Aristotle's practical science dealing with the economic, Mill's Teleology or Doctrine of Ends concerning economic goals, Wagner's setting up of an ideal to be attained, and Neville Keynes' normative economics.
4   The practical sciences of economy, including economic policy and the science of finance according to Menger, Mill's art of economic practice or Wagner's search of the way for effectively attaining economic ideals, and Sidgwick's and Neville Keynes' applied economics (Aristotle's technical science applied to the field of the economic, Aquinas' practical *ex parte rerum*, *quantum ad finem*, and *quantum ad modum sciendi*).

Only Mill's a priori science of political economy, Menger's exact orientation of theoretical research and Neville Keynes's positive economics deal with the economy in the restricted sense.

These four economic disciplines have different aims:

- the aim of the historical sciences is *to describe* past and current economic facts and to provide sources of evidence for the work of economic theory;
- the aim of the theoretical science is *to explain* and *understand* economic phenomena. It can do so by abstracting strict economic motives at a wide level of abstraction or analysing very simple economic phenomena in which non-economic motives are not present, or else, by considering all motives in more specific or more complex situations. It has to take into account so-called 'efficient causes' and also final causes. That is, it should not only deal with means given ends but also with the ends, which are the causes (or reasons) of the causes;[8]
- the aim of normative economics is *to define the desirable ends of economic actions*, *to prescribe* ends, including ethical considerations;
- the aim of the practical sciences of economics is *to achieve the defined ends*, taking into account all means that may produce the desired effects and, consequently, all motives influencing economic phenomena.

The four disciplines consequently deal with economic phenomena in different ways. They need to consider all motives, and consequently induction is present in all them. All of them deal with the economy in the broad sense, but a part of theoretical science specifically deals with the economy in the restricted sense: what is known today as positive economics. However, each discipline uses methods in different forms. I will address these differences in subsequent chapters.

The two parts of economic theory[9]

The former proposed classification of economic sciences was based on notions held by philosophers and economists before the twentieth century. How has economic thought on this subject evolved since the nineteenth century? Twentieth-century economists have considered the main division between positive and normative economics (I will come back to this topic in Chapters 8 and 9). At the same time, the art of economics has been almost completely forgotten or subsumed under positive or normative economics. This last fact has been noted by David Colander (1992). It has also been the subject of Luis Mireles Flores's dissertation (2016).

Only a few economists concerned with the topic of the nature of economics have dealt with economic theory recognizing that, among the many paradigms proposed throughout history, two have been predominant: the broad conception of economic theory that takes into account economic and non-economic motivations of economic phenomena, and the restricted positive economics.

The former has a restricted material object, economic phenomena, and a broad formal object, and considers all possible motives influencing them. In contrast, the latter – positive economics – has an ample material object, beginning with economic phenomena in Mill, but finally encompassing all human intentional actions and a restricted formal object, the analysis of human reality from the perspective of a decision to maximize the allocation of means given ends which is the instrumental maximizing rationality perspective. Economic science progressively advanced towards this second vision during the nineteenth and twentieth centuries.

In effect, as pointed out by Ronald Coase (1978: 206ff.), there are two ways to define economic science: as the study of certain types of human activities or the study of a particular approach to human choice. Israel Kirzner (1976: 17), following the work of Lindley M. Fraser (1937), calls them type A and type B definitions: the first designates a particular *department* or sector of human affairs, and the second, a concrete aspect of human actions. Robbins (1935: Chapter 1) calls them material and scarcity definitions respectively and characterizes them as 'classificatory' and 'analytical'. Phelps Brown calls these definitions 'field-determined' and 'discipline-determined' (1972: 7). Ioannides and Nielsen (2007: 7–12) have offered two alternative answers to the question about what economics is: the study of the economy and the study of a specific method and framework to this purpose. Dani Rodrik coincidently asserts (2015: 7):

> The term 'economics' has come to be used in two different ways. One definition focuses on the substantive domain of study; in this interpretation, economics is a social science devoted to understanding how the economy works. The second definition focuses on methods: economics is a way of doing science, using particular tools.[10]

These different visions of economic theory roughly correspond to Karl Polanyi's distinction between substantive and formal meanings of economic science, mentioned in the previous chapter (1971: 139–140).

The substantive definition of economics deals with the 'economy' in its broad sense, whereas the formal definition corresponds to its restricted sense. Historically, as explained, the former was the first to be adopted, followed by the latter. Buchanan favours the field-determined definition. For him, 'economists "should" concentrate their attention on a particular form of human activity, and upon the various institutional arrangements that arise as a result of this form of activity' (1987: 22). He criticizes Robbins' allocation-given scarcity definition, which he considers as applied mathematics of social engineering, and recommends concentrating on all that is related to market exchange phenomena.

As highlighted by Phelps Brown (1972: 7), the substantive 'field-determined' definition presents a twofold problem: it makes room for both rational and 'irrational' behaviour (understanding 'rationality' reductively as in accordance with the 'economic principle'), and it is concerned with the allocation of means and decisions about ends. The substantive definition is concerned with all realities falling under the ordinary name of 'economy', that is, economy in the broad sense, including rational, unpredictable and uncertain behaviours, and decisions related to means or ends, to facts or values: they should all be considered part of economic science.

This subject is indeed hard to define and to manage. To facilitate knowledge of the economy, economic science has evolved into a formal science and has been reduced nearly entirely to positive economics, which corresponds to the study of the economy in its restricted sense. Thus, it has attempted to create a specific, objective, preferably observable subject, because the 'positive science' category to which it aspires to belong focuses on this type of subject. To this purpose, it tries to avoid introspection and value judgements. Consequently, the emergence of this second paradigm, the formal vision of economics, stems from epistemological requirements.

Thus, we arrive at the definition formulated by Robbins (1935: 15): 'Economics is the science which studies human behavior as a relationship between ends and scarce means which have various applications'. That is to say, economics is the science of a specific vision of choice. In this way, economic science is turned into a formal science. It is formal because its subject of study is not a field related to material human needs or to production and distribution. It becomes a choice, any choice, to the extent that it requires adaptation of means to certain ends: it is an approach to human action. It considers ends as given. As Robbins (1935: 29; italics in the original) maintains, 'economics is not concerned at all with any ends, *as such*. It is concerned with ends in so far as they affect the disposition of means. It takes the ends as given in scales of relative valuation'. In fact, it was initially concerned only with economic phenomena viewed as an efficient distribution of resources, but it quickly applied its logic to the analysis of other human realities.

While the subject matter of economics has been expanded, its method has been narrowed: instrumental maximizing rationality attempts to be a formal logic without psychological, sociological, and moral elements. Though Robbins (1935: 83ff) tried to leave psychology aside, he recognized that it was 'half of the equation'. The very word 'utility' carries a psychological resonance. Samuelson (1938: 62; 1948: 243–253) subsequently developed his theory of revealed preference, 'dropping the last vestiges of the utility analysis'. However, the word preference itself refers to psychology. Finally, John von Neumann and Oskar Morgenstern (1944), as well as Leonard Savage ([1954] 1972), have come up with a completely formal theory of rational choice: the expected utility theory (EUT). An axiomatic theory, it states that if people are rational – in the specific sense they have been defined as such – they will behave as if they were maximizing utility. 'Well-behaved' (consistent) preferences and probabilities are assumed and the solution is exact. To achieve this, the theory contains very strict assumptions that make it even narrower than Robbins' assumptions. It leads to an oversimplification of the problem of uncertainty.

In regard to the classification of the economy presented in the previous chapter, while substantive economics is concerned with the economy in its broad sense, formal economics is concerned with the economy in its restricted sense. However, the latter applies this analysis, the 'economic principle', both to economic and non-economic realities. Gary Becker's (1976) framework and research agenda follow this trend. Coase (1978: 207) describes this process in which substantive economic science undergoes a transformation into a formal type of economics that applies to all human action. He notes that there are currently two trends at play:

> The first consists of an enlargement of the scope of economists' interests so far as subject matter is concerned. The second is a narrowing of a professional interest to a more formal, technical, mathematical analysis. This more formal analysis tends to have a greater generality. It may say less, or leave much unsaid, about the economic system, but, because of its generality, [...] economics becomes the study of all purposive human behavior and its scope is, therefore, coterminous with all of the social sciences.

Thus, economics has attempted to include all human actions from a specific perspective. Since this perspective is narrow, its knowledge is incomplete, and economics applies this incompleteness to the analysis of all intentional conduct. In this way, the logic of economics takes the place of the logic of the social sciences. As a consequence, sciences reduce their vision of rationality and this is reflected in their incorrect or even erroneous analyses. Coase (1978: 211) believes that this dualistic tendency is erroneous. He states (1978: 208):

> it by no means follows that an approach developed to explain behaviour in the economic system will be equally successful in the other social sciences. In these different fields, the purposes which men seek to achieve will not be the same, the degree of consistency in behaviour need not be the same and, in particular, the institutional framework within which the choices are made are quite different.

Albert Hirschman is also critical of this tendency. He asserts (2013: 3–4):

> there are serious pitfalls in any transfer of analytical tools and modes of reasoning developed within one discipline to another. As the economist, swollen with pride over the comparative rigor of his discipline, sets out to bring the light to his heathen colleagues in the other social sciences, he is likely to overlook some crucial distinguishing feature of the newly invaded terrain which makes his concepts and apparatus rather less applicable and illuminating than he is wont to think.

Coase additionally maintains that economic science should study other social sciences to better understand the functioning of the economic system, instead of trying to impose its logic onto these sciences. Coase was very familiar with Marshall's thought and supportive of it, and stresses Marshall's focus on studying the real economic system (see Coase 1975: 31; 1978: 206): 'firms, markets, banks and other social institutions which make up that system' (Coase nd, quoted by Medema 2018: 32). Phelps Brown (1972: 7) agrees: 'the economist's studies should be field-determined, not discipline-determined'. It seems inadequate to transform the logics of law and politics into efficiency, for example, when they should be justice and the common good. Richard Ebeling (1990: 191; italics in the original) expresses this very well:

> The economist must now truly become a *social* scientist. He can achieve this, not by superimposing his established method of analysis on other disciplines, but rather by inquiring into the methods of those other disciplines to see what useful analytical tools have been developed to grapple with problems of understanding *social* action.

Paradoxically, epistemological constraints sometimes mislead sciences. In this sense, Robert Scoon's (1943, p. 311) reflections on Robbins' definition seem far-sighted:

> I contend that, if you define economics in this way, it would include political, military, legal, medical, and all moral morals, on a utilitarian basis that is; and thus the usefulness of the definition in enabling us to distinguish economics from other disciplines disappears. Choosing is not a specifically economic activity, and the introduction of scarcity does not alter the situation.

In conclusion, I maintain that we can differentiate two notions of economic theory, one dealing with the broad notion of the economy and the other with the restricted notion, respectively called by Polanyi, substantive and formal meanings. How do I connect these forms with the Mill–Menger–Keynes' classification? The first comprises all economic theory and the second limits itself to positive economics.

It is interesting to compare these ideas with Buchanan's reflections (1987: 78). For him:

> The residual aspects of human action that are not reducible to rat-like stimuli, even in much more complex human variants, define the domain for a wholly different, wholly human, and uniquely different, science – one that cannot, by its nature, be made analogous to the positive-predictive sciences of orthodox paradigm. There is surely room for both sciences to exist in the more inclusive rubric that we call economic theory.

Buchanan's concept of 'economic theory' corresponds to my proposed notion of it. He is recognizing and putting under this umbrella not only positive economics but also a scientific treatment of all the other motives behind economic phenomena, together with the economic motives considered by positive economics.

Both conceptions of economics are connected with different forms of human rationality. Therefore, it will be interesting to analyse them from this point of view. This is the subject of the next section.

Economics and rationalities

In this section, I present another way of classifying economic sciences: by analysing the different forms of rationality that can be applied to economic phenomena. Aristotle, as already introduced in this chapter, distinguished between different forms taken on by human reason according to the subject of knowledge with which it is presented. On the one hand, the human person uses his/her reason theoretically (or speculatively). Through theoretical reason (from the Greek verb *theorein*, to contemplate), the human person knows the nature of the causes of entities.

With regard to knowledge governing proper human action, Aristotle, as already explained, distinguished between practical and poietical (or technical) rationality. Practical rationality is related to the definition of ends. Poietical or technical is that form of rationality implied in achieving results through actions. The first, the practical, asks how one should act in seeking one's own fulfilment. The second, the technical or poietical, asks what means one should employ and how one should proceed to achieve the desired external result. While practical rationality is a rationality of ends and means to the extent that it impacts ends, technical rationality is exclusively a rationality of means. The latter may be an efficient or maximizing rationality of means, or it can be indifferent to efficiency or maximization. Both rationalities appear in Figure 3.1.

Twenty-four centuries later, Weber ([1922] 1978: 24–45) distinguished four types of motives that guide social actions: instrumentally rational, value-rational, affective, and traditional. According to Weber, an action is instrumentally rational when it seeks the adequate distribution of means to obtain the actor's ends. It is value-rational when it is determined by conscious belief in

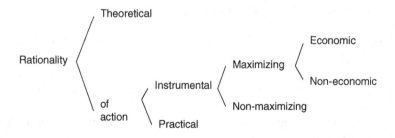

Figure 3.1 Forms of rationality.

the intrinsic value of some form of behaviour. Affective actions are guided by the actor's affects and feelings. Traditional actions are determined by adopted habit. Weber believed that, though a particular type of motive may prevail in some specific kind of rationality, almost all human action stems from several of these types. In fact, instrumental rationality is about means given ends and the other three motivations define ends; and we need means and ends to have an action. For the value-rational, affective, and traditionally guided actions, the very action is an end, independent of its consequences. One usually quoted example is voting: an individual vote does not affect the global result of the elections. Weber's instrumental rationality can be compared to Aristotle's poietic or technical rationality. The others can also be roughly compared with practical Aristotelian rationality.

As noted in the previous chapter, the economist would react by saying that value-rational, affective, and traditional motives are reducible to instrumental rationality. In the next section and in Chapter 6, I will explain the mistake in this economic way of thinking.

Milan Zafirovski (2003: 11–13) presents a list of scientific models of behaviour that follow forms of rationality different from instrumental rationality. He connects them with authors that have developed such forms of rationality (indicated in parentheses):

1   Models of behaviour guided by values (Weber, Pareto).
2   Models of behaviour governed by rules (Weber, Hayek, Veblen, Durkheim).
3   Models of affective behaviour (Weber, Schumpeter, Keynes).
4   Models of power-oriented behaviour (Marx).
5   Models of behaviour oriented towards social prestige or approval (Weber, Veblen).
6   Historical-institutional models of behaviour (Durkheim, Weber and Parsons).

Economic theory is concerned with economic phenomena, no matter if the motives implied by decisions and actions are practical or instrumental, value-driven, affective, or traditional, while the rationality of positive economics, dealing with the restricted notion of the economy, is instrumental rationality. As John Davis (2003: 27) explains in relation to the economy,

> Instrumental rationality is defined by a choice of actions that best satisfy an individual's ends or objectives however those ends or objectives may happen to be characterized. Instrumental rationality is a rationality of efficient means, and per se is completely agnostic regarding the ends those means serve.

Its essence resides in being a calculable and algorithmic way of getting from one fixed point to another.

From the point of view of the previous classification of rationality, we can also propose a typology of economic sciences coincidental with the one proposed

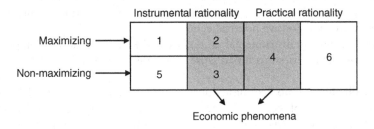

Figure 3.2 Rationality and economic sciences.

in the first section of the chapter. Figure 3.2 helps better explain the distinctions between them. Where the respective fields of 'instrumental rationality', 'practical rationality' (comprising all the other motivations), and 'economic matter' (economy in the broad sense) intersect, the following areas emerge:

1   Maximizing instrumental rationality applied to non-economic realities: though extensively present in economic journals, this is not, strictly speaking, economics, but a reductive analysis of human realities, because the subject matter is not an economic phenomenon.
2   Maximizing instrumental rationality applied to economic realities: it is Mill's a priori political economy and Menger's exact orientation of economic theory plus inductive sources of evidence, or Neville Keynes' positive economics.
3   Non-maximizing instrumental rationality applied to economic realities: it is part of Mill's allowing no economic motivations, or Menger's empirical realist orientation of economic theory.
4   Practical rationality applied to economic realities: it has three dimensions. First, we can only try to *understand* what the logic guiding the decision about ends is, that is what are the practical reasons in deciding about the ends: this is part of economic theory, a theoretical approach to a practical subject. Second, we can apply practical reason to *decide* what ends we are going to seek. This is normative economics. Third, we can use practical reason – together with economic theory – to *design* economic policies and to *implement* them. This is the art of economics or applied economics.
5   Non-maximizing instrumental rationality applied to non-economic realities: technique.
6   Practical rationality applied to non-economic realities: ethics, politics, and other practical sciences.

Given these areas, we can also analyse the distinction among economic sciences:

1   Maximizing instrumental rationality applied to economic realities (area 2) deals with the *economy in its restricted literal sense* (and also with the

economy in the broad sense given that the former is a subset of the latter).
It is *positive economics* or part of *economic theory*: it is abstract Millian or
Neville Keynes' positive political economy.

2   Non-maximizing instrumental rationality and Practical rationality applied
to economic realities in a broad sense comprise (areas 3 and 4):

- Mill allowing no economic motivations, or Menger's empirical realist
  orientation of economic theory. Menger's *Verständnis* or Sidgwick
  trying to *understand* other motives than economic motives. Part of economic theory;
- Mill's Teleology or normative economics;
- the art of economics or applied economics.

All of them need to use economic history and statistics.

On the maximizing principle

I have warned how the average economist would commonly react to the argument sustaining the literal broad notion of the economic, that is that there are
not only economic (in the restricted sense) but also non-economic motives
behind economic phenomena. The economic motive or economic principle is
'max U', that is, instrumental maximizing rationality applied to the selection of
ends in order to maximize the achievement of preferences. In agreement with
Weber, I believe that non-economic motives are other value-driven (for example,
altruism or honesty), affective (subjective desires), or sociological motives (we
have always done it this way, or everybody does it). The standard economist
would promptly reply that you can consider all these supposedly non-economic
motives as preferences, include them in a utility function and maximize it.

Which is the apparent mistake or the wrong step in economists' reasoning?
I hold that the confusion stems from equating two different notions of maximization: maximization as a 'metaphysical principle' and maximization as an
'empirical principle'. Indeed, as Bruce Caldwell (1983: 827) points out, there is
an ambiguity in economists' conceptions of maximization. A notion of maximization as a 'metaphysical' principle – universally applicable to every human
action – illegitimately and quite unconsciously transfers its universality to an
also legitimate notion of maximization as an 'empirical' principle – and is thus
falsifiable. (Here I am using the terms 'empirical' and 'metaphysical' in the sense
of propositions that are or not falsifiable respectively.) Let me shed light on
these two versions of maximization.

The first version, that is maximization as a metaphysical principle, identifies maximizing with rationality and rationality with acting intentionally.
This intention can be even against the agent's usual preferences, including
acts performed under impetuosity or akratic behaviour – weakness of will. As
Geoffrey Hodgson (forthcoming) asserts, 'apparent preference inconsistency
can be explained away by the fact that the apparently inconsistent choices are

always made at different times and in (at least slightly) different circumstances'. For example, von Mises ([1949] 1998: 39 and 241ff.) sees maximization and the concept of rationality as a general principle, the universal principle of all purposive action. In fact, he argues in *Epistemological Problems of Economics* ([1933] 1960), referring to Weber's classification of motives for social action, that all these motives are comprised in the instrumental rationality motive and can be maximized. Mises is changing Weber's underlying concept of the maximizing principle, which is empirical, transforming it into a metaphysical principle ([1933] 1960: 83–85). Becker affirms that his 'analysis assumes that individuals maximize welfare *as they conceive it*, whether they be selfish, altruistic, loyal, spiteful, or masochistic' (1993: 386; italics in the original). If to maximize means to be rational and to be rational means to have an end, it is clear that all human actions are intentional, rational, and maximizing. If we agree with this meaning of maximization, the principle is completely legitimate – but useless. This conception is discussed in the controversy between Boland (1981 and 1983) and Caldwell (1983). If you consider all motives behind actions as preferences, all actions – except actions performed under ignorance or mistake – will be maximized.

The second version is maximization as an empirical principle. This is present, for example, in von Neumann and Morgenstern (1944, as explained by Strotz 1953: 390, 393 and 397), in Savage ([1954] 1972, p. 97), and in Friedman and Savage (1948: 298 and 1952, 463 and 473). Although Savage ([1954] 1972: 20, 97) had interpreted maximization, as Sugden (1991: 757) remarks, empirically and normatively, his papers with Friedman slide towards the empirical interpretation, an explanation of real facts, admittedly imperfect, but useful as a heuristic device. To be an empirical principle means that not every human action is necessarily a maximizing action, and that there are criteria to establish if they are or not in each case. For example, a firm may or may not maximize benefits just as an individual may or may not maximize the use of his income. We may check whether they do or not, whether they behave 'rationally' or not, under a defined notion of economic rationality. Raymond Boudon's remarks are clarifying. He explains that rational choice theory uses the maximizing principle as the difference between empirically verifiable benefits and costs: 'when they [sociologists adopting the neoclassical economics' theory of rationality] speak of the Rational-Choice-Model (RCT), they mean that human action should be analysed as guided by the principle of maximizing the difference between benefits and costs' (1998: 177). He states that it should 'be recognized that social actors can have strong reasons to endorse normative beliefs, without these reasons being of cost-benefit type, and more generally, without these reasons being of the consequential type' (1998: 188).

Harvey Leibenstein (1982: 461), while defending the empirical version of maximization, calls the metaphysical principle 'tautological' because it does not make room for falsification. Leibenstein adds that this theory of maximization is mathematics, not economics, and that the postulate of universal maximizing behaviour by economic agents should be replaced by the idea of a relative response to the size of the motivation (1982: 464). I think that the following passage clarifies his position:

> The problem may be partially semantic. A lot depends on how we inter-
> pret the word utility. One can interpret utility in such a way so that all
> behavior is subsumed under some version of utility maximization. But this
> would rob the concepts of utility and maximization of real meaning. If we
> are presumed to do something which has some degree of specificity, then
> there must be something else for which it can be said we are not feeling
> the criteria of the first type of action. In other words, the idea of utility
> maximization must contain the possibility of choice under which utility is
> not maximized.
>
> (1976: 8; see also 1981 and 1982)

This position – maximization as an empirical principle – leaves space open for economic actions that are not efficient. Maximization as an empirical principle will not often adequately explain the analysed situation, but it can be useful as a normative instrument.

Let me clarify this with an example. The empirical principle of maximiza-tion will define a set of criteria to assess whether we are buying the right car: for example, price and financial conditions of the deal, servicing costs, cost of insurance and taxes, gasoline consumption, and so on. These variables will depend on the capacity needed. These economically measurable variables can be used to determine the most efficient economic transaction. In this way, we would be acting according to the restricted notion of the economy. However, men frequently like cars for other motives. We may choose – and it is often the case – to buy a car that is not economically efficient. The motives underlying this inefficient deal may be brand loyalty, social status, external appearance of the vehicle, or a specific family taste in cars. These are motives that may be behind the broad notion of the economy and falsify the maximizing empirical principle. We can set these new variables as preferences, but there will be two problems: first, we do not have elements to measure and commensurate these incommensurable variables, and second, if we manage to do it in some way, we will always do an efficient deal, and this conclusion is not useful.

Regardless of the aforementioned, both different notions, that is maximiza-tion as metaphysical principle and as an empirical principle, might coexist. Still, they must be characterized in some way, because otherwise, they might be wrongly equated. The problem is that for the former – the metaphysical prin-ciple – maximizing is equivalent to rationality, whereas in standard economics rationality, maximization is equivalent to constrained optimization – the empir-ical principle (see Drakopoulos 1991: 164). Therefore, economists must strive to free themselves from committing an ambiguity fallacy: to attribute to one version the characteristics of the other.

This potential confusion can be explained. Since David Hume, practical rationality has been reduced to instrumental rationality (see Zafirovski 2003,

Boudon 2004: 57) and, as mentioned in Chapter 1, there is a *psychological* tendency to consider instrumental rationality as maximization (Boudon 2004: 47). Then, the whole logic of human action tends to gravitate towards a specific form of rationality, that is instrumental maximizing rationality, and to consider it metaphysical and infallible. As Hollis and Sugden (1993: 5) assert, after Hume 'every problem of rational choice becomes an exercise in maximisation'. Maximization, however, does not exhaust all possibilities of human actions or economic actions.

Additionally, there is another reason that induces economists to use the maximizing metaphysical principle as if it were empirical. Once the decision is made on certain ends, it is possible to express it in terms of maximization. We can account for the decision calculating a ratio of substitution of the ends concerned. David Wiggins notes this, but he also warns that this claim is nearly vacuous because 'it does not represent a falsifiable claim about the agent's springs of action' (2002: 371). Why is it unfalsifiable? Because this notion of maximization is so wide that it is equivalent to saying that all actions have a reason, which is nearly a truism. This is different from what ordinary language means by to 'maximize' (cf. Wiggins 2002: 372). Wiggins relentlessly points out that, for him, the utility theory is not a sketch but a caricature of human decisions and actions (cf. 2002: 390). Nevertheless, if we accept a change of vocabulary, and use maximization as 'having a reason for', all we have is an a posteriori theory, but not a guide for action concerning ends. A person can have a set of preferences and fail to maximize his/her resources in order to attain these preferences. However, when we set him/her aside and look at the situation, we may interpret that he/she had a different set of preferences that he/she has maximized. If we ask him/her, he/she will tell us that we are wrong. Let him/her, not the economists, decide about his/her preferences. This is Sen's argument in his famous article 'Rational Fools' (1977). Henry Richardson explains the problem in this way:

> [P]reference-based is not a form of commensurability useful in making choices but rather a way of representing choices once made. Saving the action-guiding role of the formalistic model by supposing some finally complete articulation of reasons, of dimensions of value or goodness, and of discriminations therein, is like telling Seurat that in order to place all the figures in his masterly afternoon scene of the Grande Jatte, all he has to do is first determine where to put all the points of paint on the canvas. The solution may be logically coherent, but it is totally impracticable, and puts the cart before the horse. If our practical knowledge were perfect, we would already know what to do.
>
> (1997: 102)

This is the reason why Schoemaker (1982: 539–540, 554) qualifies the maximizing metaphysical principle as *postdictive*, in order to stress its ex-post character. Economics becomes an irrelevant theory ('trivial', says Schoemaker 1982: 540), useless for making real decisions, as also John Rawls (1971: 558) asserts. That is, a posteriori, we can describe any situation as a maximizing metaphysical situation. However, this description may be mistaken because it might not correspond to the agent's actual preferences. As Wiggins also states, 'it does not give any empirical content to the idea of maximizing anything' (2002: 371). Maximization as a metaphysical principle does not provide the way to uncover the deceit because it does not admit falsification. It is similar to the story told by Daniel Bell (referred to by Leibenstein): a general visiting Russia was impressed by the marksmanship displayed on various walls. In every instance, there was a bullet hole through the centre of the bullseye. When the general met the marksman and asked how he came to have such a good aim, he answered: 'Oh, Excellency, it's not so hard. First I shoot, and then I paint the bull's-eye' (1982: 460). In short, maximization as a metaphysical principle may work as an ex-post description, but we do not know if it is an accurate explanation and, hence, in a best-case scenario, it would only be an ex-post explanation. As Hollis and Sugden assert,

> A person whose decisions are consistent in Savage's sense acts *as if* making complicated utilitarian calculations, using measures of utility and probability to work out the expected utility of each of the acts amongst which he has to choose. But these utility and probability measures do not explain or justify choices.
>
> (1993: 7; italics in the original)

Or as Malte Dold and Mario Rizzo (2019: 9) express this:

> Explanation of decision-making by constrained maximization of a stable utility function is a metaphor and not a literal truth about how decisions are made. The preferences whose satisfaction are maximized do not exist prior to the actual choice. The preferences (and constraints) are synchronic constructs of the economist. They rationalize actual choices ex post. Thus, in principle, there is no anticipation of the individual's choice on the basis of pre-existing preferences.

In sum, maximizing is an empirical principle that only occasionally serves as a good explanation for a specific conduct. To equate maximization to rationality and intentionality might be a philosophical but not an economic principle, and it goes against the common usage of language.

This discussion has been resumed by Daniel Hausman in his 2012 book *Preference, Value, Choice, and Welfare*. Though they make up only a section of a chapter, I believe the ideas upheld here are crucial. I will need to come back to them in Chapter 7.

Conclusion

Economics' main objective is to deal with real economic problems. This is why we need a whole set of economic sciences. We need history and statistics

as the *materia prima* of all economic sciences. We need positive economics to
identify specific economic causes. We need to consider other causes of economic phenomena. We need normative economics to fix our economic ideals,
and we need the art of economics to achieve them. These sciences have their
corresponding tasks, aims and methods:

- statistics and economic history provide information; they *describe* and provide elaborated information needed by economic theory;
- economic theory *explains* and *understands*. It explains taking into account
economic causes (positive economics) and non-economic causes, and
understands reasons or final causes;
- normative economics *prescribes* ideals or ends;
- the art of economics or applied economics *designs* policies to achieve those
ideals through means and *implements* them.

In the next chapters, I will develop the nature, aims, relations, and method of
these economic sciences and their roles. We will see that, though separable, they
are closely interrelated, given, as John Gerring expresses it, 'the *inextricability* of
theory, values, and evidence' (2010: 90; italics in the original).

Notes

1 (Essay V of his *Essays on Some Unsettled Questions of Political Economy* (London: Parker,
  1844), published in the *London and Westminster Review* in 1836, and a second edition
  reprinted in 1874 with minor changes).
2 I used the 1844 version of the Essay published in volume 4 of the *Collected Works
  of John Stuart Mill*, University of Toronto Press, 1967 (reprinted by Liberty Fund,
  2006), and the 1882 publication by Harper & Brothers of the eighth edition of the
  System of Logic (Longmans, 1872), which is the most frequently consulted because
  it is the last version corrected by Mill. I took the information about the previous
  publication of the Essay from the introduction to it on p. 309.
3 On 'idealization', see Ernan McMullin 1985.
4 That is, in contemporary terms, he is 'externalist' in relation to the definition of the
  objects of desire. There are reasons that are independent and previous to desires. See,
  for example, John Searle 2001.
5 For a summary appraisal of this point, see for example the note of Gilles Campagnolo
  in Menger 2011: 138.
6 I will not delve here into the difficult topic of the position of the 'German Historical
  School'. I think that Schumpeter's understanding of the *Methodenstreit* ([1954]
  2006: Part 4, chapter 4) was balanced, and that Dimitris Milonakis and Ben Fine
  (2009: chapter 5, 6.3 and 13.2) are doing a good job of their analysis of the Historical
  School.
7 In his memoir of Marshall, Maynard Keynes recounts that he met Wagner at
  Marshall's house (Keynes 1934: 357).
8 Additionally, today, positive economics has both a descriptive and an explaining role
  (as considered by Neville Keynes), but it is usually used to try to predict and prescribe.

If you want to maximize your utility or your financial earnings, for example, you should buy this portfolio of goods or assets. It is normative not about the ends, but about the best way to attain ends. For Neville Keynes, this role would be included in the art of economics.

9   This and the following two sections partially draw on R. Crespo 2013a and 2013b.
10   He affirms that he uses the term 'economics' in the second sense. It will consequently be useful to take his vision into account in the chapter on positive economics.

References

Ackrill, J. L. (1981). *Aristotle the Philosopher*. Oxford: Clarendon Press.

Aquinas, T. (1949). *De Veritate*, in *Quaestiones Disputatae I*. Torino-Rome: Marietti.

Aquinas, T. (1950). *Summa Theologiae*. Pars Prima et Prima Secundae. Torino-Rome: Marietti. English translation: www.newadvent.org/summa/1014.htm#article16.

Aristotle (1984). *The Complete Works of Aristotle*, edited by Jonathan Barnes. Princeton: Princeton University Press.

Backhouse, R. E. and S. Medema (2009). 'Retrospectives: On the Definition of Economics', *Journal of Economic Perspectives*, 23/1: 221–233.

Becker, G. (1976). *The Economic Approach to Human Behavior*. Chicago: Chicago University Press.

Becker, G. (1993). 'Nobel Lecture: The Economic Way of Looking at Behavior'. *Journal of Political Economy*, 101/3: 385–409.

Boland, L. (1981). 'On the Futility of Criticizing the Neoclassical Maximization Hypothesis'. *American Economic Review*, 71/5: 1031–1036.

Boland, L. (1983). 'The Neoclassical Maximization Hypothesis: Reply'. *American Economic Review*, 73/4: 828–830.

Boudon, R. (2004). 'Théorie du choix rationnel, théorie de la rationalité limitée ou individualisme méthodologique: que choisir?'. *Journal des Economistes et des Etudes Humaines*, 14/1: 45–62.

Boudon, R. (1998). 'Social Mechanisms without Black Boxes'. In: P. Hedström and R. Swedberg (eds.), *Social Mechanisms. An Analytical Approach to Social Theory*. Cambridge: Cambridge University Press, pp. 172–203.

Buchanan, J. M. (1987). Economics. Between Predictive Science and Moral Philosophy. College Station: Texas A&M University Press.

Caldwell, B. J. (1983). 'The Neoclassical Maximization Hypothesis: Comment'. *American Economic Review*, 73/4: 824–827.

Coase, R. (1975). 'Marshall on Method'. *Journal of Law and Economics*, 18/1: 25–31.

Coase, R. (1978). 'Economics and Contiguous Disciplines'. *Journal of Legal Studies*, 7/2: 201–211.

Colander, D. (1992). 'Retrospectives: The Lost Art of Economics'. *Journal of Economic Perspectives*, 6/3: 191–198.

Crespo, R. F. (2013a). *Philosophy of the Economy. An Aristotelian Approach*. Dordrecht: Springer.

Crespo, R. F. (2013b). 'Two Conceptions of Economics and Maximisation'. *Cambridge Journal of Economics*, 37/4: 759–774.

Davis, J. B. (2003). *The Theory of Individual in Economics*. London: Routledge.

Dold, M. F. and M. J. Rizzo (2019). 'Old Chicago against Static Welfare Economics' (April 3). *Journal of Legal Studies* (forthcoming). Available at SSRN: https://ssrn.com/abstract=3411308. Accessed 20 June 2019.

Drakopoulos, S. A. (1991). *Values and Economic Theory. The Case of Hedonism.* Avebury: Aldershot.

Ebeling, R. M. (1990). 'What Is a Price? Explanation and Understanding'. In: D. Lavoie (ed.), *Economics and Hermeneutics.* London and New York: Routledge, pp. 177–194.

Fraser, L. M. (1937). *Economic Thought and Language.* London: A & C Black.

Friedman, M. and L. J. Savage (1948). 'The Utility Analysis of Choices Involving Risk'. *Journal of Political Economy*, 56/4: 279–304.

Friedman, M. and L. J. Savage (1952). 'The Expected-Utility Hypothesis and the Measurability of Utility'. *Journal of Political Economy*, 60/6: 463–463.

Gerring, J. (2010). 'Review of Julian Reiss's *Error in Economics: Towards a More Evidence-Based Methodology.* London: Routledge, 2007, 272pp'. *Erasmus Journal for Philosophy and Economics*, 3/1: 89–92.

Hausman, D. M. (2012). *Preference, Value, Choice, and Welfare.* Cambridge: Cambridge University Press.

Hirschman, A. O. (2013). 'Political Economics and Possibilism'. In: Albert O. Hirschman, *The Essential Hirschman*, edited and with an introduction by Jeremy Adelman. Afterword by Emma Rothschild and Amartya Sen. Princeton and Oxford: Princeton University Press, pp. 1–34.

Hodgson, G. M. (forthcoming). 'Are Rumours of the Death of Max U Exaggerated?' In: *Is There a Future for Heterodox Economics?* Cheltenham: Edward Elgar.

Hollis, M. and R. Sugden (1993). 'Rationality in Action'. *Mind*, NS, 102/405: 1–35.

Ioannides, S. and K. Nielsen (2007). 'Economics and the Social Sciences: Synergies and Trade-Offs'. In: I. Starvos and K. Nielsen (eds.), *Economics and the Social Sciences. Boundaries, Interaction and Integration.* Cheltenham and Northampton: Edward Elgar, pp. 7–12.

Keynes, J. M. (1934). 'Alfred Marshall, 1842–1924'. *Economic Journal*, 34/135: 311–372.

Keynes, J. N. ([1890] 1955). *The Scope and Method of Political Economy.* Fourth Edition. New York: Kelley and Millman.

Kirzner, I. M. ([1960] 1976). *The Economic Point of View.* Kansas City (KS): Sheed and Ward.

Leibenstein, H. (1976). *Beyond Economic Man.* Cambridge (MA): Harvard University Press.

Leibenstein, H. (1981). 'Microeconomics and X-Efficiency Theory: If there Is No Crisis, There Ought To Be'. In: D. Bell and I. Kristol (eds.), *The Crisis in the Economic Theory.* New York: Basic Books, pp. 97–110.

Leibenstein, H. (1982). 'On Bull's-Eye: Painting Economics'. *Journal of Post-Keynesian Economics*, 4/3: 460–465.

Madison, R. D. (2011). *First Philosophy: Aristotle's Concept of Metaphysics*, ProQuest, UMI Dissertation Publishing (3 September 2011).

Mäki, U. (2002). 'The Dismal Queen of the Social Sciences'. In: U. Mäki (ed.), *Fact and Fiction in Economics. Models, Realism and Social Construction.* Cambridge: Cambridge University Press, pp. 3–32.

Marshall, A. ([1890–1920] 1962). *Principles of Economics* (Eighth Edition, 1920). London: Macmillan.

McMullin, E. (1985). 'Galilean Idealization'. *Studies in History and Philosophy of Sciences*, 16/3: 247–273.

Medema, S. G. (2018). 'Between LSE and Cambridge: Accounting for Ronald Coase's Fascination with Alfred Marshall', https://papers.ssrn.com/sol3/papers.cfm?abstract_id=3250358. Accessed 11 November 2018.

Menger, C. ([1883] 1985). *Investigations into the Method of the Social Sciences with Special Reference to Economics*, Ed. Louis Schneider, Transl. Francis J. Nock. New York and London: New York University Press (*Untersuchungen über die Methode der Socialwissenschaften und der Politischen Oekonomie insbesondere*, Ducker & Humblot, Leipzig).

Menger, C. ([1883] 2011). *Recherches sur la méthode dans les sciences sociales et en économie politique en particulier* (trans. Gilles Campagnolo). Paris: Éditions EHESS.

Menger, C. (1889). 'Grundzüge einer Klassifikation der Wirtschaftswissenschaften'. *Jahrbücher für Nationalökonomie und Statistik*, ed. J. Conrad, New Series, Jena: Gustav Fisher, XIX: 465–496.

Menger, C. (1960). 'Toward a Systematic Classification of Economic Sciences'. In: Louise Sommer (transl. and ed.), *Essays in European Economic Thought*. Princeton: D. van Nostrand, pp. 1–38.

Mill, J. S. ([1844] 2006). *Essays on Some Unsettled Questions of Political Economy* (Essay V: 'On the Definition of Political Economy; and on the Method of Investigation Proper to It'). In *Collected Works of John Stuart Mill*, vol. 4. Indianapolis: Liberty Fund.

Mill, J. S. (1882). *A System of Logic, Ratiocinative and Inductive*. Eighth Edition. New York: Harper & Brothers.

Milonakis, D. and B. Fine (2009). *From Political Economy to Economics*. London: Routledge.

Mireles Flores, L. (2016). *Economic Science for Use: Causality and Evidence in Policy Making*. Doctoral thesis, Erasmus University, Rotterdam.

Mises, L. v. [1933] 1960. *Epistemological Problems of Economics*. Princeton: D. van Nostrand (*Grundprobleme der Nationalökonomie*. Jena: Gustav Fisher).

Mises, L. v. [1949] 1998. *Human Action. A Treatise on Economics*. Auburn (AL): Ludwig von Mises Institute (The Scholar's Edition).

Phelps Brown, E. H. (1972). 'The Underdevelopment of Economics'. *Economic Journal*, 82/325: 1–10.

Polanyi, K. (1971). 'Aristotle Discovers Economy'. In: George Dalton (ed.), *Primitive, Archaic, and Modern Economies. Essays of Karl Polanyi*. Boston: Beacon Press, 78–115.

Rawls, J. (1971). *A Theory of Justice*. Cambridge (MA): Belknap Press of Harvard University Press.

Richardson, H. (1997). *Practical Reasoning about Final Ends*. Cambridge: Cambridge University Press.

Robbins, L. C. (1935). *Essay on the Nature and Significance of Economic Science*. Second Edition. London: Macmillan.

Rodrik, D. (2015). *Economic Rules*. Oxford: Oxford University Press.

Samuelson, P. A. (1938). 'A Note on the Pure Theory of Consumer's Behaviour'. *Economica*, 5/17: 61–71.

Samuelson, P. A. (1948). 'Consumption Theory in Terms of Revealed Preference'. *Economica*, 15/60: 243–253.

Savage, L. J. ([1954] 1972). *The Foundation of Statistics*. New York: Dover.

Schoemaker, P. J. H. (1982). 'The Expected Utility Model: Its Variants, Purposes and Limitations'. *Journal of Economic Literature*, 20/2: 529–563.

Schumpeter, J. A. ([1954] 2006). *History of Economic Analysis*. London: Routledge e-edition.

Scoon, R. (1943). 'Professor Robbins' Definition of Economics'. *Journal of Political Economy*, 51/4: 310–320.

Searle, J. R. (2001). *Rationality in Action*. Cambridge (MA) and London: MIT Press.

Sen, A. (1977). 'Rational Fools: A Critique of the Behavioral Foundations of Economic Theory'. *Philosophy and Public Affairs*, 6: 317–344.

Sidgwick, H. (1887). *The Principles of Political Economy*. Second Edition. London: Macmillan.

Smith, A. ([1776] 1828). *Inquiry into the Nature and Causes of the Wealth of Nations*. Book IV, Introduction, J. R. McColluch. Edinburgh, Printed for A. Black and W. Tait, 1828.

Strotz, R. H. (1953). 'Cardinal Utility'. *American Economic Review*, 43/2: 384–397.

Sugden, R. (1991). 'Rational Choice: A Survey of Contributions from Economics and Philosophy'. *Economic Journal*, 101/407: 751–778.

Van Laer, H. (1956). *The Philosophy of Science*. Pittsburgh: Duquesne University and Louvain: Editions E. Nauwelaerts.

Von Neumann, J. and O. Morgenstern (1944). *Theory of Games and Economic Behavior*. Princeton: Princeton University Press.

Wagner, A. (1886). 'Wagner on the Present State of Political Economy'. *Quarterly Journal of Economics*, 1/1: 113–133.

Weber, M. ([1922] 1978). *Economy and Society*. edited by G. Roth and C. Wittich. Berkeley and Los Angeles: University of California Press (*Wirtschaft und Gesellschaft*, 1922).

Wiggins, D. (2002). *Needs, Values, Truth*. Third Edition. Amended. Oxford and New York: Oxford University Press.

Zafirovski, M. (2003). 'Human Rational Behavior and Economic Rationality'. *Electronic Journal of Sociology*, 11–13: www.sociology.org/content/vol7.2/02_zafirovski.html. Accessed 8 February 2013.

4 Empirical data, measurement, and statistics

The first set of 'economic sciences' considered by Menger is the 'historical sciences of economics', which comprise statistics and economic history ([1883] 1985: Appendix 4, and 1960: passim). They provide elements needed by economic theory and the rest of economic sciences. In the previous chapter, I have adopted them as the first of the economic sciences.

In the concluding section of the previous chapter, I emphasized the close link that exists among the different economic sciences. I affirmed that statistics and economic history describe facts, thus providing information to economic theory. However, this information is not just any information. It has to be relevant information and this entails that facts are conceptually related to a theory.[1] As Reiss (2008: xix) remarks, in the context of a specific inquiry, we cannot neatly distinguish between evidence and theory.

We can consider a progressive degree of connection between data and theory: from almost pure data to the design of experiments and the discernment of relevant evidence, which typically implies the use of econometric tools. That is, the boundaries between describing and explaining, between providing useful information and economic theory, are not clear but blurry. Let us recall, as mentioned in the previous chapter that, for example, for Menger, although featuring different perspectives of analysis (formal object), the exact and the empirical realistic orientation of theoretical economics usually work together ([1883] 1985: 67). In this chapter I will focus on measurement and index building – which constitute one statistical method – and I will address topics more closely related to theory in the next chapters. It will be clear that not only theory but also values are intermingled in data analysis. This fact also implies the necessary presence of experts in data selection and elaboration. However, the expert will play a crucial role not only in this step but also in the following steps –which I will consider in the next chapters – as well as in putting together the necessary tools to offer adequate evidence. Therefore, I will leave for later (Chapter 10) a review of the ideas about expertise and my view on it.

In the chapter, I will first define some concepts related to the concerned topic: empirical data, phenomena, evidence, statistics, probability, and measurement. Second, I will examine the scope and limits of a necessary statistical tool, measurement. Third, I will describe the difficulties involved in index building, which is a useful statistical device. Finally, I will analyse the theoretical background and value assumptions implicit in building the Human Development Index, which will be offered as an example.

Some philosophical definitions

The first step in this chapter is to define the relevant concepts related to the first set of disciplines: statistics, and economic history.[2] The elements provided by these sciences are used in two ways. First, theory is not constructed ex nihilo. There are always, even in the most theoretical and abstract positions, empirical elements nourishing it. History is or should be taken into account because it is *magistra vitae*, that is life's teacher. This is why it is relevant for economic studies to learn economic history. Second, all economic theories need empirical testing. Throughout the history of the development of ideas on methodology, there were only a few thinkers who sustain an extreme apriorist position. There are only a few incontrovertible economic principles that are abstract and general. That is, empirical elements intervene both in inductive inferences and in testing hypotheses.

The most 'primitive' empirical elements are empirical data, observational or experimental, that are facts from which we can draw inferences. Data, however, though 'primitive', are not purely given, because they are searched through senses, instruments or experiments and are consequently somehow conditioned by them. Senses, instruments or experiments capture data, but these data are insignificant until we conceptualize them. There is always at least a 'pre-theoretical' framework behind them. We look for data through observation or experiments with the purpose of building or verifying hypotheses. There is an observer or experimenter that looks for data, gathers them or designs experiments, and has adequate skills to identify data relevant to the subject being investigated and to the aim of the investigation. Empirical data enable inductive inferences, providing (or not) evidence about scientific hypotheses. Let us expand this explanation.

It may prove convenient to clarify the meaning of two concepts: phenomena and evidence. For James Bogen and James Woodward (see Bogen and Woodward 1988 and Woodward 1989: 393), as already advanced in Chapter 1 (endnote 3), phenomena are stable and general features of the world that are beyond data, and that can be explained and predicted by general theories. Theories, for them, are not about data, but about phenomena. Phenomena, explains Bogen (2009), are processes, causal factors, effects, facts, regularities, and other pieces of ontological furniture, often unobservable. This implies that knowledge goes beyond mere observation; mere observation only helps us arrive at the knowledge of those kinds of phenomena. Inferring phenomena involves data elaboration. In agreement with Bogen and Woodward (1988), and quoting them, Nancy Cartwright (1989: 169) states that 'nature is full, not only of data, but of phenomena as well'. Julian Reiss states about phenomena (2014: 134):

Phenomena, that is, objects and events of scientific interest in the form in which they appear to us, are […] co-produced by reality and the idiosyncrasies of our particular points of view such as details of our perceptual apparatus, expectations formed by upbringing and culture, local and historical details of the conditions under which the observation was made and so on.

That is, not only theoretical frames but also the observer's idiosyncratic characteristics affect data.

Reiss (2015: 33ff.) considers two notions of evidence: 'supporting evidence' – a sign of the truth of a hypothesis –, and 'warranting evidence' – criteria defining the amount and kind of evidence that we need to warrant the hypothesis to a certain degree. Here again, the expert's skill is relevant. Concerning experiments, Martin Deutsch states: 'the decisive intuition of the experimenter […] is really the ability to *recognize relevance* in the evidence present by the experiment' (1959: 102; italics in the original).

Induction is the process of inferring generalizations from empirical data. There are different degrees of certainty in these generalizations, depending on the nature of the matter generalized. There are almost necessary matters, such as the gravitational force or the quantitative equation of money, and other more or less contingent matters such as weather, tides, or future annual inflation. We can infer almost universal laws about necessary matters, as the gravitational law, and we can consequently calculate the speed of a falling ball with certainty. However, we can only induce more or less limited generalizations about contingent matters. Probability is an instrument that expresses the degree of contingency of inductive inferences, from 1 (certainty) to 0 (complete uncertainty).

There are two types of induction, essential induction about necessary maters and enumerative or 'Baconian' induction about contingent matters.[3] When Mill defines Political Economy or Menger speaks about the exact orientation of theoretical research, they are looking for essential inductions. However, they both recognize the limited abstract character of these branches of knowledge, given the contingent character of their subject. The reason for this is obvious. The human realm is particularly contingent. A multiplicity of motives drives human actions: 'each person is a world of its own', with its proper identity, physical and social environment, and characteristics. In addition, humans are free. Personal and social routines and uses instil stability and predictability. However, surprises are always around the corner.

Consequently, all inductive devices concerning contingent matters, that is to say, most human matters, are imperfect. This does not mean that we will never be able to move close to the truth about economic generalizations. However, they will always remain generalizations. We should strive to achieve a progressively better knowledge of reality. This can be facilitated by combining different inductive tools and circumscribing the analysis to particular contexts or problems where we have a satisfactory knowledge of the relevant variables.

Statistics is a systematic study of empirical data. In its first step, it collects them. Then it conceptualizes, classifies, and works on them. We can distinguish a 'descriptive statistics' and an 'analytical statistics'. That is, statistics does not limit itself to gathering data but it also detects and classifies phenomena and provides evidence. Statistics usually works with quantitative characteristics of data. The way of determining these quantitative properties of facts is measurement, according to a measurement theory. Therefore, behind measures there are theoretical concepts and practical decisions depending on the measurement theory adopted, and the criteria and skills of the institution or person that measures. The quantitative characteristics measured and used by statistics may stem from direct or indirect observation or from experiments.

Coming back to Menger, for him, statistical and historical sciences deal with the individual, which is not, he clarifies, the singular, but the concrete: for example, a definite nation or a concrete economy ([1883] 1985: 37 nt. 3). Economic history is not a mere compilation of information, but a complete study that provides a consistent picture of the facts under study.[4] The same applies to statistics. Menger states: 'Uncritical compilations, or merely superficial arrangements of statistical material lacking higher unity, do not come within the domain of scientific description' ([1883] 1985: 38 nt. 7). He adds:

'Statistics as a science' can never be merely a method. What is commonly called '*the theory of statistics*' is usually by its nature the *methodology* (so-called theory of cognition!) of this science. More correctly only the results of a truly *theoretical* consideration of statistical material, the *laws* of the co-existence and the succession of social phenomena, should be designated as *theoretical*-statistical knowledge and the totality of these should be designated as theoretical statistics.

([1883] 1985: 38 nt. 7; italics in the original)

Neville Keynes discusses if statistics is a science, a method or an instrument of scientific inquiry. He supports the first view. However, he states:

the statistician rightly, and even necessarily, performs the function of interpreting results. [...] He applies his statistics [...] within the domain of some particular science; and it may be added that unless he has an adequate knowledge of that science, not only will he probably go astray in his interpretation, but the very facts themselves are not likely to be suitably selected or arranged.

([1890] 1955: 337)

For Neville Keynes, statistics not only has a descriptive role, but it also suggests empirical laws, it checks deductive results and elucidates and interprets particular phenomena. He devotes 20 pages to explaining the precautions that should be taken into account when using statistics in economics ([1890] 1955: 351–370). That is, many years before the emergence of econometrics, both Menger and

Neville Keynes had entertained some ideas and harboured worries that would be tackled by this discipline: they perceived the necessary link between statistics and economic theory.

In this chapter, I will briefly revise measurement and indexes, which are sources of evidence, their strengths, and weaknesses. It will be clear that it is easier to obtain adequate data when we restrict the research to particular contexts than try to cover all phenomena; that there are theoretical and value commitments involved in these tasks; and that expert judgement will prove necessary to construct and appraise these data

On measurement[5]

Before dealing with measurement, it is pertinent to note that, given the nature of the economy, qualitative methods are not negligible: they are a way of discovering possible relevant variables influencing economic phenomena, especially non-economic variables. This is why, for example, qualitative psychological research may be highly useful to detect them. This is the right place to come back to economic history. Though 'history repeats itself', two historical events are never exactly identical. However, they show tendencies that may alert us about the variables, economic and non-economic, intervening in the event under study. In my personal experience, I have learned a lot from the world and domestic economic history. We can use analogy to infer which variables might be relevant to the present situation. History helps experts make forecasts.

Moreover, quantitative historical and current data are especially adequate to study economic phenomena because these phenomena have quantitative characteristics or are expressible in quantitative terms. In addition, quantitative information and methods allow rigorous work in an uncertain realm.

A first step in quantitative work is choosing and measuring the relevant variables. It is impossible to be theoretically neutral when choosing variables. The idea that theoretical notions influence the meaning and perception of scientific evidence has garnered widespread acceptance in the history and philosophy of science. As the first step in this influencing process, contemporary philosophers of science believe that there are no 'neutral' data because a scientific theory always stands 'behind' them, guiding the selection and the method used to analyse or measure data. Second, on a deeper level, a metaphysical preconception 'supports' scientific theory, influencing its perspective and formulation.

Concerning the presuppositions of underlying data, French scientist Pierre Duhem is one of the earliest thinkers to note the theoretical commitments behind empirical scientific investigation. In his view, the outcome of any experiment in physics is the result of observation interpreted on the basis of the theories held by the observer. When using their instruments, physicists, chemists, and physiologists 'implicitly admit the accuracy of the theories, justifying the use of these pieces of apparatus as well as of the theories giving meaning to the abstract ideas of temperature, pressure' ([1906, 1954] 1998: 259–260).

In *The Logic of Scientific Discovery* (1934), Karl Popper wrote that 'even for even singular statements, there are always *interpretations of the "facts" based on theories*' ([1959] 2000: 423, italics in the original). Popper holds that any descriptive statement contains universals, which are hypotheses or conjectures. Indeed, for him, 'universals cannot be correlated with any specific sense-experience' (id.: 95) – because 'they transcend experience' (id.: 424); these propositions cannot be verified. Then, a scientific community's convention is required to establish an empirical basis (id.: Chapter 5).

In 1958, Norwood Russell Hanson coined the expression *theory-ladenness* in his well-known statement: 'seeing is a "theory-laden" undertaking' (1958: 19). Thomas Kuhn and Paul Feyerabend also uphold this view. Despite the relevant differences in the notions supported by the authors mentioned above (see, e.g. Heildelberger 2003), a certain influence of theory in observations and experiments remains undisputed and clear. This influence may be conceptual or semantic – the meaning of observational terms is (partially) determined by theory – or 'perceptual', stemming from a theoretical cognitive bias of the observer. In 1951, Willard van Orman Quine challenged the analytic-synthetic distinction, arguing that empirical propositions cannot be isolated from their associated theories. More recently, empiricist Bas van Fraassen (1980: 81) has also supported theory-ladenness (see Monton and Mohler 2012). Jim Bogen explains that 'by Bayes' theorem, the conditional probability of the claim of interest will depend in part upon that claim's prior probability. [...] One's use of evidence to evaluate a theory depends in part upon one's theoretical commitments' (2013: 11).

Values are also present in the selection and appraisal of the amount of necessary evidence. Since Max Weber ([1904] 1949), there is no doubt about the presence of values in the choice of a scientific research problem (see Reiss and Sprenger 2014). Values are also present in the determination of the amount of evidence needed to infer a scientific conclusion. A classic paper on the role of values in science is Richard Rudner's (1953). His argument is based on the impossibility of a complete empirical induction. For Rudner, accepting or rejecting a hypothesis always implies a mistake risk, since it will never be completely verified, due to the intrinsic imperfection of inductive inferences. Scientists must judge how much evidence is enough to accept or reject a hypothesis, and this will depend on their assessment of the degree of ethical seriousness of the possible mistake, which entails a value judgement (1953: 2–3) – accepting or rejecting a hypothesis involves an ethical decision, because it may be wrong. I will come back to the topic of values in science in Chapter 8.

As mentioned, I will use a case to exemplify the presence of conceptual definitions and values in measurement. An extensive discussion has taken place regarding the relevance, construction, merits, and weaknesses of indexes such as the Human Development Index (HDI). Much of this discussion goes beyond the issue of technique and involves careful decisions such as, for example, what dimensions should be taken into account in evaluating development and what weights should be assigned to each of these dimensions. These decisions assume a definition of concepts such as development and a reflection upon its under-lying values. Here is an example of how facts and values are entangled in a measuring instrument such as an index.[6] However, let us first introduce some notions about measurement and then move on to the logic and usefulness of indexes.

Measuring involves describing reality through its quantitative proper-ties. When measuring, we assign numbers to the quantitative properties of an empirical system in such a way that a certain equivalence is established between this system and the numerical system. Numbers can also be assigned to qualita-tive properties, using conventions that allow them to be expressed numerically.

Why do we measure? As previously mentioned, human beings face a contin-gent, uncertain world, where different individuals with different idiosyncrasies and ends make present and future actions unpredictable. A widely regarded way to manage this unpredictable human future is to transform practical aspects of human or social action in a technical way. This has been an ancient desire of human beings. The earliest testimony to this ambition is expressed in Plato's dialogue *Protagoras*. He searches for a decision-making process that can save us from the contingency of 'luck'. Aristotle realized that customs and routines are means that help consolidate a predictable tendency (see, e.g. *Nicomachean Ethics* VII, 10, 1152a 26–27). Social pressure, laws, and organizations produce predictable behaviours. All these means are often gathered under the label of 'institutions' in a broad sense.

The alignment of qualitatively different motives or ends influencing human actions is facilitated by reducing their different qualities to a common quan-tity. Numbers are homogeneous and pragmatic. As Theodore Porter (1995: 86) asserts, 'numbers are the medium through which dissimilar desires, needs, and expectations are somehow made commensurable'. Expressing realities in numbers facilitates decisions. Porter (1995: 8) also states, 'quantification is a way of making decisions without seeming to decide'. How, then, could we reduce choice about qualitative features to a quantitative calculation? This is the question raised by Plato. When asked: which science will save us from the unpredictable contingency?, he replied: 'the science of measurement' (*Protagoras*, 356e). Human beings strive for security, and measurement helps encourage it. Martha Nussbaum accurately notes that:

> What we need to get a science of measurement going is, then, an end that is single (differing only quantitatively): specifiable in advance of the *techne* (external); and present in everything valuable in such a way that it may plausibly be held to be the source of its value.
>
> (2001: 179)

Institutions apply standards, procedures, and measurement devices. Once the crucial step of making conceptual and practical definitions is advanced, institutions establish technical processes to obtain them. Given that often these technical aspects impact on practical aspects, the process of designing technical procedures is not accomplished directly but requires further adjustments.

Table 4.1 Types of scales

Scale	Nominal	Ordinal	Ratio	Absolute
Description	Assigned codes	Attribute ranking	Ratio between magnitudes of the same type	Reason between a magnitude and its standard unit
Example	Man / Woman Black / White Married / Single Goodness / Beauty	Happiness / Goodness/ Satisfaction	Indexes (Price, Income, ...)	Length in Cm., Weight in Kg.

Let us return to conceptual notions about measurement. Measurement validity and reach depend on the existence and nature of the relationship between the numbers and that which is being measured (Michell 2005). A measurement is direct when it refers to actual quantities, and it is indirect if it denotes conventions for measuring qualitative elements. It is thus useful to understand the different types of possible 'fits' between means and realities being measured. Measurements assume that the rules expressed by certain types of scales are adequate for what is being measured. These scales are organized systematically in Table 4.1.

Nominal Scale: All realities examined are equal, and there is no inherent reason for precedence.

Ordinal Scale: There is only a possibility of establishing equality and a hierarchical order, but no cardinal quantitative difference.

Ratio and Absolute Scale: The cardinal differences correspond to real differences; these scales validly undertake numerical operations.

The different types of scales convey the nature of measured realities, which leads to different measurement forms. From right to left:

• first, quantitative realities, such as distance, weight and sales, can be measured by using cardinal numbers and conventionally defining a unit measurement – metres, kilos, units sold, or revenues. Mathematical operations can be performed with these units;

• second, we can measure the evolution of these real quantities using ratios between compared values – for example, the evolution in price levels. A standard value is defined for the base period – for example, 1960 price level = 100 – to turn the ratio into a cardinal scale. The resulting numbers become meaningful in relation to the base;

• third, the ordinal scale. Economics often works with this type of measurements. Numbers can be assigned to ordinal values – first, second, and so on;

• fourth, there are finally other characteristics of beings that cannot be put in an order from least to greatest or vice versa, that is cannot be ranked, such as gender, ethnicity, or marital status (see Boumans and Davis 2009: 152). These realities can be ranked on the basis of a specific criterion. This is the case with the dimensions considered by the HDI.

As a result, faced with numbers, we must determine what type of reality they belong to in order to understand their reach and limitations.

In considering these different kinds of scales, as Patrick Suppes (2000: 550) asserts, 'extensive quantity' – or cardinally measured quantity – allows for addition, while 'intensive quantity' – as expressed in ordinal scales – does not allow for addition. Thus, we need to transform ordinal scales into cardinal scales in order to obtain an operative tool. Cardinal scales are more operative than ordinal scales because they allow mathematical operations that can be performed with numbers. Cardinal scales make options commensurable. However, the ordinal-cardinal transformation implies conventional decisions as well as the ordering of nominal scales. Maynard Keynes explains this clearly:

> The objective quality measured may not, strictly speaking, possess numerical quantitativeness, although it has the properties necessary for measurement by means of correlation with numbers. The values which it can assume may be capable of being ranged in an order [...]; but it does not follow from this that there is any meaning in the assertion that one value is twice another value [...] It follows that equal intervals between the numbers which represent the ratios do not necessarily correspond to equal intervals between the qualities under measurement; for these numerical differences depend upon which convention of measurement we have selected.
>
> (1921: 46–47)

These difficulties may be instances of what Reiss (2008: 64) calls the 'fundamental problem of measurement': the value of a variable and the veridical character of the measurement procedure are both mutually dependent and there is no independent variable; ergo, we cannot solve the equation. In other words: in order to know the value of a variable, we need to know that the measurement procedure associated with it is veridical, but in order to be able to check whether the procedure is veridical, we need to know the value of the variable. Reiss (2008: Chapter 4) does a good job of analysing different positions about measurement and proposes a solution to the 'fundamental problem of measurement' based on Hasok Chang's 'coherentist theory of measurement' (Chang 2004).

For Marcel Boumans (2015: ix), the problem of measurement is more characteristic of 'field sciences' (sciences that are based on data that do not come from 'clean and controlled environments', which he calls 'laboratories'). He mainly deals with economics in that book (2015) and suggests that model building should consider all possible relevant variables in order to obtain reliable measurements. However, for the reasons already mentioned – that can be summarily expressed in the contingency of the human realm – these models will never be perfect, and we need expert skills to build them and to acquire a comprehensive understanding of economic phenomena (Boumans 2015: Chapters 3–5). Boumans also contemplates different methods to improve the accuracy of experts' work. Indexes exhibit these same difficulties. Let us now turn our attention to them

On indexes

Indexes are useful measurement tools of statistics. Index numbers may provide a homogeneous representation of multiple factors. However, the fact that index numbers are composed of heterogeneous variables gives rise to limitations. We can create a dimensionless index with values from 0 to 1 to rank different categorical values. To do so, for example, some indexes calculate the ratio among the values assigned to each category, find the extreme values of each and then calculate the average of the ratios obtained. We simply add up natural numbers, which can be assumed to represent, for example, the overall attractiveness of some products. However, this ranking is based on conventions and assumptions.[7] In this respect, Alain Desrosières (2008: 10) remarks that quantification implies attaining a consensus on how to measure: 'to postulate and to build a space of equivalence allowing quantification and thus measurement is at the same time a political and a technical act' (2008: 13). We have first a convention and only then a measure. What is incommensurable is made commensurable by adopting a conventional standard unit for each incommensurable variable, calculating the value of the variables according to these units and adding a weighted proportion of the values of all the variables (Boumans 2001: 326 and Mary Morgan 2001: 240). This means that we accept, inter alia, the assignment of weights for each variable as indicated in the index number formula. The weight must be the 'due' weight (Morgan 2001: 240).[8] This is not easy task when the categories to be weighted are qualitatively different (see H. Spencer Banzhaf 2001). Even though this process has proved useful, we are aware that minor changes in the composition of the index might change the ranking results.

This capacity to handle index numbers might lead to index manipulation. Clearly demonstrating the criteria used in index building can best help avoid deceit. This shows how technical aspects of measurement are intertwined with judgemental practical aspects: beliefs and values affect technical decisions about how to compose the index. Roy G. D. Allen (1951: 100ff.) emphasizes the technical problems involved in the choice of items, the choice of formula, and the choice of base periods. However, these technical problems also involve values. Oskar Morgenstern, for example, specifically referring to indexes, considers technical problems and recognizes 'that we are here confronted with a political as well as an economic problem' (1963: 192). The way in which we count has political consequences. Boumans (2015: 4–14) deals extensively with Morgenstern's ideas. Morgenstern distinguishes mere data (mere information collected) from 'observations', which are guided by theory. Given the complex nature of the economic stuff, theory is inexact, 'constructed and invented'

(1963: 88). For him, this inexactness downplays the accuracy of data selection and variables. The mentioned model-based procedure proposed by Boumans (2015) is aimed at overcoming this problem. For all that, accuracy is almost unachievable in this realm.

This accounts for a certain mistrust and resistance towards indexes. Sen, for example, was initially very critical about constructing a human development index, because he insisted on defending human individuality, that is the heterogeneous character of human individuals which is absent in an index, as in any statistical generalization (see, for example, 1999: 76–77). However, it is important to reach middle ground on this issue: there is a trade-off between considering human heterogeneity and the feasibility of analysing human affairs. Although reducing qualitative concepts to quantitative measures will always be imperfect, we need these measures. Numbers conceal realities, and relevant meanings are lost in the process of commensuration, but numbers are still very useful. Let us now turn to the example, the construction of the HDI.

In 1990, the United Nations Development Program (UNDP) published its first annual *Human Development Report* (*HDR*) introducing the HDI. This Index was inspired by Sen's Capability Approach (CA), which underlines the importance of ends (capabilities) over means (e.g. income). The HDI adopted *measurands* for three specific capabilities: health, education, and a decent standard of life. The *measurands* are respectively life expectancy, literacy and school enrolment, and income. The three dimensions are equally weighted into the Index, to track progress in the level of human development of countries or to monitor them over time. Despite its recognized 'vulgarity',[9] the HDI provides a better alternative to assess a country's development than through per capita national income. Deeply based on the CA, HDI's project leader, Mahbub ul Haq, planned to use this Index to delineate a new concept of well-being and create accessible well-being measures based on this conception. Sen, who was one of the main consultants on *HDR 1990*, at first did not see the point of a crude composite index such as the HDI. Haq instead maintained: 'We need a measure of the same level of vulgarity as GNP – just one number – but a measure that is not as blind to social aspects of human lives as GNP is' (UNDP 1999: 23). More recently, Sen (2009: 226) has agreed with this.

The HDI has evolved over the years to increase its quality and capacity to express real human development. This improvement derives from the need to answer different criticisms of the index and from the UNDP's initiative to make it more effective.[10] In this sense, it is important to consider the 2010 *Human Development Report*. In the introduction to the report, Sen maintains that, despite being a 'crude' index, the HDI did what it was expected to do: to go beyond commodities and income in the assessment of development. He adds that 'new tables continue to appear in the steady stream of Human Development Reports, and new indices have been devised to supplement the HDI and enrich our evaluation' (UNDP 2010: vi).

As rightly emphasized by Sen, human capabilities are incommensurable. Practical reason, as conceptualized in the previous chapter, is the appropriate manner for dealing with incommensurable categories. Through it, we can obtain an ordinal ranking by comparing different capabilities.[11] We cannot commensurate income, longevity, and literacy because they are measured in different units. We can only compare them (the task of practical reason), rank them for a specific situation, and extract some conclusions. These conclusions will be practical judgements involving beliefs about value priorities. These judgements cannot be organized without values. What is the meaning of the index number comprising these three dimensions? The index number determines a unique rank stemming from a comparison and makes it legitimate for any country, time and situation; then it decides on *measurands* and assigns extreme numerical values to them in order to construct a ratio scale of each dimension; finally, it adds up the resulting numerical weighted values. In the case of the HDI, variables are assigned weights of one-third. We are applying ratios to ordinal categories and adding their weighted numerical values (see Boumans and Davis 2009: 152; Finkelstein 1982: 19). At the same time, we are aware that the result is based on a convention established through the exercise of practical reason and public discussion.

Sudhir Anand and Sen (1994: 2) note that there is a loss of information when using an aggregate number (a 'scalar') for a set of numbers representing individual circumstances (a 'vector'). In the same vein, they (2000) affirm that the domain of the *Human Development Report* is much wider than what is captured by the HDI. As the first *Human Development Report* claims, 'The index is an approximation for capturing the many dimensions of human choices. It also carries some of the same shortcomings as income measures' (UNDP 1990: 1). This is also emphasized by Sen when he speaks of the HDI as a 'measure with the same level of crudeness as the GNP' (1999: 318, nt. 41).

Another problem with the HDI is that it uses averages, not distributions, thus concealing possible internal differences. Disregarding internal inequalities implies a particular evaluative position. Anand and Sen consider this criticism, but they also contend (1994: 2) that 'a distribution-sensitive scalar measure would continue to involve some loss of information, since there is no way of capturing the entire wealth of knowledge embedded in a set of numbers in one real number'. The Inequality-adjusted Human Development Index (IHDI) – a new index included in the 2010 *Human Development Report* – avoids this weakness of the HDI. As this Report asserts,

> the HDI can be viewed as an index of 'potential' human development (or the maximum level of HDI) that could be achieved if there was no inequality) while the IHDI is the actual level of human development (accounting for inequality). The difference between the HDI and the IDHI measures the 'loss' in potential human development due to inequality.
>
> (UNDP 2010: 87, see also 217)

It is indeed interesting to analyse these losses and their differences among countries and dimensions.

Further problems with index numbers are technical and related to data accuracy and homogeneity. The need for simplicity may work against realism. Given all the aforementioned difficulties, why then do we adopt index numbers? We do it because they are still highly useful. We must accept that measuring always implies simplification. Boumans (2001) explains Irving Fisher's account of index numbers and their inconsistencies, as described by Ragnar Frisch, Abraham Wald, and Wolfgang Eichhorn. However, as Boumans (2001: 336) remarks, the strength of Fisher's account is not based on his emphasis on theory but on the instrumental or pragmatic usefulness of this tool. In addition, Fisher conceded that it is an imperfect tool. We do not look for complete axiomatic consistency but rather for the best balance between theoretical and empirical requirements (2001: 316) and for the best possible approximation. Assessing the adequacy of this approximation goes beyond mathematical consistency (2001: 341). It is a question of reasonable consensus. Boumans (2005: 151) thus asserts: 'Practical issues require a different set of rules than axiomatic problems. This means that the rigour applied in solving practical problems will inevitably be different to the rigour in an axiomatic system'. We are thus giving up consistency and adopting comparability.

Index numbers, then, are measurement tools that prove useful for pragmatic objectives. Let us recall Plato's thinking about the usefulness of measurement for practical purposes. The definition of a practical purpose is obviously not valueless. As noted, the limitations of the HDI have been well recognized and the index has been defended on practical grounds. Regardless of its limitations, the HDI is a worthy instrument. This is eloquently expressed by Paul Streeten (1994: 235; italics in the original):

> It is clear that the concept of human development is much deeper and richer than what can be caught in *any* index or set of indicators. This is also true of other indicators. But, it might be asked, why try to catch a vector in a single number? Yet, such indexes are useful in focusing attention and simplifying the problem. They have a stronger impact on the mind and draw public attention more powerfully than a long list of many indicators combined with a qualitative discussion. They are eye-catching.

Sakiko Fukuda-Parr, who was head of the Human Development Report Office between 1995 and 2006, is more sceptical. She thinks that the absence of freedom indicators leads us to misperceive development as equivalent to social development plus economic growth: 'the human development concept has been trapped inside its reduced measure' (2003: 307). Summing up, the HDI has to be taken as no more than a guide to be handled with care and refined through technical improvements and theoretical and practical reason. Policymakers should always be prepared to go beyond the simple index and analyse its components in search of possible improvement. This does not imply, however, that we should do away with the HDI. Indeed, the practical aim of the HDI fits perfectly with the idea of it as a normative model of development, a model that will require continuous improvement. In other words, a presumably simple measuring instrument becomes a normative, value-laden device. In the next section, I will elaborate on these values.

Theory and values in the HDI

In this section, we claim that the HDI presupposes theoretical definitions and practical decisions that are insufficiently explicit and justified, and that these concepts and practical arguments call for more adequate definitions in order to improve the quality of the Index as well as for the sake of a 'fairer play'.[12] At this point, I wish to make clear that I am not saying that the HDI's theoretical and practical aspects were insufficiently studied by those who built the Index. I cannot claim to know this. What I mean to say is that these studies have not been sufficiently recorded in HDI-related documents, that is in the *HDRs*.

Initially, the practical decision involved in building the HDI is selecting the dimensions of well-being – education, health, and a decent standard of living – and their corresponding measurable variables: life expectancy, literacy, and income (the last as a proxy for the other capabilities). Although sensible, the reasons for this selection were not accounted for in *Human Development Reports*. As Sabina Alkire (2007: 89) asserts referring to poverty researchers, 'the problem is that they do not make explicit their reason for making a particular choice of dimensions'. References to this decision appear in the first *HDR*:

> Human development is a process of enlarging people's choices. The most critical of these wide-ranging choices are to live a long and healthy life, to be educated and to have access to resources needed for a *decent* standard of living. Additional choices include political freedom, guaranteed human rights and personal self-respect.
>
> (UNDP 1990: 1 and 10)

> [...] at all levels of development, the three *essential* ones [choices] are for people to lead a long and healthy life, to acquire knowledge and to have access to resources needed for a decent standard of living. If these *essential* choices are not available, many other opportunities remain inaccessible.
>
> (UNDP 1990: 10)

> People are the real wealth of a nation. The basic objective of development is to create an enabling environment for people to enjoy long, healthy and creative lives. This may appear to be a *simple truth*. But it is often forgotten in the immediate concern with the accumulation of commodities and financial wealth.
>
> (UNDP 1990: 9, my italics in the three quotations)

As the last passage indicates, defining these goals appears to be a *simple truth*. But this is not trivial; it has to be justified. The Report also states that its choices are *essential*, and that income should enable a *decent* standard of living. The 1993 Report adds:

> The three dimensions of the HDI relate to one or many capabilities that they are expected to capture. Thus, longevity captures the capability of leading a long and healthy life. Educational attainments capture the capability of acquiring knowledge, communicating and participating in the life of the community. Access to resources needed for a decent standard of living captures the capability of leading a healthy life, guaranteeing physical and social mobility, communicating and participating in the life of the community (including consumption).
>
> (UNDP 1993: 105)

That is, life expectancy, literacy, educational enrolment, and per capita income are supposed to capture these capabilities. These are, however, mere assertions. We need to uncover their underlying reasoning.

Concerning life expectancy, the *HDR* 1990 explains:

> The use of life expectancy as one of the principal indicators of human development rests on three considerations: the intrinsic value of longevity, its value in helping people pursue various goals and its association with other characteristics, such as good health and nutrition. The importance of life expectancy relates primarily to the value people attach to living long and well.
>
> (UNDP 1990: 11)

Evidently, this intrinsic value of longevity is a practical truth. However, its relation to other goals and their characteristics requires further development.

Another practical decision is used to define knowledge. The *Human Development Report* (UNDP 1990: 12) contends that literacy is a person's first step in learning and knowledge building, but it recognizes it should also take into account other variables (as future reports did by adding enrolment).

Concerning the third key component of human development, 'command over the resources needed for a decent life', it is recognized that using per capita income as an indicator has strong limitations, because it leaves aside non-tradable goods and services and the distorting effects stemming from exchange rate anomalies, tariffs and taxes (UNDP 1990: 12). Furthermore, 'the income component of the HDI has been used as an indirect indicator of some capabilities not well reflected, directly or indirectly, in the measures of longevity and education' (Anand and Sen 2000: 86; see also 99 and 100).

However, it would be a strong assumption to say that income is an indirect indicator of other capabilities (other than health and education), because it would mean that income can 'buy' these capabilities, and that their values are lower than those of education and life expectancy. As the first *HDR* recognizes, 'there is no automatic link between income growth and human progress' (UNDP 1990: 10).

In addition, the use of logarithms for the income scale has two effects: first, it decreases the weight of the highest incomes; second, logarithm average tends to increase when income is more equally distributed. The first effect entails the decision to reduce the impact of the highest incomes on development (Anand and Sen 2000: 87). The second effect seems to entail a preference for equality (Anand and Sen 1994: 3). Therefore, though at a first glance the use of logarithms might seem to be only a technical decision, it has practical consequences.

Applying a logarithm to life expectancy is even more debatable. Life has intrinsic value, and the last years of life cannot be considered less valuable than others. Anand and Sen (1994: 5), however, also believe that life expectancy can also be viewed as useful for other objectives, in which case reducing inequalities may prove relevant. Individuals would have to be considered as group members. In this case, however, data quality will not allow for potential index improvement.

Despite these limitations, health, literacy and income still remain sensible dimensions for assessing human development. Of course, people from different cultural backgrounds may believe that education or income, and even longevity, are not so important, and value other things, for example family links, or religious faith, which cannot be bought. They might indeed consider the Index as expressing the ideals of Western Enlightenment. For example, Seyed Hadi Arabi (2016), basing his arguments on Islamic philosophers Avicenna and Mulla Sadra, stresses the importance of otherworldly well-being, wisdom, and ethical virtue. Thus, we need to consider whether the simplification assumed in erasing cultural specificities could turn the HDI into an illegitimate tool.[13] In any case, taking these cultural specificities into account or not is a matter of practical decisions that need to be discussed. As Alkire (2007: 101) says, 'in the case of the HDI, the authors assumed that people across cultures, regions, ages, genders, ethnicities, and even across sources of diversity, valued survival, income, and basic education'. She calls these suppositions 'normative assumptions'. However, she warns that the strength of these normative assumptions is deeply limited 'unless the authors transparently communicate their assumptions in order to catalyse public discussion or scrutiny of these issues' (2007: 101). Practical reason indicates that, when creating an index, you need to make decisions about variables. It is hard to know whether you have made the best possible decision, but if its basis is 'collaborative, visible, defensible, and revisable' (Alkire 2002: 77), it is justifiable. Thus, we need to establish a decision-making process. Otherwise, we would have an insufficiently illustrated practical decision: a practical decision without practical science.

The second practical decision was to assign equal weights to the three variables. This also sounds feasible, but the arguments are not presented in the Reports.[14] They only include a statement that all three of the HDI components are equally important and thus deserve equal weight (UNDP 1991: 88).

Within the confines of education, the decision to assign two-thirds of this dimension of the Index to adult literacy and one-third to the combined gross enrolment is also a practical decision. With regards to enrolment, the decision to assign the same weight to primary, secondary, and tertiary education also counts as a practical judgement not explained in the Report. Bagolin and Comim identify this assumption as an example of issues not effectively addressed:

> Education represents 1/3 of the index weight. Higher education has the same weight as fundamental education. It is almost frivolous to question if higher education has the same intrinsic value as fundamental education. It is also possible to ask why income, that represents all standard of living aspects, goes through a diminishing return to scale in the HDI and why the same does not apply to education? Could higher education be considered a basic capability?
>
> (Bagolin and Comim 2008: 25)

In addition, the 2009 Report (UNDP 2009: 205–206) recognizes that combined gross enrolment ratios can hide important differences among countries associated with differences in quality, grade repetition, and dropout rates. This simplification also entails practical consequences. The 2010 *Human Development Report* introduced changes in order to enhance considerations of this dimension. Instead of using literacy and enrolment as indicators of knowledge, it uses mean and expected years of schooling. This appears to better reflect the current situation of education because it implicitly considers potential school dropout.

Martha Nussbaum interestingly notes, with respect to her criticism of Sen for his reluctance to make substantive commitments:

> The use of capabilities in development is typically comparative merely, as in the Human Development Reports of the UNDP. Thus, nations are compared in areas such as health and educational attainment. But concerning what level of health service, or what level of educational provision, a just society would deliver as a fundamental entitlement to all its citizens, the view is suggestive, but basically silent.
>
> (Nussbaum 2003: 35)

In effect, the HDI only determines the extreme values of the variables, and does not define threshold values, analogous to, for example 'poverty or indigence lines'. This might be legitimate but would entail a detailed explanation of why extreme values are preferred.

In sum, we must explicitly justify the practical decisions we make. If we fail to employ values that are not rationally founded, we run the risk of being accused of exhibiting ideological bias. The HDR's first issue explicitly declares that its orientation 'is practical and pragmatic [...]. Its purpose is neither to preach nor to recommend any particular model of development' (UNDP 1990: iii). However, the HDR consistently uses the words 'should' and 'must': values are present and need to be explicitly justified. This justification calls for a definition of value concepts and decisions, a task of theoretical and practical reason.

All in all, the HDI relies on theoretical definitions and practical decisions that are insufficiently explicit or discussed in the Reports. Broader specification of these definitions and their underlying arguments would improve the quality of the Index. As Ingrid Robeyns (2005b) argues, even a short explanation of why and how dimensions are selected could prove extremely valuable.

Another index introduced in the 2010 *Human Development Report*, the Multidimensional Poverty Index (MPI), considers more variables. It captures multiple deprivations at the individual level across the same dimensions as the HDI: health, education, and standard of living. It uses data from household surveys. The MPI determines thresholds for the three dimensions, introducing new indicators. It combines the multidimensional headcount ratio (the proportion of analysed population that is under the threshold) and the intensity of poverty (the proportion of indicators in which people are deprived). 'The basic intuition is that the MPI represents the share of the population that is multidimensionally poor, adjusted by the intensity of the deprivations suffered' (UNDP 2010: 222). The MPI uses nutrition and child mortality as indicators of health, years of schooling and children enrolled as indicators of education, and access to services and assets (cooking fuel, toilet, water, electricity, floor, etc.) as criteria for establishing the minimum standard of living.

The 2010/2011 Human Development Research Paper broadens the rationale for selecting the new indicators and their weights. Regarding dimensions, it indicates (Alkire and Santos 2010: 9–10) that their selection has relied on mechanisms such as *participatory exercises*; the use of some *enduring consensus* – particularly surrounding human rights and the Millennium Development Goals (MDGs); *theories* – such as many philosophical or psychological accounts of basic needs, universal values, and human rights; and, finally, a binding constraint – *whether the data exist*.

This Research Paper obviously acknowledges that values are involved in the choice of the dimensions. Then, selection procedures are typical of practical science. In the same vein, the paper sufficiently argues, based on a 'reasoned consensus', for the choice of indicators and the determination of weights. Procedures include participatory processes, expert opinion informed by public debate, and survey questions. It explicitly states that 'the relative weights on different capabilities or dimensions that are used in society-wide measures are value judgments' (Alkire and Santos 2010: 16).

I welcome this initiative that responds to some of the critiques and suggestions presented in this chapter. Far from invalidating criticism, I believe this conclusion actually validates them, because it means that the UNDP is actually taking action in line with my claims. However, as the Report recognizes (UNDP 2010: 118):

> fully realizing the human development agenda requires going much further. Putting people at the center of development is more than an intellectual exercise – it means making progress equitable and broad-based, enabling people to become active participants in change and ensuring

that achievements are not attained at the expense of future generations. Meeting these challenges is not only possible but necessary – and more urgent than ever.

The 2016 *Human Development Report* (UNDP 2016: 9) did not add dimensions to the indexes. It recognizes that though 'freedom of agency' is an integral part of human development, the HDI focuses on well-being on account of the challenges involved in measuring agency. However, it exhibits an increasingly comprehensive analysis of the components of true human development. Additionally, new indicators appeared, the *Millennium Development Goals* in 2000, and the *Sustainable Development Goals* in 2015.[15]

Summing up, regardless of the specific contents of the *Human Development Reports*, the aim of this section was to show, in the manner of a case study, how the HDI clearly demonstrates that both theoretical definitions and practical evaluative judgements are embedded in the index-building technique. The HDI is actually built on a series of assumptions that are based on value-driven or practical elements. It has yet to answer several questions: Why are these three variables chosen? Why are they given equal weight? Does selected data accurately represent these variables? The answers are statements rather than explanations. In short, the HDI is built upon a range of unexplored assumptions about the dimensions of human development.

Conclusion

In this chapter, I have analysed the role of statistics and economic history in the examination of empirical economic data and the detection of economic phenomena. I have stressed the theoretical and value-laden character of these tasks. Though a measurement may seem innocuous in relation to theory and values, it is heavily loaded with them. Obviously, the interpretation of economic history holds more assumptions than present measures. This fact entails the inevitable role of experts in the first set of economic sciences, which I will explore more extensively in Chapter 10. What has become clear is that in order to achieve an adequate measurement, we need to put the conceptual definitions and values involved on the table and discuss them.

I conceive practical reason as the way of discovering and deciding about these values. The field has all the characteristics of the subject matter of practical sciences: it is 'context-dependent and sensitive to local conditions'; it is 'much more inexact than a laboratory science' (Boumans 2015: 174); it needs a 'considered judgment' (Elgin 1996), analogous to clinical practice (Boumans 2015: Chapter 5). Evaluating the specific method for doing this is beyond the possibilities of this book. I will come back to the role of the expert in this sense in Chapter 10. It would be sensible to take into account Susan Haack's warning: 'we shouldn't allow the fact that probabilistic and statistical evidence is expressed in precise numerical terms to distract us from asking whether it is strong or weak, reliable or unreliable, truth-indicative or misleading' (2018: 518). We need an honest expert to recognize this.

It may be concluded that the link between these economic sciences and other economic disciplines lies in a necessary mutual cross-interaction between them, especially with economic theory. The art of Political Economy also needs the information provided by statistics and history.

Notes

1 As von Wright (1971: 1) affirms, 'the Discovery and description of facts cannot always be conceptually separated from a theory about them and is often an important step towards an understanding of their nature'.

2 In addition to the sources quoted, these definitions are based on Runes' (1942), Lacey's (1996), and Bunge's (2003) dictionaries, as well as the *Concise Routledge Encyclopedia of Philosophy* (Craig and Craig, eds., 2000).

3 As rightly John Maynard Keynes (1921: 274 – Notes on Part III) remarks, this distinction is already present in Aristotle and Bacon uses both forms of induction. However, the modern use of the term 'Baconian' corresponds to enumerative induction.

4 Raymond Aron (1959: 21) also states that 'historical knowledge is not a simple accumulation of facts': facts and interpretations are intertwined in historical investigation.

5 In this and the following section I draw material from Crespo (2013: Chapter 6).

6 On this, also see the example provided by Julian Reiss (2008: Chapters 3 and 4) and Reiss (2013: Chapter 8).

7 They are non-additive qualities: see, e.g. M. R. Cohen and E. Nagle (1934: 296).

8 She explains (2001: 240):

> Index number formulae conceived as measuring instruments are based on the strategy of aggregating in a way that allows each individual element to be assigned its due weight in the whole. Such a 'weighted average' strategy provides a solution to a general problem in economics, namely that many concepts refer to aggregates of things which may be considered homogeneous in the dimension of prices or money value, but are nonhomogeneous in another dimension, namely amounts consumed or produced. The solution is to use weights to overcome the problem of how to average in a manner that takes account of both amounts and values.

9 Cf. UNDP (1999: 23) and Richard Jolly (2005: 126).

10 For a review of this criticism, see Elizabeth Stanton (2007: 16–28) and Izete Bagolin and Flavio Comim (2008: 17–22).

11 Scales of measurement in the social and behavioural sciences are nominal or ordinal (Finkelstein 1982: 26).

12 These theoretical and practical insights are part of what Makiko Harrison calls (2002: 37) 'outside criteria' needed to operationalize a theory of well-being. In this section I draw material from Crespo (2012).

13 The 2016 HDR (UNDP 2016) insists on 'Universalism' as a key to human development. This fact makes more urgent a careful argumentation about the components of human development.

14 For Lucio Esposito and Enrica Chiappero-Martinetti (2008: 3; italics in the original), 'the act of *not* giving weights – equivalent indeed to the assignation of

identical weights to each dimension – is itself a subjective decision motivated by the value judgment that those dimensions are equally valuable. [...] In the literature [...] the possible meanings of the statement 'dimension h is more important than dimension k have not critically been searched for'.

15 Mary Morgan and Maria Bach (2018) appraise their pros and cons as compared to the HDI, and their relation with values and politics.

References

Alkire, S. (2002). *Valuing Freedoms. Sen's Capabilities Approach and Poverty Reduction.* Oxford: Oxford University Press.

Alkire, S. (2007). 'Choosing Dimensions: The Capability Approach and Multidimensional Poverty'. In: N. Kakwani and J. Silber (eds.), *The Many Dimensions of Poverty.* New York: Palgrave Macmillan, pp. 89–119.

Alkire, S. and M. E. Santos. (2010). 'Acute Multidimensional Poverty: A New Index for Developing Countries', Human Development Research Paper 2101/11.

Allen, R. G. D. (1951). *Statistics for Economists.* London: Hutchison.

Anand, S. and A. Sen. (1994). 'Human Development Index: Methodology and Measurement', *Occasional Papers*, 12, Human Development Report Office, New York.

Anand, S. and A. Sen. (2000). 'The Income Component of the Human Development Index'. *Journal of Human Development*, 1/1: 83–106.

Arabi, S. H. (2016). 'Well-Being Orthodox Theories and Islamic Views'. *International Journal of Social Economics*, 43/2: 190–204. https://doi.org/10.1108/IJSE-01-2013-0019.

Aristotle (1984). *The Complete Works of Aristotle*, edited by Jonathan Barnes. Princeton: Princeton University Press.

Aron, R. (1959). 'Evidence and Inference in History'. In: D. Lerner (ed.), *Evidence and Inference.* New York: Free Press of Glencoe, pp. 19–47.

Bagolin, I. and F. Comim (2008). 'Human Development Index (HDI) and Its Family of Indexes: An Evolving Critical Review'. *Revista de Economia*, 34/2: 7–28.

Banzhaf, H. S. (2001). 'Quantifying the Qualitative: Quality-Adjusted Price Indexes in the United States, 1915–61'. In: J. L. Klein and M. S. Morgan (eds.), *The Age of Economic Measurement*, HOPE Annual Supplement, pp. 345–370.

Bogen, J. (2009). 'Saving the Phenomena' and Saving the Phenomena', http://philsci-archive.pitt.edu/archive/00004554/01/Sumitted_'Saving'-Saving.doc. Accessed 19 January 2010.

Bogen, J. (2013). 'Theory and Observation in Science'. In: E. Zalta (ed.), *The Stanford Encyclopedia of Philosophy*, http://plato.stanford.edu/entries/science-theory-observation/. Accessed 28 June 2014.

Bogen, J. and J. Woodward (1988). 'Saving the Phenomena'. *Philosophical Review*, 97/3: 303–352.

Boumans, M. J. (2001). 'Fisher's Instrumental Approach to Index Numbers'. In: J. L. Klein and M. S. Morgan (eds.), *The Age of Economic Measurement*, HOPE Annual Supplement, pp. 313–344.

Boumans, M. J. (2005). *How Economists Model the World into Numbers.* Abingdon: Routledge.

Boumans, M. J. (2015). *Science Outside the Laboratory.* Oxford: Oxford University Press.

Boumans, M. J. and J. B. Davis . (2009). *Economic Methodology*. Amsterdam: Amsterdam School of Economics, History and Methodology Group.

Bunge, M. (2003). *Philosophical Dictionary.* Enlarged Edition. Amherst: Prometheus.

Cartwright, N. (1989). *Nature's Capacities and Their Measurement.* London and New York: Oxford University Press.

Chang, H. (2004). *Inventing Temperature.* Oxford: Oxford University Press.

Cohen, M. R. and E. Nagle (1934). *An Introduction to Logic and Scientific Method.* New York: Harcourt Brace.

Craig, E. and E. Craig (eds.)(2000). *Concise Routledge Encyclopedia of Philosophy.* London: Routledge.

Crespo, R. F. (2012). 'Practical Reasoning in Economic Affairs: The HD Index as a Case Study'. In: J. C. Caldas and V. Neves (eds.), *Facts, Values and Objectivity in Economics.* Abington and New York: Routledge, pp. 158–179.

Crespo, R. F. (2013). *Philosophy of the Economy. An Aristotelian Approach.* Dordrecht: Springer.

Desrosières, A. (2008). *L'argument statistique, I. Pour une sociologie historique de la quantification.* Paris: Presses de l'École des mines.

Deutsch, M. (1959). 'Evidence and Inference in Nuclear Research'. In: D. Lerner (ed.), *Evidence and Inference.* Glencoe (IL): The Free Press of Glencoe, pp. 107–138.

Duhem, P. ([1906, 1954] 1998). 'Physical Theory and Experiment'. In J. A. Cover and M. Curd (eds.), *Philosophy of Science: the Central Issues.* New York: W. W. Norton, 1998, pp. 257–279, from Pierre Duhem, *The Aim and Structure of Physical Theory* (transl. P. P. Wiener, Princeton University Press, 1954; original: *La théorie physique. Son objet et sa structure.* Paris: Chevalier et Rivière. Online at www.ac-nancy-metz.fr/enseign/philo/textesph/duhem_theorie_physique.pdf. Accessed 3 July 2014.

Elgin, C. Z. (1996). *Considered Judgment.* Princeton: Princeton University Press.

Esposito, L. and E. Chiappero-Martinetti. (2008). 'Multidimensional Poverty Measurement: Restricted and Unrestricted Hierarchy among Poverty Dimensions', *Oxford Poverty and Human Development Initiative (OPHI) Working Paper,* 22, www.ophi.org.uk/pubs/OPHI_WP22.pdf. Accessed 8 January 2010.

Finkelstein, L. (1982). 'Theory and Philosophy of Measurement'. In: P. H. Sydenham (ed.), *Handbook of Measurement Science,* vol. 1. New York: John Wiley, pp. 1–30.

Fukuda-Parr, S. (2003). 'The Human Development Paradigm: Operationalizing Sen's Ideas on Capabilites'. *Feminist Economics,* 9/2–3: 301–317.

Haack, S. (2018). 'Proof, Probability, and Statistics: The Dangers of "Delusive Exactness"'. In: *Evidence in the Process* (Atelier, Spain: 2018), pp. 497–521; University of Miami Legal Studies Research Paper No. 18–38. Available at SSRN: https://ssrn.com/abstract=3287440

Hanson, N. R. (1958). *Patterns of Discovery.* Cambridge: Cambridge University Press.

Harrison, M. (2002) 'From Theory to Measurement to Policies: Operationalising the Capability Approach to Well-Being'. *Measurement in Physics and Economics Discussion Paper Series,* 18/02, LSE.

Heidelberger, M. (2003). 'Theory-Ladenness and Scientific Instruments in Experimentation'. In: H. Radder (ed.), *The Philosophy of Scientific Experimentation.* Pittsburgh: University of Pittsburgh Press, pp. 138–151.

Jolly, R. (2005). 'Interview by Thomas Weiss', United Nations Intellectual History Project, www.unhistory.org/CD/PDFs/Jolly.pdf. Accessed 23 June 2016.

Keynes, J. M. (1921). *Treatise on Probability.* London: Macmillan.

Keynes, J. N. ([1890] 1955). *The Scope and Method of Political Economy.* New York: A. M. Kelley & Millman.

Lacey, A. R. (1996). *A Dictionary of Philosophy.* Third Edition. London: Routledge.

Menger, C. ([1883] 1985). *Investigations into the Method of the Social Sciences with Special Reference to Economics,* Ed. Louis Schneider, Transl. Francis J. Nock. New York and London: New York University Press (*Untersuchungen über die Methode der Socialwissenschaften und der Politischen Oekonomie insbesondere,* Ducker & Humblot, Leipzig).

Menger, C. (1960). 'Toward a Systematic Classification of Economic Sciences'. In: L. Sommer (transl. and ed.), *Essays in European Economic Thought.* Princeton: D. van Nostrand, pp. 1–38.

Michell, J. (2005). 'The Logic of Measurement: A Realistic Overview'. *Measurement,* 38: 285–294.

Monton, B., and C. Mohler. (2012). 'Constructive Empiricism'. In: E. N. Zalta (ed.), *The Stanford Encyclopedia of Philosophy,* http://plato.stanford.edu/entries/constructive-empiricism/. Accessed 28 June 2014.

Morgan, M. (2001). 'Making Measuring Instruments'. In: J. L. Klein and M. S. Morgan (eds.), *The Age of Economic Measurement,* History of Political Economy Annual Supplement to Volume 33. Durham (NC) and London: Duke University Press, pp. 235–251.

Morgan, M. and M. Bach (2018). 'Measuring Development – from the UN's Perspective'. In: M. Alacevich and M. Boianovsky (eds.), *The Political Economy of Development Economics: A Historical Perspective,* History of Political Economy Annual Supplement to Volume 50. Durham (NC) and London: Duke University Press, pp. 193–210.

Morgenstern, O. (1963). *On the Accuracy of Economic Observations.* Princeton: Princeton University Press.

Nussbaum, M. C. (2001). 'The *Protagoras*: A Science of Practical Reasoning'. In: E. Millgram (ed.), *Varieties of Practical Reasoning.* Cambridge (MA) and London: MIT Press, pp. 153–202.

Nussbaum, M. C. (2003). 'Capabilities as Fundamental Entitlements: Sen and Social Justice'. *Feminist Economics,* 9/2–3: 33–59.

Plato (1997). *Complete Works.* Edited by John M. Cooper and D. S. Hutchison. Indianapolis: Hacket.

Popper, K. R. ([1934] 1959, 2000). *The Logic of Scientific Discovery.* New York: Hutchison; London: Routledge (*Logik der Forschung,* translated by the author).

Porter, T. (1995). *Trust in Numbers.* Princeton: Princeton University Press.

Quine, W.v.O. (1951). 'Two Dogmas of Empiricism'. *Philosophical Review,* 60/1: 20–43.

Reiss, J. (2008). *Error in Economics.* Abingdon: Routledge.

Reiss, J. (2013). *Philosophy of Economics. A Contemporary Introduction.* Abingdon: Routledge.

Reiss, J. (2014). 'Struggling over the Soul of Economics: Objectivity versus Expertise'. In: C. Martini and M. Boumans (eds.), *Experts and Consensus in Social Science.* Dordrecht: Springer, pp. 131–153.

Reiss, J. (2015). *Causation, Evidence, and Inference.* New York and Abingdon: Routledge.

Reiss, J. and J. Sprenger. (2014). 'Scientific Objectivity'. In: E. N. Zalta (ed.), *The Stanford Encyclopedia of Philosophy,* https://plato.stanford.edu/entries/scientific-objectivity/. Accessed 30 September 2018.

Robeyns, I. (2005). 'The Capability Approach: A Theoretical Survey'. *Journal of Human Development*, 6/1: 93–114.

Rudner, R. (1953). 'The Scientist *Qua* Scientist Makes Value Judgments'. *Philosophy of Science*, 20: 1–6.

Runes, D. D. (ed.) (1942). *The Dictionary of Philosophy*. New York: Philosophical Library.

Sen, A. (1999). *Development as Freedom*. Oxford: Oxford University Press.

Sen, A. (2009). *The Idea of Justice*, Cambridge (MA): Belknap Press of Harvard University Press.

Stanton, E. (2007). 'The Human Development Index: A History', Working Paper Series 127, Political Economy Research Institute, University of Massachusetts, Amherst.

Streeten, P. (1994). 'Human Development: Means and Ends'. *American Economic Review*, 84/2: 232–237.

Suppes, P. (2000). 'Measurement, Theory of'. In: E. Craig (ed.), *Concise Routledge Encyclopedia of Philosophy*. London: Routledge.

United Nations Development Program (UNDP). (1990). *Human Development Report 1990*. Oxford: Oxford University Press.

United Nations Development Program (UNDP). (1991). *Human Development Report 1991*. Oxford: Oxford University Press.

United Nations Development Program (UNDP). (1993). *Human Development Report 1993*. Oxford: Oxford University Press.

United Nations Development Program (UNDP). (1999). *Human Development Report 1999*. Oxford: Oxford University Press.

United Nations Development Program (UNDP). (2009). *Human Development Report 2009*. Basingstoke and New York: Palgrave Macmillan.

United Nations Development Program (UNDP). (2010). *Human Development Report 2010*, 'The Real Wealth of Nations: Pathways to Human Development'. New York: Palgrave Macmillan.

United Nations Development Program (UNDP). (2016). *Overview Human Development Report 2016: Human Development for Everyone*, online, http://hdr.undp.org/sites/default/files/HDR2016_EN_Overview_Web.pdf. Accessed 24 July 2018.

Van Fraasen, B. (1980). *The Scientific Image*. Oxford: Oxford University Press.

Von Wright, G. H. (1971). *Explanation and Understanding*. London: Routledge and Kegan Paul.

Weber, M. ([1904] 1949). '"Objectivity" in Social Science and Social Policy'. In: Max Weber. *The Methodology of the Social Sciences*, ed. by E. Shils and H. Finch. New York: Free Press, pp. 50–112.

Woodward, J. (1989). 'Data and Phenomena'. *Synthese*, 79/3: 393–472.

5 Economic theory I
Some philosophical concepts

In Chapter 3, I argued that the aim of economic theory is *to explain* and *understand* economic phenomena. As Boudon states, 'explaining a social phenomenon means identifying its causes' (1998: 172). The causes, as already explained, are of at least two types: the efficient – the means to produce the phenomenon –, and the aim, reason, or end – that is the final cause of it. We need a reason that triggers the actions that produce the phenomenon. In that chapter (3), following the ideas of Mill, Menger, and Neville Keynes, I maintained that social scientists and, specifically, theoretical economists should try to identify both types of causes. I distinguished between explaining by efficient causes and understanding the final causes. However, the term 'explanation' can also be used in a more general sense to include both causes.

Positive economics, which is, in fact, today's economic theory, concentrates on the means, and consequently on efficient causes because it considers ends as given. It applies the economic principle, that is, it explains the economic action as an action targeted at making an efficient – maximizing – use of means, and it prescribes how to perform it, because today's positive economics does not only assume an explaining role but also tries to predict and to prescribe. If you want to maximize your utility or your financial earnings, you should buy this portfolio of goods or assets. It is normative not in terms of ends, but in terms of the best way to attain ends. For Neville Keynes, this role would be included in the art of economics.

However, economic theory does not exhaust itself in positive economics. It should also try to identify the reasons for the actions taken, given that other motivations than the economic principle could motivate non-efficient, economic actions. Chapter 3 describes Menger's definition of the goal of economic theory as including not only cognition but also *understanding* of the ends of phenomena, that is, knowing their final causes. In Chapter 1, I maintained that economic theory should be an 'interdisciplinary' enterprise – defining interdisciplinarity in this case as the conceptual integration of explaining causes and understanding reasons or ends. I also stated that there is no conflict between a 'positive' and an 'interpretivist' approach: they can coexist and work together, in mutually enriching ways.

In this first chapter about economic theory, I will introduce some philosophical concepts. First, I will discuss the notions of explanation, causality, and types of causes, because economists are increasingly interested in the causes of economic phenomena. These are broad topics of which I will only be able to provide some definitions.

Then, I will introduce the notion of 'abduction' because, like all sciences, economics uses this method aimed at postulating hypotheses. Despite its fallibility, abduction becomes necessary because all sources of evidence used by the economist are imperfect and he/she consequently needs a special craft to 'abduct' adequate hypotheses that are postulated in models.

In the next chapters, I will respectively concentrate on positive economics and on economic theory dealing with ends.

Explanation and causes

The aim of economic theory and positive economics is to explain economic phenomena. However, what is an explanation, or what does it mean to explain? To explain is to offer an account, to show the reason why, or the process of how something happens. It is, as Reiss (2013: 19) states, an answer to why-questions. In effect, to ask why something happens is generally to ask the cause of it. However, there are different 'whys' and different theories of what an explanation is. In addition, human and social phenomena, given the complex nature of the human realm, cannot be explained by universal laws, as the 'classical' covering-law model of explanation has intended, and there is usually more than one cause behind social phenomena.

This is not a book on explanation and causality. I cannot describe and discuss all the theories of explanation and causality that have been proposed throughout the history of philosophy, especially in the twentieth century. I will focus on theories that particularly apply to social phenomena – especially economic – and on those that claim that there are true existent causes. I agree with Reiss that 'to explain a specific economic event is to cite its causes; to explain a general economic phenomenon is to describe the causal mechanism responsible for it', and I also agree with him that 'causal explanations cannot be successful unless they are true' (2013: 120).

Mill speaks about explaining by causal tendencies (1882: Book 3, Chapter X), Menger's exact orientation towards theoretical investigation looks for the reason (*Grund*) of phenomena, and Neville Keynes says that Political Economy must reach beyond description 'and discover laws of causal connexion' ([1890] 1955: 176). He adds ([1890] 1955: 224):

> while the pure theory assumes the operation of forces under artificially simplified conditions, it still claims that the forces whose effects it investigates are *verae causae* in the sense that they do operate, and indeed operate in a predominating way, in the actual economic world.

That is, the three authors on whom I have based the classification of economic phenomena and economic sciences – Mill, Menger, and Neville
Keynes – understand that explaining is to show or demonstrate the cause of
the concerned phenomenon. The claim, in addition, has a metaphysical flavour.
That is, causes are not psychological feelings inspired by the mere regularity
of some events, but they really exist in the external world. Nancy Cartwright
(1989: 170), though arguably, equates Mill's concept of tendency with her concept of capacity – a stable cause –, which has a metaphysical commitment.[1,2]
In the case of Menger, the Aristotelian metaphysical influence on this point is
clear. Neville Keynes' statement quoted above speaks for itself about this metaphysical orientation: *verae causae* operating in the actual world.

Causality was strongly present as a real property of substances in the whole
history of Western philosophy until the seventeenth century. A milestone in its
rejection was Hume's idea of causality. He emptied it of ontological significance by reducing it to a conjunction or regularity of two events, a position
that faces serious problems.[3] However, while from an empiricist position such
as Hume's this regularity is all there is, from a realist metaphysical view this
regularity is a sign of a possible, actually existent causal force. We do not see or
touch causality: we understand it through what we see or touch, and through
other proceedings.[4] Moreover, as Reiss (2015: 62) states, 'the markers of causal
relationships are, in most cases, not straightforwardly observable, just like the
causal relationships themselves'. However, for a reduced vision of the scope of
human reason such as Hume's, we cannot capture the essences or causes that are
'behind' empirical data. As we saw in the last chapter, this is not right, because
theoretical notions are embedded in these data: causes are somehow present in
data. Robert M. MacIver has stated many years ago:

> Causal knowledge is always inferential, never immediate. The causal nexus,
> like every other relationship between data, is not itself a datum. It can never
> be vindicated by perception or by any of the devices that come to the aid
> of perception. The assertion of any relationship, no matter how simple or
> obvious, involves the appeal to reason, and its establishment is a scientific
> *construction*.
>
> (1942: 203; italics in the original)

However, for an epistemic realist approach, this construction is based on data
and expresses something really existent: reason passes through data and captures
real existent causes. Evidence and data are 'marks' or 'symptoms' of causality
(Reiss 2015: 60ff.). Observations are evidence on the basis of which we infer
causes (cf. Reiss 2015: 189.). That is, for a realist account of it, causality is
not something built up by reason but discovered by reason. Maynard Keynes
thinks that

> we are capable of direct knowledge about empirical entities that goes
> beyond a mere expression of our understanding or sensation of them. [...]

[W]e are capable, that is to say, of direct synthetic knowledge about the nature of the objects of our experience.

([1921] 1973: 292–293)

He describes his view of the scientific process in a paper titled 'Science and Art', read to the Apostles on 20 February 1909:[5]

> He [the scientist] is presented with a mass of facts, possessing similarities and differences, arranged in no kind of scheme or order. His first need is to perceive very clearly the precise nature of the different details [...] He [then] holds the details together clearly before his mind and it will probably be necessary that he should keep them more or less before his mind for a considerable time. Finally, he will with a kind of sudden insight see through the obscurity of the argument or of the apparently unrelated data, and the details will quickly fall into scheme or arrangement, between each part of which there is a real connection.

This, however, is not an easy task, especially when looking for causes of human and social phenomena. Yet, the difficulty of the task does not mean that causes are not real.

Hume's reduction of the concept of causation to a law-like relation of cause-and-effect events (not the production of the effect as a result of the intrinsic capacity of the cause) and it's consequent consideration of causality as a psychological phenomenon have left an impact on the philosophy of science and on current science.

In the twentieth century, prevailing views in science did not set out to explain but only to predict, which led to an instrumentalist or pragmatist version of science – employed by scientists such as Ernst Mach, Pierre Duhem, and Henri Poincaré.[6] The axioms of geometry, Poincaré asserts, are 'conventions' ([1906]1925: 66). For Mach, the concept of 'atom' is a provisional help. Scientific theories are mere tools for making empirical predictions. However, this perspective entails a lacking notion of science. The logical or neopositivist current holds an ultra-empiricist position that discards metaphysical knowledge. This was the case with founders Moritz Schlick or Rudolf Carnap, but also with more recent philosophers of science such as Carl Hempel, whose covering law model provides explanations that are not necessarily based on real causes.[7] To base all knowledge only on experience, leaving aside any intellectual intuition stemming from it, however, is an unfeasible program. As Alfred North Whitehead (1929: 54–55) affirmed,

> the modern doctrine, popular among scientists, is that science is the mere description of things observed. As such it assumes nothing, neither an objective world, nor causation, nor induction [...] The conclusion is that science, thus defined, needs no metaphysics [...] in that sense science loses its importance.

Twentieth-century history of the philosophy of science is the history of a quest for the foundations of science that has failed to attain its goal. Hempel (1950: 61–62) himself recognizes the problems of the neopositivist empiricist program and argues for the need for a deeper knowledge through theories (1966: 70). As Stephen Körner (1984: 53) argues, the analytical philosopher who condemns the metaphysician often condemns himself implicitly. Craig Dilworth (2006: 183) cleverly asserts,

> From an epistemological point of view, to limit science to the investigation of phenomena and their formal relations would be to deny the relevance of the principles of substance and causality to modern science – which have here been shown to be part of its essence. This would mean giving up the quest of making phenomena understandable in a broader perspective, and at the same time losing a source of inspiration regarding how new phenomena or laws might be discovered.

As a result, he complains of the empiricist denial of metaphysics and calls for a reinstitution of metaphysics. Rejecting metaphysics implies denying ontological realism. Aristotelian tradition, instead, while it does not necessarily always hold a scientific realism (the position that maintains that all unobservable scientific concepts are real), does hold an ontological realism, a logical-semantic realism and, to some extent, an epistemic realism relative to the contingency of the concerned matter. With respect to ontological realism, Edward Craig states: 'The basic idea of realism is that the kinds of things which exist, and what they are like, are independent of us and the way in which we think about them' (1998: 105).

Logical-semantic realism states that propositions about entities – in respect to which there is an ontological commitment – are true (or false) if the conditions of truth in these propositions hold (or not) determinatively, objectively, and independently of our knowledge capacities. As Mäki affirms, 'semantic realism is the thesis that the thesis contained in scientific theories are genuine, *true or false*, statements about the real world and that they have a truth value irrespective of whether we are able to determine it' (1998: 406; italics in the original).

Logical-semantic realists support the idea of objective criteria of truth. That is, there exists a causal order in reality independent of our knowledge (or not) of it. Consequently, while sometimes the nature of the subject does guarantee the accuracy of knowledge, the attempt at knowing is worthwhile, since there is a causal order in reality that we can try to capture through an intellectual intuition motivated and aided by empirical data. That is, depending on the subject, we can also take an epistemic realist stance. Epistemic realism holds:

> that the Xs that are claimed to exist are also knowable. Different forms of *epistemological realism* presuppose some versions of ontological realism and semantic realism and add to them the idea of being known or being knowable. Epistemological realism says of some existing X that facts about X are

known or can be known, implying that knowers have epistemic access to *X*, that there is no veil separating the cognitive subject and the existing object.

(Mäki 1998: 407; italics in the original)

An Aristotelian realist philosopher would maintain that there is a gradation of the capacity for knowledge depending on the necessary or contingent character of the subject studied

Immanuel Kant cast a sceptical doubt on epistemic realism. For him, intuition does not penetrate the nature of things. Kant speaks about a *noumenon*, that is, 'a thing which must be cogitated not as an object of sense, but as a thing in itself (solely through the pure understanding)'. For him, 'the possibility of such noumena is quite incomprehensible, and beyond the sphere of phenomena, all is for us a mere void' (*Critique of Pure Reason*, Second Part, Book II, Chapter III, 'Of the Ground of the Division of All Objects into Phenomena and Noumena', 1982: 97). As Whitehead maintains, 'Kant drove a wedge between science and the speculative Reason because science is about phenomena, not about unknowable noumena' (1929: 60).

Reason then does not play an intuitive but a 'constructivist' role, constructive of the object of knowledge through a priori categories – one of which is a determinist and universal causality (*Critique of Pure Reason*, Book II, Chapter II, section 3, second analogy) – and judgements. This places science on weak ground, given that it ultimately relies on the very reason that builds it, not on reality. Thus, Kant does not provide the foundation that science was looking for. Agnosticism cuts off every possible path towards this foundation. It seems then that we should renounce agnosticism and look again at intuition if we want to find such a foundation.

By the second half of the twentieth century, realist theories of causality start to re-emerge.[8] Indeed, despite Kantian critiques of causality, scientists have always, sometimes unconsciously, looked for causes: 'causality never really went away: scientists' claims were always intended to inform policy, experiment and technology, and such applications require causation, rather than mere association' (Illari, Russo and Williamson, 2011: 3).

The recognition of real causes and their role in explanation lies at the core of Cartwright's message (e.g. 1989). She opposes Hume's reduction of causality to mere regularity of association: 'The generic causal claims of science are not reports of regularities but rather ascriptions of capacities, capacities to make things happen, case by case' (Cartwright 1989: 2–3). She also opposes covering-law explanations because they do not consider causes; they only include the singular case within a general covering law. The following statement by Cartwright (1989: 211) is clear:

I chose deliberately the Aristotelian language of matter, form, and function because these terms are fundamental to a preliminary description of phenomena that appear in my image of science. This language is a thread to the neo-Humean covering-law theorist, and it is meant as such.

When speaking about matter, form, and function, Cartwright recalls the Aristotelian doctrine about explanation and causes. She is not alone in reviving this doctrine. Let me briefly introduce it.

According to Aristotle, explanation is based on causes; for him, causes are really existent, and the ontological and explicative priority of them belongs to the end, 'that, for the sake of which a thing is done', later called 'final cause'. In *Metaphysics* (I, 3–7), Aristotle reviewed the earlier Greek tradition on the nature of investigations into any reality or events, which focused on a search for underlying causes. Proper knowledge hinges on knowing the causes or why something happens. He then elaborated on his pluralist stance on causality (*Physics* II, 3 and 7; *Metaphysics* I, 10 and V, 5): 'a doctrine of four becauses' (Ackrill 1981: 36), finding answers to these questions: What is this made of? Why is this thing and not another? Who made it? And for the sake of what is this made? Later they were respectively called material, formal, efficient, and final causes. Aristotle introduced this doctrine in *Physics* (II, 3 194b 16–35; see also *Metaphysics* I, 3, 983a 26–33):

> In one sense, then, (1) that out of which a thing comes to be and persists is called 'cause' – e.g., the bronze of the statue [...]. In another sense (2) the form or the archetype, i.e., the statement of the essence, and its genera, are called 'causes' [...]. Again (3), the primary source of change or coming to rest; e.g., the man who gave advice is a cause, the father is the cause of the child [...]. Again (4) in the sense of end or 'that for the sake of which' a thing is done.

This last cause is a *telos* (an end which is a perfection), and Aristotle views it as the primary cause: 'First is evidently the one we call for the sake of something' (*Parts of Animals* I, 639b 14). The final cause is ontologically prior to and triggers the action of the efficient cause. As Aristotle states, 'generation is for the sake of substance, not substance for the sake of generation' (*Parts of Animals* I, 640a 18–19). Without an end, there is no action in either the natural or human realms. Aristotle asserts: 'Nature does nothing in vain. For all things that exist by nature, exist for an end' (*On the Soul* II, 12, 434a 31–33).

The final cause also comes first in an explanation. Johnson (2005: 167) explains, 'the cause for the sake of which is not an efficient cause [...] [It] provides the explanation of the end-oriented activity which necessitates "efficient causal" (moving and material) processes'. Aristotle argues that the final cause must be determined first (*Parts of Animals* I, 639b 11–21). Johnson (2005: 180) elaborates, 'an explanation of a natural kind has to specify not just, and not first, the capacities, but rather the activities and that for the sake of which the capacities exist and become active'.[9] For Aristotle, 'explanation cannot even begin until the for the sake of which has been identified [...] To put it into ontological terms: were there no for the sake of which, there would be no powers, potentials, or mechanisms' (Johnson 2005: 185 and 186; see also Falcon 2012: 7–9). Consequently, the teleological explanation is the ultimate explanation, and it is necessary for a full explanation. In Chapter 3 I have noted that Mill also puts the determination of the end at the beginning of the scientific process.

Nonetheless, while Aristotle regards the final cause of an event as the 'primary' (*Metaphysics* I, 3 983a 25–26) cause and explanation, he also considers the possibility of an event with no final cause: in this case, the primary cause is efficient, amounting to its explanation (*Metaphysics* VIII, 4, 1044b 13–15; he uses an eclipse as example).[10]

Aristotle's thinking on explanation and causes is also flexible, as he considers several degrees of necessity/contingency and universality/particularity in causal explanation, depending on the reality to be explained – 'generic effects should be assigned to generic causes, particular effects to particular causes' (*Physics* II, 3, 195b 25–26) – and depending on the explainers' concerns (*Physics* II, 2, 194a 36 – b7; Sorabji 1980: 58–59). Additionally, one or a combination of all four kinds of causes may be more appropriate, also depending on the phenomenon to be explained. However, as noted earlier, the 'primary cause' (*Physics* II, 2, 194a 20; *Metaphysics* I, 3, 983a 25–16) – the final cause – remains the priority. This cause is intimately related to the formal cause because the nature or essence (formal cause) of something corresponds to its end (final cause). Such, for example, is the case of the *ergon* (function) argument to determine the definition of *eudaimonia* in *Nicomachean Ethics* (I, 7; see Johnson 2005: 218–222; Reeve 1995: 123–124).

One reason for the flexibility in Aristotle's account of causes is that, for him, necessity is not absolute but hypothetical. Events are generated by a conditional convergence of causes that do not always occur simultaneously. He states that 'some cases, moreover, we find that, at least, for the most part, and commonly, tend in a certain direction, and yet they may issue at times in the other or rarer direction' (*On Interpretation* IX, 19a 20–23), and that 'those things that are not uninterruptedly actual exhibit a potentiality, that is, a may be or may not be. If such things may be or may not be, events may take place or not' (*On Interpretation* IX, 19a 10–13).

A second reason for contingency lies in causes acting from outside. Aristotle considers luck (*týche*) and spontaneity (*automáto*) (*Metaphysics* XII, 3, 1070a 6–7; cf. also VII, 7, 1032a 12–13). Both terms express an event that results from coincidence (*apo symptômatôn: Physics* II, 8, 199a 1–5). However, does coincidence rule out causality? Aristotle's answer is 'no'; lucky or spontaneous events have causes, but they are indefinite: 'that is why chance is supposed to belong to the class of the indefinite and to be inscrutable to man' (*Physics* II, 5, 197a 9–10). Causes acting from outside might be unexpected because they are not known, or because they are known but cannot be shielded. The former are a source of contingency. The latter are not, because though undesired, they are known. There are concurrent causes that interfere in the action of other causes.

Aristotle's emphasis on a causal explanation does not mean that he did not take into account other purposes of science. Depending on the subject, he stressed the relevance of data collection, the usefulness of predictions, and the normative – technical or ethical – role of some sciences. Yet, while keeping in mind other purposes, he viewed causal explanation as the most important.

In conclusion, Aristotle holds a pluralist view of causality as a way of explaining, but he does not reduce the role of sciences to explanation. He stresses the priority of the final cause. This cause has fallen into oblivion in recent philosophy, even more than the concept of cause. However, we need to understand the final cause before looking for efficient causes: without ends, means do not make sense; without individual or social preferences, there are no economic actions. As MacIver states, 'without goals or motives there are no *social* phenomena. Without some knowledge of goals and motives, there is no understanding of social phenomena' (1942: 331; italics in the original). I will focus on explanation by final cause in Chapter 7. All in all, the flexibility, plurality, and consideration of the contingent nature of the human realm exhibited in Aristotle's position about causality make it especially apt to adopt it in the analysis of human and social causation.

Coming back to contemporary thinking, Reiss (2015: 4–15) does a nice job of explaining the problems of present-day neo-Humean accounts of causality: regularity accounts (John Mackie), probabilistic accounts, process accounts (Wesley Salmon), counterfactual accounts (David Lewis), and interventionist accounts (James Woodward). He then explains realist theories – Anscombe's radical causal pluralism, and causal power theories – and finally presents his theory – the 'inferentialist theory of causation' (2015: 16–22).

I have maintained that economists – like most scientists – are naturally realists about causes.[11] I have shown that Mill (as originally interpreted by Cartwright), Menger, and Neville Keynes searched for causes. Current economists also want to know the causes of economic crises; they need to know the relation between causes and effects to predict what will happen; and they need to know causes to suggest, prescribe, or even implement adequate policies. They do not care about metaphysical problems, but they actually use real causes in all their works. Rodrik's recent book (2015; and see also his article 2018: 277–278), for example, continuously describes the need to seek out the causes of economic phenomena as the task of the economist and the aim of models. This is why I support realist theories.

Aristotle's insights serve as inspiration for Elizabeth Anscombe's ideas on causality. I believe that the latter also adequately explain economic phenomena, because, on the one hand, she thinks that all phenomena have causes but, on the other hand, she maintains that these causes are not necessary. She 'refuse(s) to identify causation as such with necessitation' ([1971] 1981: 133). This refusal involves an argument both against determinism and in favour of indeterminism. Anscombe distinguishes between being determined in the predetermined and determinate senses. What has happened is determined once it happens, and this is obvious (this is the sense in which Aristotle asserts that the past and present are necessary). What she is concerned with is predetermination. Here she proposes this distinction: there are non-necessitating causes, or causes 'that can fail of [their] effect without the intervention of anything to frustrate it', and necessitating causes, or causes that can only be frustrated by interference. For example, tetanus is a necessitating cause of death because without treatment it is not possible for one who has tetanus to survive. Indeterminism, then, is the thesis that not all physical effects are necessitated by their causes. This does not mean, however, that indeterminate effects have no causes ([1971] 1981: 144). For Anscombe, additionally, sustaining indeterminism is relevant for the human realm. She ([1971] 1981: 146) asserts:

> The truth of physical indeterminism is thus indispensable if we are to make anything of the claim to freedom. But certainly it is insufficient. The physically undetermined is not thereby 'free'. For freedom at least involves the power of acting according to an idea, and no such thing is ascribed to whatever is the subject (what would be the relevant subject?) of unpredetermination in indeterministic physics.

That is, for her, contingency in the human realm goes beyond physical indeterminism. The human source of cause is human will, which is free.

Cartwright also distinguishes between necessitating and non-necessitating causes. She refers to Anscombe's non-necessitating causes when she asserts that 'the exercise of a capacity need not occur universally upon triggering even when nothing interferes' (2007: 20; cf. also 2, 4, 50–51). She gives a physical (the quantum capacity of an excited atom to emit a photon) and a 'human' example: 'triggering my irritability *can* produce anger but it *may not* [...] It may even happen that the capacity is there all my life and never exercised' (2007: 20; italics in the original). This kind of cause evidently entails a difficulty for scientific explanation and an even greater one for prediction. Cartwright supports a notion of nondeterministic singular real causes, and she holds that scientific explanation is the knowledge of these causes. Cartwright explains in her book *The Dappled World*:

> [The thesis that] I am most prepared to defend, follows Aristotle in seeing natures as primary and behaviours, even very regular behaviours, as derivative. Regular behaviour derives from the repeated triggering of determinate systems whose natures stay fixed long enough to manifest themselves in the resulting regularity.
>
> (1999: 149)

Cartwright asks: 'What facts then are they that make our capacity claims true?' She answers (1999: 72):

> [T]he best worked out account that suits our needs more closely is Aristotle's doctrine on natures [...]. Capacity claims, about charge, say, are made true by facts about what it is in the nature of an object to do by virtue of being charged. To take this stance of course is to make a radical departure from the usual empiricist view about what kind of facts there are.

The reference to Aristotle's doctrine on causes is explicit. Nature is the essence, which is the formal cause of substance. This essence, as already explained, is oriented towards an end (the cause for the sake of which) that triggers the action of the efficient cause. However, Cartwright recognizes that it is more difficult to discover social capacities.[12] Similar ways of thinking about causes as real existent – though not necessarily manifested – are developed by philosophical currents, considering them as 'powers' (e.g. Mumford and Anjum 2011, Groff 2008, Witt 2008).

Positive economics is only concerned with the efficient cause because it takes the final cause as given. How do we detect this cause? I have argued that it is not directly observed, but uncovered or discerned by the mind through signs or symptoms of it. In the next chapter, I will maintain that the aim of experiments, econometrics, and economic models is to help discover these causes of economic phenomena. This discovery helps us explain and predict them, as well as design policies. This discovery involves an abductive process: abduction plays a relevant role in this task. I will explain it in the next section.

On abduction[13]

Although Aristotle discussed abduction under the name of *apagoge* (in *Posterior Analytics* I, 13), the modern view of abduction was first formulated by American polymath philosopher Charles S. Peirce. Two meanings can be discerned in his use of the term. First, he considers abduction as a type of logical inference. While deduction infers a result from a rule and a case, and induction infers a rule from the case and the result, abduction infers the case from the rule and the result. So understood, abduction can be identified with the fallacy of affirming the consequent. Thus, its result can only be conditionally accepted.

In a second sense, Peirce sees abduction as a way of arriving at scientific hypotheses. He formulates it as ([Peirce 1958] 5.189):

- the surprising fact C is observed;
- but if A were true, C would be a matter of course;
- hence, there is a reason to suspect that A is true.

The conception implied in this second formulation is more general than the first. A might be a case or a hypothetical rule (see Niiniluoto 1999). However, Peirce states that, given that the fallacy of affirming the consequent remains, this process of discovery and hypotheses postulation constitutes the first step of scientific research. That is, abduction in this second sense is a heuristic method assisted by a set of criteria formulated by Peirce. For him, hypotheses should be explanatory (Peirce 1958: 5.171, 5.189, 5.197), economical (Peirce 1958: 6.395, 6.529, 8.43), and capable of being tested in experiments (Peirce 1958: 2.96, 2.97, 4.624, 5.597, 5.634, 8.740). Peirce (1958: 2.756–760) distinguishes three forms of induction: 1) crude induction, that is everyday life empirical generalizations; 2) quantitative induction, that is statistical induction; and 3) qualitative induction, 'the collaborative meshing of abduction and retroduction, of hypothesis conjecture and hypothesis testing' (Rescher 1977: 3). This abduction corresponds to its second formulation and 'retroduction [to] the process of eliminating hypotheses by experiential/ experimental testing' (Rescher 1977: Ibid.).

In common examples of abducting reasoning, explanations often point to causes: 'we want to know the cause' (Peirce 1958: 7.198; see also 2.204, 2.212, 2.213, 3.395, 3.690, 7.221). Let us consider this example in Aliseda (2006):

> You observe that a certain type of clouds (nimbostratus) usually precede rainfall. You see those clouds from your window at night. Next morning you see that the lawn is wet. Therefore, you infer a causal connection between the nimbostratus at night, and the lawn being wet.

There is a background knowledge that helps in identifying the explanation, and consequently, the cause. The final aim of scientific knowledge according to Peirce is, as Nicholas Rescher remarks and argues, 'the actual truth' (Rescher 1977). Still, David Boersema (2003) contends that Peirce takes into account not only metaphysical (causal) aspects in his account of explanation but also epistemological and axiological elements, in the context of a broad theory of inquiry. However, the need for retroduction as a second step in Peircean qualitative induction implies that abduction in its second sense is a way to suggest hypotheses or possible explanations pointing to true causes, but not a sufficiently justified way of accepting them as true.

Nevertheless, IIkka Niiniluoto (1999) asserts that Pierce considers 'an extreme case of abductive inferences' that are 'irresistible or compelling' and come to us 'like a flash' (Peirce 1958: 5.181). In these cases, Niiniluoto contends, 'for Peirce [abduction] is not only a method of discovery but also a fallible way of *justifying* an explanation' (Niiniluoto 1999, italics in the original). That is, the strength of this flash would produce a change of the epistemic state of the agent.

Niiniluoto thus distinguishes the process of suggesting hypotheses embodying a 'weak conception' of abduction and the justification of the hypotheses as a 'strong conception' of it. He equates the latter to an 'Inference to the Best Explanation' (IBE): 'in the strong interpretation, abduction is not only an inference to a potential explanation but to the *best explanation*' (Niiniluoto 1999, italics in the original). In short, the weak conception is the best way of arriving at hypotheses, but does not justify them. The strong conception, in turn, is a fallible way of justifying explanations. This latter conception implies a change in the epistemic state of the agent by which she accepts the hypothesis, acquiring new knowledge (Thagard 1978). Obviously, this acceptance does not mean that the hypothesis is infallible: it is just an accepted hypothesis.

Peter Lipton (2004) regards IBE as a tool to explore, generate, and justify hypotheses. Eleonora Cresto (2002 and 2006) proposes conceiving IBE as a complex process which proceeds in two steps: the abductive stage and, after testing, the selective stage, in which the epistemic state of the agent changes. Developing ideas from Isaac Levi, Cresto applies IBE to the expected utility theory, considering the epistemic virtues of simplicity (or parsimony), unification power, fertility, testability, economy, and accuracy as essential elements of her proposal. Similarly, Harman (1965) proposes simplicity, plausibility, and explanation power as criteria for judging the hypotheses, while Thagard (1978) emphasizes consilience (how much a theory explains), simplicity, and analogy. In turn, Lipton (2004) mentions unification, elegance, and simplicity as virtues leading to what he calls the 'loveliest explanation'. According to him, this 'loveliest explanation' ultimately becomes the 'likeliest explanation'. In addition to empirical adequacy, which is required but not sufficient, other epistemic virtues come into play in the whole IBE process. Each particular context determines the weight assigned to virtues in the epistemic utility calculus. For example, as Maynard Keynes contends, vagueness may be more virtuous than precision when dealing with the complex social realm. For him, elegance and simplicity may be misleading and economy may be a vice instead of a virtue. Rodrik (2015: 179) also distinguishes between 'simple' and 'simplistic' when referring to the characteristic of good models. This is compatible with Peirce's thought: for him 'simplicity' does not imply a 'simplified' hypothesis, but 'the more facile and natural, the one that instinct suggests, that must be preferred' (Peirce 1958: 6.477). Criteria selection is a key point in the process of postulating hypotheses (and, eventually, justifying them). Economic models also aspire to simplicity, unification power, fertility, testability, economy, and accuracy. In the next chapter, I will show how abduction applies to economics.

Conclusion

In this chapter, I have presented a realist Aristotelian and neo-Aristotelian position regarding causality and causation. I have argued that it conforms to the notion of causality that economists need and employ. Then, I briefly explained the meaning of abduction, a method for formulating hypotheses in science. These elements lie at the basis of the arguments that I will develop in the next chapters about economic theory.

Notes

1 Cartwright has been criticized for her interpretation of Mill. Christoph Schmidt-Petri (2008) argues that Cartwright's capacities are significantly different from Mill's tendencies, which he also believes to be problematic for Mill's entire thinking. According to Schmidt-Petri, Mill uses the concept of tendency for entirely practical methodological reasons rather than for metaphysical reasons (2008: 292). Hence, they do not support Cartwright's realist view of capacities (2008: 298). The key question is: are real causes internally consistent with Mill's Humean-like context? Cartwright (1989: 178–179), in her reply to Schmidt-Petri (2008b), has admitted that she was possibly wrong in applying her concept of capacity to Mill. Geach (1961: 103), on whom Cartwright's interpretation of Mill is based, argues that Mill,

confronted with the facts, was obliged to affirm the existence of these real tendencies. But he complains that this doctrine is incompatible with Hume's invariable-succession theory. He adds that Mill's tendencies are very close to Aquinas' doctrine of *inclinationes* or *appetites* in nature –interestingly, because these *inclinationes* are also very close to Cartwright's capacities of nature (cf. Geach 1961: 104–105).

2 In Crespo (2013: 18) I argued for this metaphysical commitment.

3 For a criticism of Hume's conception of causality, see Reiss (2013: Chapter 5), who also provides examples of its failures when applied to economic phenomena.

4 In Crespo (2013: 25) I maintained that the cause may be assimilated to what Aristotle calls a 'common sensible': 'objects which we perceive incidentally through this or that special sense, e.g. movement, rest, figure, magnitude, number, unity' (*De Anima* III, 1, 425a 16–17). This perception is the basis of abstract knowledge of concrete causes and is complemented by it.

5 Quoted by R. Skidelsky ([1983] 1994: 159).

6 For a history of the empiricist and realist positions in the last centuries, see Dilworth (2006, Chapter 1).

7 For an overview of logical positivism, logical empiricism, the attack against this 'received view' and the responses, see Wade Hands (2001, Chapter 3). Hands states:

> According to classical empiricism and early logical positivism, scientific theories *do not explain at all*; the scientific domain is the domain of empirical observation and the purpose of a scientific theory is to reliably describe those empirical observations. The commonsense view of science that science should 'explain' what we observe in the world by uncovering deep, underlying, not directly observable, causal mechanism, is a view that is alien to strict empiricism; 'in science there are no depths; there is surface everywhere' (Carnap, Hahn and Neurath 1929: 8).
>
> (2001: 85; italics in the original)

8 A hallmark of this rehabilitation was Mario Bunge's 1959 book.

9 According to G. H. von Wright, for Aristotle (as well as for Hegel), 'explanation consists in making phenomena teleologically intelligible rather than predictable from knowledge of their efficient causes' (1971: 8).

10 Von Wright (1971: 170) states: 'Although there is a strong emphasis on teleology in Aristotle and in "Aristotelian" science, by no means all explanations characteristic of their way of thinking are teleological'.

11 As Stephen Mumford and Rani Lill Anjum affirm, 'only philosophers worry about it but everyone else believes in causation' (2011: 1). *Causation* is the *production* of an effect by its cause(s), and *causality* is usually understood as the *relationship* between cause and effect. However, in the Aristotelian conception it can be causality without causation, that is, without an effect, because the cause is an inner capacity that may or not act.

12 She asserts:

> The natural thought about the difference between the most fundamental capacities studied in physics and the capacities studied in economics is that the economic capacities are derived whereas those of fundamental physics are basic. Economic features have the capacities they do because of some underlying

social, institutional, legal and psychological arrangements that give rise to them. So the strengths of economic capacities can be changed, unlike many in physics, because the underlying structures from which they derive can be altered.

(2007: 54)

That is, she is not denying causality, but the stability of causes; and she is maintaining the context-dependence of capacities in economics. This is in line with the conception of economic models that I will uphold in the next chapter.

13 In this section and the following chapter, I draw material from Tohmé and Crespo (2013).

References

Ackrill, J. L. (1981). *Aristotle the Philosopher*. Oxford: Clarendon Press.

Aliseda, A. (2006). *Abductive Reasoning. Logical Investigations into Discovery and Explanation*. Dordrecht: Springer.

Anscombe, G. E. M. ([1971] 1981). 'Causality and Determination'. In: *The Collected Philosophical Papers of G. E. M. Anscombe*, vol. 2: *Metaphysics and the Philosophy of Mind*. Oxford: Basil Blackwell, pp. 133–147.

Aristotle (1952). *On the Generation of Animals*. Translated by Arthur Platt. Oxford: Oxford University Press.

Aristotle (1952). *Posterior Analytics*. Translated by G. R. G. Mure. Oxford: Oxford University Press.

Aristotle (1954). *Nicomachean Ethics*. Translated and introduced by Sir David Ross. Oxford: Oxford University Press.

Aristotle (1958). *Politics*. Edited and translated by Ernest Barker. Oxford: Oxford University Press.

Aristotle (1972). *De Partibus Animalium I*. Translated with notes by D. M. Balme. Oxford: Oxford at the Clarendon Press.

Aristotle. (1995). *The Complete Works of Aristotle. The Revised Oxford Translation*. Sixth Edition with corrections. Edited by Jonathan Barnes. Princeton: Princeton University Press.

Boersema, D. (2003). 'Peirce on Explanation'. *Journal of Speculative Philosophy*, 17/3: 224–236.

Boudon, R. (1998). 'Social Mechanisms without Black Boxes'. In: P. Hedström and R. Swedberg (eds.), *Social Mechanisms. An Analytical Approach to Social Theory*. Cambridge: Cambridge University Press, pp. 172–203.

Bunge, M. (1959). *Causality. The Place of the Causal Principle in Modern Science*. Cambridge (MA): Harvard University Press.

Carnap, R., H. Hahn and O. Neurath (1929). 'The Scientific Conception of the World: The Vienna Circle', reprint 1973. Dordrecht: D. Reidel Publication.

Cartwright, N. (1989). *Nature's Capacities and Their Measurement*. Oxford: Oxford University Press.

Cartwright, N. (1999). *The Dappled World. A Study of the Boundaries of Science*. Cambridge: Cambridge University Press.

Cartwright, N. (2007). *Causal Powers: What Are They? Why Do We Need Them? What Can Be Done with Them and What Cannot?*, Centre for Philosophy of Natural and Social Science. London School of Economics and Social Science. Technical Report

04/07. www.researchgate.net/publication/48910977_Causal_powers_what_are_they_why_do_we_need_them_what_can_be_done_with_them_and_what_cannot. Accessed 8 August 2018.

Cartwright, N. (2008). 'Reply to Christoph Schmidt-Petri'. In: Stephan Hartmann, C. Hoefer and L. Bovens (eds.), *Nancy Cartwright's Philosophy of Science*. London: Routledge, pp. 303–304.

Craig, E. (1998). 'Realism and Antirealism'. In: E. Craig (ed.), *Routledge Encyclopedia of Philosophy*, vol. 8, Abingdon: Routledge, pp. 115–119.

Crespo, R. F. (2013). *Theoretical and Practical Reason in Economics. Capacities and Capabilities*. Dordrecht: Springer.

Cresto, E. (2002). 'Creer, inferir y aceptar: una defensa de la inferencia a la mejor explicación apta para incrédulos'. *Revista Latinoamericana de Filosofía*, 28/2: 201–230.

Cresto, E. (2006). *Inferring to the Best Explanation: A Decision Theoretic Approach*, PhD thesis, Columbia University.

Dilworth, C. (2006). *The Metaphysics of Science*. Dordrecht: Springer.

Falcon, A. (2012). 'Aristotle on Causality'. In: E. N. Zalta (ed.), *The Stanford Encyclopedia of Philosophy*, http://plato.stanford.edu/entries/aristotle-causality/. Accessed 24 July 2013).

Geach, P.T. (1961). 'Aquinas'. In: E. G. Anscombe and P.T. Geach (eds.), *Three Philosophers*. Oxford: Basil Blackwell, pp. 64–125.

Groff, R. (2008) (ed.). *Revitalizing Causality*. Abingdon: Routledge.

Hands, D. W. (2001). *Reflection without Rules. Economic Methodology and Contemporary Science Theory*. Cambridge, New York, Melbourne: Cambridge University Press.

Harman, G. H. (1965). 'The Inference to the Best Explanation'. *Philosophical Review*, 74/1: 88–95.

Hempel, C. (1950). 'Problems and Changes in the Empiricist Criterion of Meaning'. *Revue Internationale de Philosophie*, 11: 41–63.

Hempel, C. (1966). *Philosophy of Natural Science*. Englewood Cliffs (NJ): Prentice-Hall.

Illari, P. M., F. Russo and J. Williamson. 2011. 'Why Look at Causality in the Sciences? A Manifesto'. In: P. M. Illari, F. Russo and J. Williamson (eds.), *Causality in Sciences*. Oxford: Oxford University Press, pp. 3–22.

Johnson, M. R. (2005). *Aristotle on Teleology*. Oxford: Oxford University Press.

Kant, I. ([1787] 1982). *The Critique of Pure Reason. Encyclopedia Britannica*.

Keynes, J. M. ([1921] 1973). *A Treatise on Probability, The Collected Writings of John Maynard Keynes*, vol. 8. London: Macmillan.

Keynes, J. N. ([1890] 1955). *The Scope and Method of Political Economy*. Fourth Edition. New York: Kelley and Millman.

Körner, S. (1984), *Cuestiones fundamentales de filosofía*. Barcelona: Ariel (*Fundamental Questions of Philosophy*, Penguin 1969).

Lipton, P. (2004). *Inference to the Best Explanation*, Second Edition. London: Routledge.

MacIver, R. M. (1942). *Social Causation*. Boston: Ginn and Co.

Mäki, U. (1998). 'Aspects of Realism about Economics'. *Theoria*, 13/2: 301–319.

Mill, J. S. (1882). *A System of Logic, Ratiocinative and Inductive*, Eighth Edition. New York: Harper & Brothers.

Mumford, S. and R. A. Anjum. (2011). *Getting Causes from Powers*. Oxford: Oxford University Press.

Niiniluoto, I. (1999). 'Defending Abduction'. *Philosophy of Science*, 66, Supplement (Proceedings): S436–S451.

Peirce, C. S. (1958). *Collected Papers of Charles Sanders Peirce*. Cambridge (MA): Harvard University Press.

Poincaré, H. ([1906] 1925). *La Science et l'Hypothèse*. Paris: Flammarion.

Reeve, C. D. C. (1995). *Practices of Reason*. Oxford: Clarendon Press.

Reiss, J. (2013). *Philosophy of Economics. A Contemporary Introduction*. Abingdon: Routledge.

Reiss, J. (2015). *Causation, Evidence, and Inference*. New York and Abingdon: Routledge.

Rescher, N. (1977). *Peirce's Philosophy of Science. Critical Studies in His Theory of Induction and Scientific Method*. Notre Dame (IN) and London: University of Notre Dame Press.

Rodrik, D. (2015). *Economic Rules*. Oxford: Oxford University Press.

Rodrik, D. (2018). 'Second Thoughts on Economic Rules'. *Journal of Economic Methodology*, 25/3: 276–281.

Schmidt-Petri, C. (2008). 'Cartwright and Mill on Tendencies and Capacities'. In: S. Hartmann, C. Hoefer and L. Bovens (eds.), *Nancy Cartwright's Philosophy of Science*. London: Routledge, pp. 291–302.

Skidelsky, R. ([1983] 1994). *John Maynard Keynes: Hopes Betrayed. 1883–1920*. New York: Penguin Books.

Sorabji, R. (1980). *Necessity, Cause and Blame. Perspectives on Aristotle's Theory*. London: Duckworth.

Thagard, P. R. (1978). 'The Best Explanation: Criteria for Theory Choice'. *Journal of Philosophy*, 75/2: 76–92.

Tohmé, F. and R. F. Crespo (2013). 'Abduction in Economics: A Conceptual Framework and Its Model'. *Synthese*, 190: 4215–4237.

Von Wright, G. H. (1971). *Explanation and Understanding*. London: Routledge and Kegan Paul.

Whitehead, A. N. (1929). *The Function of Reason*. Boston: Beacon Press.

Witt, C. (2008). 'Aristotelian Powers'. In: R. Groff (ed.), *Revitalizing Causality*. Abingdon: Routledge, pp. 129–138.

6   Economic theory II
Positive economics

In this chapter, I will deal with positive economics, the science that studies economic phenomena from a restricted economic point of view, that is the perspective adopted by the second concept of economics described in Chapter 3: a method of applying maximizing instrumental logic to economic phenomena as defined in Chapter 2. It is, in Dani Rodrik's words, a logic of efficiency (2015: 186, 192).[1] Its primary purpose, within economic theory, is to explain. However, it also attempts to predict, a rather challenging task given the uncertainty deriving from complex economic phenomena. As Rodrik (2015: 185) asserts, 'often we can neither guess which among many plausible changes will actually take place, nor be confident about their relative weights in the ultimate outcome. In such instances, economics demands caution and modesty rather than self-confidence'. In Chapters 1 and 3, I argued that economic theory should be broader than positive economics, incorporating the consideration of the actual final causes of economic phenomena. This, I proposed, should be a *conceptual* (in the sense of going beyond a mere sociological or organizational task) interdisciplinary work. Sometime in the future, economic theory might become a new science considering both efficient and final causes. New economic currents as behavioural economics are already undergoing this process.

I reject the developments that apply the restricted economic logic to other human phenomena on the assumption that they are not part of positive economics (though often presented as such).[2] I have argued in Chapter 3 that they are reductive analyses of other human realities. I agree with Coase and Hirschman, among others, in their rejection of these attempts. Various studies that have succumbed to the widespread practice of misusing these terms are published in economic journals. I believe that their usual partiality in explaining non-economic phenomena would make them unsuitable for publication in journals on topics around education, politics, family matters, law, or religion. I also think that economic phenomena are so complex and difficult to understand, while at the same time so relevant for the world, that it is unfortunate that many intelligent people devote a lot of time to other topics and, worse, apply inappropriate methods to these subjects.[3] I recognize that it is a debatable issue because I do not deny that economic logic inserts a quota of 'rationality' into other fields: efficiency is indeed a virtue. However, efficiency is not everything and often it is not the main explanatory criterion in those fields. Actually, it is difficult to avoid falling into mistakes when following these misguided reductionist views. Be that as it may, I am interested in economic phenomena and will concentrate on economists' work on them.

In Chapter 4, I focused on measurement issues. I will not dwell here on the disadvantages of other methods of gathering evidence such as natural, laboratory, and thought experiments, nor will I deal with the limitations of econometrics.[4] I will take these problems for granted and focus on how the economist works using these instruments.

Uncovering causes

The social and human world is a complex world. Although the logic of efficiency may frequently prevail, a plethora of specificities of human beings and societies, individuals' free will, 'irrational' impulses, spontaneous unpredictable decisions, and so on make the task of discovering causes difficult and very much context dependent. In the face of this situation, the work of positive economics is limited. It can be applied to simple and pure economic phenomena – which are very scarce – or it calls for a very strong ceteris paribus condition largely limiting any conclusion. Explanations provided by positive economics will be at best approximate; its hypotheses will be only imperfectly verified; there will always be a margin of error. Its predictions will be decidedly determined by the nature of the phenomena to be predicted and the particular circumstances. Thus, economic policy recommendations must be very prudent and should also take into account specific contextual situations. Therefore, Rodrik (2015) insists on the context dependence of models. He asserts (2015: 45):

> unlike a rock or a planet, humans have agency; they choose what they do. Their actions produce a near infinite variety of possibilities. At best, we can talk in terms of tendencies, context-specific regularities, and likely consequences [...] Economics deals with the real world and is much messier than that [mathematics].

Actually, identifying 'non-economic' causes will contribute to the task of explaining, predicting, or prescribing. A lot of economic phenomena are not efficient from a restricted economic point of view. However, this does not mean that positive economics is completely useless. Its logic can be applied in many cases. In most instances, for example, an increase in money supply will translate to lower interest rates and, given a stable velocity of circulation, this will lead to an increase in the level of transactions and/or prices. Lower interest rates will promote an increase in investment and/or consumption. In a country such as Argentina, where people are used to being wary of inflation, mere signals of monetary expansion or of domestic currency devaluation immediately affect inflation expectations and consequently increase the speed of circulation, thus reinforcing the inflation tendency. In more stable countries, it will have a lesser effect because people are used to stability. It will not be easy to precisely predict the final effect on all variables, but the knowledge of these causal relations and their relative weight – often highly context dependent – will simplify the task. However, getting to know the final effect requires introducing non-economic motives such as social psychology in this case.

When uncovering causes, given the difficulty involved in this process, we have to consider all possible tools that can help us detect them: observation of regularities, though they can be spurious regularities or only a few; calculi of probability, though only probable and not a sign of necessary dependency between events; the study of mechanisms' processes, though sometimes there are no processes, or of interventions' effects, though it is not always possible to intervene; and consideration of what would happen in the absence of the presumable cause, though sometimes the cause does not make a difference. All these means can provide us, albeit imperfectly, with signs of the presence of causes. Statistics, experiments, and econometric studies are tools or methods – also imperfect – based on the above-mentioned sources of evidence, which assist in the task of inferring causes (what has been called 'evidential pluralism about causation'; see Reiss 2015a: 190). Reiss points out the problems of laboratory experiments (2013: Chapter 10, 193), randomized controlled trials (2013: Chapter 11; 206–207), econometrics (2013: Chapter 9, 172), and mechanisms (2013: Chapter 6; 115).[5] All these sources and methods are imperfect because they largely apply induction to contingent realities. We cannot infer universal statements from data on contingent matters. Contingency is essentially not universal. This is very well expressed by Reiss (2015a: 154): 'there is always an inductive gap between evidence and hypothesis: no amount of evidence will be sufficient for the hypothesis or "prove" it in the sense of logically entailing it'.

Additionally, we can wonder whether all these sources of evidence for detecting causes share a common concept of cause. Reiss' (2015a: 191ff.) answer is negative, which would really be a problem if it were true. He is probably right. The word 'cause' is commonly misused and it probably means different things to the econometrician, the statistician, the theorist, and the practical economist (cf. Reiss 2015a: 196).[6] Consequently, in my view, the key to inferring the real causes of economic phenomena lies in the work of the experienced economist who skilfully combines the 'signs' of 'causes' provided by all available methods that can be applied to the study of the concerned phenomenon, again, in order to abduct the real causes. I think that the title of Cartwright's (2007b) book *Hunting Causes and Using Them* adequately describes the economist's job description: he/she should be a chaser – and user – of causes. This is not an easy undertaking since it implies continuously going back and forth from data and experience to theory in order to progressively improve economic models and identify causes. In addition, this economist should be honest and recognize that his/her conclusions are fallible, provisional, and context dependent. There is a strong moral dimension in the economist's task.

I will describe the work of the economist trying to explain past or current economic phenomena. It is harder to predict than to explain, because in explaining the causes of phenomena, causes have already acted and thus, they can presumably be known. In predicting, we can only consider economic causes and some predictable non-economic causes, making other causes difficult to identify in the context of an uncertain future. In the previous chapter, I introduced the Peircean concept of 'abduction'. As in all empirical sciences, the work of the economist includes a large number of abductive inferences. Abduction looks for possible causes involved in hypotheses. The skilled or expert economist usually employs abduction, though often unconsciously. The literature on its use by experts is huge. I will deal with it in the last chapter. The remainder of this chapter will be devoted to explaining my vision about the nature and aims of models: models are 'signs' of causes that they aim to discover. Next, I will discuss the role of abduction in the work of the positive economist.

Good models: 'models as signs' as good economic models[7]

Maynard Keynes wrote to Harrod in the already quoted letter: 'Good economists are scarce because the gift for using "vigilant observation" to choose good models, although it does not require a highly specialised intellectual technique, appears to be a very rare one' (1973: 296). He refers to the art of choosing or developing adequate models to fit the specific context. Rodrik also speaks about 'good models' whose 'critical assumptions approximate the real world' (2015: 29), those which are 'relevant and applicable' (2015: 73; cf. 185). For him, 'the discipline [economics] advances by expanding its library of models and by improving the mapping between these models and the real world' (Rodrik 2015: 5). He regards models as fables, but fables that apply to particular situations (cf. 2015: 21). There is a connection between good models and their close approximation to reality, displaying causal links.

Models can be theoretical or empirical; they can be aimed at merely describing a phenomenon, at explaining or at predicting it. That is, there are many different models with diverse functions. I have professed that economists are great realists: they want to capture some truth in reality because they know that truth is relevant to the accuracy of economic policies. Truth is useful. This is the main message that Harry Frankfurt tries to convey in his bestseller *On Truth* (2006). Therefore, it could be said that the most useful models for economists are those that help infer the true causes of phenomena.

There is an implicit agreement among social scientists about what makes a 'good model'. Through Internet research, interviews with colleagues and ideas extracted from academic papers I have identified an adequate framework for a good model, which I will convey here. A good model brings to light some aspects of reality previously unproved or unnoticed. The conclusions of a good model should match the available data about the situation concerned. In an International Monetary Fund publication, under the section 'Back to Basics', Sam Ouliaris (2011) has asserted:

What makes a good economic model? Irrespective of the approach, the scientific method (lots of sciences, such as physics and meteorology, create models) requires that every model yield precise and verifiable implications about the economic phenomena it is trying to explain. Formal evaluation involves testing the model's key implications and assessing its ability to reproduce stylized facts. Economists use many tools to test their models, including case studies, lab-based experimental studies, and statistics. [...] No economic model can be a perfect description of reality. But the very process of constructing, testing, and revising models forces economists and policymakers to tighten their views about how an economy works.

Paul Teller (2009: 235) states that 'science accomplishes veridical accounts through the use of models', but he underscores that we accept a statement as true when it is 'true enough', relative to our needs and interests (2009: 236). Thus, when speaking of good models, it is essential to maintain a balance between the model's link with reality and the necessary simplification (isolation and idealization) in order to focus on specific dimensions or aspects of reality.

R. I. G. Hughes, for example, points to the importance that models maintain a correspondence with reality when he asserts that 'the characteristic – perhaps the only characteristic – that all theoretical models have in common is that they provide representation of parts of the world, or of the world as we describe it' (1997: S325). On the other hand, Joan Robinson (as do many others) points to the balance between realism and simplification when she remarks (1971: 141):

> It is easy enough to make models on stated assumptions. The difficulty is to find the assumptions that are relevant to reality. The art is to set up a scheme that simplifies the problem as to make it manageable without eliminating the essential character of the actual situation on which it is intended to throw light.

Over the years, there have been different types of models (Morgan 2012) and different explanations about their nature, their role, and the way in which they are built. This topic has been extensively explored by philosophers of economics, who have reached varied positions. Indeed, models are considered, inter alia, as methods to investigate stable, real causes (Cartwright 1999); as mediators between theory and data (Haavelmo 1944, Morrison and Morgan 1999); as surrogate systems (Mäki 2011); as vehicles for testing theories; as thought experiments; as conceptual explorations (Hausman 1992); as open formulas or frameworks for formulating hypotheses (Alexandrova 2008: 200; Guala 2005: Chapter 7); as 'credible worlds' (Sugden 2000 and 2009); as a means of communication or storytelling (Dow 2002: 96–98; Morgan 1999: 178ff., Morgan 2012); as 'epistemic warfare' (Magnani 2012); or as analogies (Hesse 1966; McMullin 1968). These positions attempt, to a greater or lesser extent, to explain and capture some truth about the phenomena under examination.

Here I apply a conceptual instrument, that is a specific conception of signs, for assessing whether a model is a good model, specially focusing on their capacity to reveal the causes of economic phenomena. I base my proposal on the realist conception of signs held by ancient and long-overlooked Portuguese thinker João, or Joannes, Poinsot (1589–1644), who wrote *Tractatus de signis* (*Treatise on Signs*). Poinsot, also known as John of St. Thomas, was a leading representative of the so-called Coimbricenses (from Coimbra, Portugal), a group of seventeenth-century logicians who developed a highly elaborated theory of signs. Let us keep in mind that the medieval period saw the introduction of a very rich theory of semiotics (see Meier-Oeser 2003).

For Poinsot, a sign is 'that which represents something other than itself to a cognitive power' (1985: 25). He thus classifies signs in this way (1985: 27):

> [I]nsofar as signs are ordered to a [knowing] power, they are divided into formal and instrumental signs; but insofar as signs are ordered to something signified, they are divided according to the cause of that ordering into natural and stipulative and customary. A formal sign is the formal awareness which represents of itself, not by means of another. An instrumental sign is one that represents something other than itself from a pre-existing cognition of itself as an object, as the footprint of an ox represents an ox. And this definition is usually given for signs generally. A natural sign is one that represents the nature of a thing, independently of any stipulation and custom whatever, and so it represents the same for all, as smoke signifies a fire burning. A stipulated sign is one that represents something owing to an imposition by the will of a community, like the linguistic expression 'man'. A customary sign is one that represents from use alone without any public imposition, as napkins upon the table signify a meal.

Table 6.1 illustrates this classification.

According to Poinsot's conception, words (such as 'fire') are considered instrumental and customary or conventional signs, while thoughts or concepts (such as the concept of fire) are formal and natural signs of the captured reality. Poinsot's formal sign directly applies to a real reference. Leo Apostel (1961: 15) argues that 'the mind needs in one act to have an overview of the essential characteristics of a domain'. This is performed by a 'formal sign'.

Table 6.1 Poinsot's classification of signs

According to its relationship to its meaning.	– Natural: smoke and concept of fire. – Conventional: the word 'fire' or drawing of a flame.
According to its relationship to what is represented: with the cognoscente.	– Formal: deals directly with what it represents. – Instrumental: smoke and word 'fire'.

This conceptual framework is in accordance with some current ideas about models. Mäki (2011) distinguishes between the model ('the imagined world, possessing the characteristics provided by the set of idealizing assumptions and missing characteristics of real-world situations') and the description of the model (mathematical, verbal, geometric). In the same vein, Pierre Salmon (2000 and 2005) distinguishes between

- the real world with all its complexity;
- the isolated or 'target system' (i.e. the aspect of the real world, isolated from its context, that we try to explain and understand);
- the model or the 'model described'; and
- the description of the model, or the 'describer model'.

An additional step in assessing or building a good model would be to ensure that the 'describer model' actually serves as an instrumental and customary representation or sign, and that the 'model described' is a formal and natural sign of the real connections between the variables of the isolated target system.

If we accept the last step proposed for building a good model, the described model should bring the knower to the real connections concerned in a way that allows him to understand them directly. We do not need to fix our attention on the model per se but rather directly grasp the relation between concepts that it *expresses*. In this way, knowledge 'passes through models' towards the known relation. For example, using a golf metaphor, a good stroke depends highly on continuing the swing down with a good 'follow through'. Just as if you stop the swing, the stroke is ineffective, so too, if knowledge is stopped at the model itself, it will be ineffective as well. Rodrik states that models 'open our eyes to counterintuitive possibilities and unexpected consequences' (2015: 46), and that economics becomes a useful science when models 'enhance our understanding of how the world works and how it can be improved' (2015: 83).

One may ask, however, whether the belief in this relation is true, that is, whether it is strictly speaking knowledge.[8] This is a distinctive characteristic of my vision of a 'good model'. Models, however, are fallible. As such, their truth depends on the empirical existence of the concepts that they denote and of the relations that they postulate. In other words, are the concepts denoted by the model actually related in the way expressed by the model? If the answer is affirmative, the model is true. The aim of scientific inquiry is to determine the truth of the model. Here, since abduction is fallible, retroduction – testing – becomes necessary. Econometrics tries to provide a bridge between data and the model in order to accept, reject, or refine it.[9]

Finally, what kind of relation does a 'good model' express? I have asserted that most economists are realists. However, I acknowledge that some economists only aim to know which variables are 'determined' (and hence 'explained' but not necessarily really caused) by the model and which are not. However, I hold that a 'good model' must go beyond merely showing which variables are determined and seek to uncover the real causes at play in the situation under analysis. Why? Because correlation without causation makes for very imperfect knowledge and economists want to accurately predict and propose dependable economic policies. Thus, Cartwright (2009: 20) asserts: 'the function of a model is to demonstrate the reality of a capacity' (which for her is a stable cause). In the same vein, Reiss (2001: 295) has maintained that 'only if a model represents a capacity, will it be informative about a real situation'.

For Henry Veatch, a scientific hypothesis 'leads to a recognition of a causal order underlying and making intelligible the connections between the various objects of knowledge' (1952: 330). For him, these hypotheses 'would seem to be instruments for intending the causal order and structure of what is given in experience' (1952: 331). I indeed think that this is what economists should look for in models. Larry Boland (1989: Chapter 6 and 2010) claims that 'every model can be seen to be positing a causal mapping'. This is the describer model. He adds that 'every explanation of observed events [...] implies a conjectured cause-effect relationship' (2010: 536). The simplification that a 'good model' entails should be then aimed at detecting the relevant causes. Caterina Marchionni suggests that 'some of the unrealistic elements of economic models serve the function of fixing the *causal* background' (2006: 426, my italics). I have noted that the importance of discovering causes is present throughout Rodrik's book.

Must all models express causation? Not all types of models need to reveal causation. Beyond all possible kinds of models, however, there is a reason why the social field recommends the search for causes. Whatever conception we hold about the connection of events within the social field, that is teleological connections, reasons for action, intentional causation (Searle 2001), there is growing agreement about what in ordinary language we would call 'cause'. This is why it seems that expressing or revealing a cause, while not being a necessary condition, is a sufficient and convenient condition for good models. At this point, it may prove useful to listen to other economists. For example, Kindleberger asserts (1965: 40):

> An economic model is a statement of relationships among economic variables. Its purpose is to illustrate causal relations among critical variables in the real world, stripped of irrelevant complexity, for the sake of obtaining a clearer understanding of how the economy operates, and in some formulations, in order to manipulate it.

The verbs 'to operate', and 'to manipulate' actually refer to causes.[10] Paul Romer, in his 2016 controversial paper 'The Trouble with Macroeconomics', uses the verb 'to cause' nine times and complains about what he calls 'post-real models' (2016: 4ff.). A good model that uncovers causes will prove adequate for explanation, prediction, and policymaking. However, we may broadly hold that a 'good model' should postulate a hypothesis about the causes at work in the analysed situation. Perhaps Anna Alexandrova's (2008: 396) proposal for models as 'open formulae' is too 'weak', but it comes close to my idea. She argues that 'models are used as suggestions for developing causal hypotheses that can be tested by an experiment'. I would say that 'good models' postulate testable causal hypotheses.

Next, we must prove this hypothesis. We must take into account that, given the local and complex character of the social field, we may easily make mistakes. In fact, there is a trade-off between precision and accuracy (see Paul Teller 2008). We must then perform an empirical verification. As Aristotle asserts in *Generation of Animals* (concerning his observations with regard to the generation of bees) 'credit must be given rather to observation than to theories, and to theories only if what they affirm agrees with the observed facts' (III 10, 760b 31). Through testing, we carry out a process of adapting models to the specific situations concerned. As Maynard Keynes maintains, 'the specialist in the manufacture of models will not be successful unless he is constantly correcting his judgment by intimate and messy acquaintance with the facts to which his model has to be applied' (1973: 300).

Harold Kincaid (2008, pp. 596–597, italics in the original) explains,

> If we have evidence that a model with unrealistic assumptions is picking out the causes of certain effects, then we can to that extent use it to explain, despite the 'irrealism'. If I can show that my *insight* is that a particular causal process is operative, then I am doing more than reporting a warm feeling. If I can show that the same causal process is behind different phenomena, then *unification* is grounded in reality. If I can provide evidence that I use my model as an *instrument* because it allows me to describe real causes, I can have confidence in it. Finally, if I can show that the causes postulated in the model are operative in the world, I can begin to provide evidence that the model really *does* explain.

The term 'insight' used by Kincaid is often used by Maynard Keynes with reference to intellectual apprehension (see my paper 2008). It is also used by Kuipers (1961: 132): 'Senses and intellect both play an active part in our shaping of the model and consequently in our obtaining an *insight* into the phenomena which cause us to try and find explanations' (my italics). 'Good models' produce an intellectual apprehension of or insight into a possible cause.

In sum, albeit fallibly, models should identify causes in order to apprehend them. They need to be fine-tuned through a verification process. Although I recognize that data are theory laden and value laden, I maintain that to 'test, test and test' (Hendry 1980: 403) is the only way to refine causal apprehension. However, what is the model formulation process? This is the subject of the next section.

The work of the economist

Maynard Keynes wrote to Roy Harrod in 1938:

> It seems to me that economics is a branch of logic; a way of thinking [...] one cannot get very far except by devising new and improved models. This requires, as you say, 'a vigilant observation of the actual working of our system'. Progress in economics consists almost entirely in a progressive

improvement in the choice of models [...] Economics is a science of thinking in terms of models joined to the art of choosing models which are relevant to the contemporary world. [...] The object of a model is to segregate the semi-permanent or relatively constant factors from those which are transitory or fluctuating so as to develop a logical way of thinking about the latter, and of understanding the time sequences to which they give rise in particular cases.

(Keynes 1973: 296, letter to Harrod, 4 July 1938)

Though Rodrik (2015) does not quote these Keynes' ideas on models, in his 2018 paper he affirms: 'Had I been familiar with this quote from Keynes before I wrote the book, I might have chosen not to spend the effort!' (2018: 277). For Rodrik, the essential work of the economist is to choose appropriate models or develop new models adapted to specific circumstances (2015: passim), capturing 'the most relevant aspect of reality in a given context' (2015: 11). The reason for this is the complexity and contingency of the social life (2015: 67, 116): 'there are few immutable truths in economics' (2015: 148). Rodrik applies Isaiah Berlin's famous metaphor to economists, splitting them into two camps: hedgehogs and foxes. Berlin quotes the Greek poet Archilochus' saying, 'the fox knows many things, but the hedgehog knows one big thing' (1953: 1). Hedgehog economists think that there is always one way of resolving an economic problem, regardless of context, while fox economists will answer, 'it depends' (2015: 175). Rodrik favours fox economists. In the same train of thought, he supports Albert Hirschman's criticism of some scholars' compulsive tendency to look for all-encompassing theories that discard real-world contingencies (2015: 145). Hirschman coined the telling expression 'monoeconomics' and criticized its claims (1981: 3).

Models are central devices used by economists. Statistics; natural, laboratory, and thought experiments; and econometric tools are elements that contribute to formulating and refining models in an iterative process going back and forth. The economist develops this 'craft' through practice and experience (cf. Rodrik 2015: 83, 112, 184). Rodrik also speaks of the need for 'good judgment' in selecting models (2015: 21).

I will add that abduction is an essential component of economic analysis, both theoretical and practical, because abduction lies behind model selection. This craft or good judgement of the economist is the skill of abducting models from background theoretical knowledge, data, experiments, and whatever sources of evidence to which the economist has access: 'good judgment, evidence from other sources and structured reasoning' (Rodrik 2015: 24).

Models are often written in mathematical language but, regardless of their formal expression, they use metaphors, analogies, and pieces of intuition to motivate their assumptions and to give support to their conclusions (see Frigg 2006).[11] In dealing with ongoing economic processes, agents and analysts must generally evaluate whether a given situation bears a significant resemblance to instances observed or studied in the past, and whether this warrants somehow applying the 'lessons' drawn from those experiences. Judging 'whether some pasts are good references for the future' becomes a particularly hard task when the economy undergoes important changes. Simplicity in the Peircean sense, explanatory power, coherence, and testability are rather unconsciously considered in this abduction of possible explanatory models.

The retroductive phase also involves problems implying abductive-like decisions. As obvious as it may sound, it must be recognized that there is a gap between the formulation of a question to be answered through measurement and the actual measurement providing the right answer. The difference arises from the fact that problems are qualitative, while data are quantitative. In consequence, rough data (which are the quantitative counterparts of qualitative concepts) must be organized according to the qualitative structure to be tested. That is, we must seek to find a correspondence between theory and data. So, for example, economic theory draws a crucial distinction between ordinal and cardinal magnitudes in the characterization of preferences. But once measurement is involved, we must assume that the theoretical relational structure is homomorphic to a numerical structure (Krantz et al. 1971). This implies that if there is a database holding numerical observations about the behaviour of a phenomenon or a system, we might want to infer the properties of the qualitative relational structure to which the numerical structure is homomorphic.

Of course, several factors may hinder this task:

- the syntactic representation of the qualitative structure can be somewhat ambiguous (Barwise and Hammer 1994);
- although the observations fall into a numerical scale, the real world is too noisy, allowing only a statistical approximation;
- the complexity of the phenomena may be exceedingly high. Thus, only rough approximations may make sense.

These factors, which preclude a clear-cut characterization of the observations, leave ample room for arbitrary differences. In this sense, the economist's and the econometrician's intuition and experience will determine the limits of arbitrariness in an abductive-like fashion. As an example, consider the question 'Did a specific economy grow last year?' To provide an answer, first, one has to clearly define what exactly does it mean when you say that an economy is growing and which variables can be used to measure such a growth phenomenon. According to economic theory, economic growth is usually measured as the per cent rate of increase in national income. But in order to answer the question, an economist has to define what real-world data will represent national income; that is he/she has to embed the available data in the theoretical framework. In this case, the national product is an available variable which is easy to measure and is considered (theoretically) equivalent to national income. Therefore, it is easy to check out whether the specific economy grew or not. But if the case poses a question such as 'Did welfare increase in the last 20 years?', the procedure will be far less simple. How do we define welfare and, moreover, how do we make the concept operational? This is where the economist's intuition is brought into play. Although theoretical concepts may be lacking, a set of alternative models of the notion of welfare and its evolution over time should be provided in order to check out which one better matches real-world data. Once the question is settled, it is possible to consider developing a theory formalizing the properties satisfied in the chosen model. That is, when the abducting process is completed, the theory-building phase can start.

Inferences that allow economists and econometricians to detect patterns in reams of data cannot be called mere statistical inductions. They are more the result of a detective-like approach to scarce and unorganized information, where the goal is to get clues out of unorganized data bases of observations and to disclose hidden explanations that make them meaningful. In other words: it is a matter of making guesses, which can later be put into a deductive framework and tested with statistical procedures. So far, it seems that it is just an 'artistic' feat, which can only be performed by experts.

Paola D'Orazio (2017: 417–419) has shown the relevance of abduction for agent-based macroeconomic models which use big data. John Davis (2018) has also discussed the role of abduction in these models and in agent-based computational economics. He contrasts 'standard economics' – which has stable principles – with these two currents, showing the closed methodological approach used by the former and the open approach adopted by the latter. Abduction is an open form of inference. Davis calls the latter approach a 'social science model of economics' and shows how it evolves alongside the world it investigates and vice versa, while in standard economics this mutual interaction does not happen. Mickey Peled (2019) shows the role of weak abduction (in contrast with strong abduction or IBE) in the formulation of monetary policy. In addition, I have maintained together with my colleague Fernando Tohmé (Tohmé and Crespo 2013) that abduction is also present in some of the steps of standard economic theories.

Economists work with a set of general rules. When a surprising or abnormal fact appears, or when the economist wants to explain a phenomenon that has not already been explained, or wants to study the possible effect of a given action, the first step is to try to come up with an explanation according to those rules. By a surprising or abnormal event, we mean one that we usually ignore. As Gabbay and Woods (2005: 85) assert, 'abduction is triggered by the irritation of ignorance'. This irritation may be weak or strong. It is weak when we presume that the event can be explained by our previous knowledge (rules, theories, models). In contrast, it is strong when we do not find in our previous knowledge any possible explanation. Weak ignorance or abnormal/surprising events often lead to selective abduction, while strong ignorance prompts creative abduction: 'the researcher develops a new model that he or she claims better accounts for the "deviant" observations' (Rodrik 2015: 64). The economist has to either select from a portfolio of models or create a new model.

The best explanation is obtained by narrowing down the possible hypotheses until only one of them remains. In this process, the economist uses information on similar situations as well as the features of the specific case to capture simple and coherent hypotheses and models.

Let us give a brief systematization of this reasoning process in economics. We may distinguish the following steps:[12]

1   An abnormal/surprising/ignored triggering event is detected, requiring an explanation.
2   The event is carefully described.
3   Some stylized facts are extracted from the description.
4   Situations sharing the same stylized facts are given particular attention.
5   Possible explanations based on a theory, a modified theory, a combination of theories (sometimes supposing a decision about possibly competing theories), or a completely new theory are imagined.
6   Formal expressions – models – capturing the relations deemed essential in the explanation of the relevant stylized facts, according to the previous step, are formulated.
7   Only those combinations of deductive chains and inductive plausibility that are both externally valid and internally coherent are chosen, discarding other possibilities.
8   This provides an original coherent explanation/s of the event.
9   The conclusions are tested.

Abduction especially underlies steps 3, 4, 5, and 7. Steps 6 and 7 are mostly deductive. Step 9 is inductive and retroductive. The whole process is a Peircean qualitative inductive process (in the already mentioned sense defined by Rescher (1977: 3), but it generally also uses instrumental assumptions. The so-called *as if* arguments are continuously used in economics.

Good economists display a 'guess' instinct ([Peirce 1931–1958]: 6.476– 477) in these scientific processes. This is no mysterious miracle but an intellectual intuition, stemming from a theoretical framework or background knowledge, experience, and hard work with theories, models, and data. This induces good economists to foresee a set of possible successful models. Combining this gift with hard empirical work, economists often overcome the problem of underdetermination of theories by formulating local or context-dependent theories. Context dependence is a characteristic feature of the 'inference to the best explanation' (IBE) (Cresto 2006; Day and Kincaid 1994). However, economists always try to improve their models. This is because, given the fluctuating ontological condition of the economic material, a close approximation to reality is required. The analogies sometimes work and sometimes do not. Old or conventional theories may be misleading. Model improvement, however, is limited. On the one hand, the frequent urgency of decisions that cannot wait for further investigation, and the economy of research (Rescher 1977: 65ff., extensively quoting Peirce), actually lead to accepting the conclusions as fallible though reasonable inferences to the best explanation. On the other hand, the mentioned quantification, conceptual, institutional, data accuracy, calculation and even presentation issues also prompt us to accept a sufficiently proved, fallible conclusion as a good one.

Conclusion

In this chapter, I did not delve into the imperfections of all the sources of evidence of positive economic work.[13] They are very well explained, for example, by Reiss (2013 and 2015a). I have taken them for granted. However, despite these limitations, I have attempted to provide a positive outlook by focusing on the conditions and strategies for developing good positive economics.

Models are the main tool of positive economics. The key to building good models – models that are close to reality and uncover the causes of economic phenomena – lies in the flexibility to select or construct models adapted to the specific context concerned. This requires a special craft or expertise on the part of the economist, as well as good judgement to discern the most appropriate models. Abduction, the logic of formulating hypotheses, underlies this expertise. The economist abducts a model taking into account the evidence provided by a plethora of sources and instruments: statistics, thought, natural and lab experiments, econometrics, and so on. All of them are imperfect devices but provide clues to finding the causes that models should help capture. Reiss (2015a and 2015b) also assigns a key role to judgement in his theory of inference from evidence to hypotheses, given the highly context-dependent characteristics of causal claims, and the necessity of basing our inferences on a plurality of sources of evidence.

In the next chapter, further contributing to improving the economist's task, I will consider non-economic causes that affect economic phenomena.

Notes

1   This chapter will take Rodrik's book (2015) especially into account. He is a prominent practicing academic economist open to new developments in the field. This book echoes my criticisms of economists' modelling practice, considers insights from philosophers of economics and maintains a balanced and clever position towards positive economics. As Emrah Aydinonat (2018a: 211) states, this book 'presents a rare opportunity for economists and philosophers of economics to engage in mutually beneficial exchange that could improve our understanding of the power and limits of economics, and the rights and wrongs of the dismal science'.

2   As stated in Chapter 3, Rodrik adopts the idea that economics is a method and considers applying this method to other human realities as part of economics. However, he recognizes that 'economists do get careless and make claims that are broader than their economist licenses really allow'. He acknowledges that 'questions of justice, ethics, fairness, and distribution' [...] 'cannot be evaluated solely on grounds of efficiency' (2015: 194).

3 I think the following statement by Charles Taylor against 'formalisms like utilitarianism' applies to these people: 'we find masses of researchers engaging in what very often turns out to be futile exercises, of no scientific value whatever, sustained only by the institutional inertia of a professionalized discipline' (1985: 231).

4 On these limitations, see, for example, Boumans (2015: Chapter 4).

5 The problems of laboratory experiments, especially of external validity, have generated extensive discussion. Guala (2005) is a must in this sense. See also Santos (2010). The validity of the conclusions in randomized controlled trials has also been abundantly discussed. Reiss (2013: 115) thinks that mechanistic explanations do not apply in economic models that are highly idealized.

6 For the meaning of causality in econometrics, see K. Hoover (2001: Chapter 7 and 2004).

7 In this section I draw material from Crespo (2012).

8 According to a long-standing philosophical tradition, knowledge is by definition a true belief. From the days of Plato to the present, knowledge is, for most scholars, 'JTF', that is, justified true belief (see, for example, R. K. Shope, 'Propositional Knowledge'. In: J. Dancy and E. Sosa (1992), *A Companion to Epistemology*, Oxford: Blackwell, or M. Steup, 'The Analysis of Knowledge'. In: E. N. Zalta (ed.), *The Stanford Encyclopedia of Philosophy*, http: //plato.Stanford.edu/entries/knowledge-analysis/). Thus, the least we can assign to knowledge is to be 'factive' (to presuppose the truth), that is, if we know that *p*, then it is the case that *p*. We cannot know something that is not a fact. This does not portray our intelligence as infallible. If the known proposition is not true, an epistemic state of mere belief will emerge, different from an epistemic state of knowledge. Keynes asserts: 'Thus knowledge of a proposition always corresponds to certainty of rational belief in it and at the same time to actual truth in the proposition itself. We cannot know a proposition unless it is in fact true' ([1921] 1973: 11). Closer to Keynes than Plato or contemporary philosophers, Bertrand Russell affirms: '[S]ome propositions are true and some false, just as some roses are red and some white; that belief is a certain attitude towards propositions, which is called knowledge when they are true, error when they are false' (1904: 523).

9 This description of econometrics corresponds to a vision of it as inspired or guided by theory. The founding of the Econometric Society in 1931 marks the 'official' birth of Econometrics, a discipline aimed at relating economics, mathematics, and statistics. The Cowles Commission for Research in Economics began its econometric research in 1932. The work carried out in these institutions, mainly theory based, set the perspective from which econometrics has been developed during its early history. This perspective can be summarized as follows: economic theory inspires the construction of a model, then we gather the relevant data for the models' variables to estimate the unknown parameters and, finally, the model is tested. That is, econometrics – a joint work of economic theory and statistics – helps assess whether economic theory is right or not. It tries to connect this theory with empirical reality. However, given the limitations of economic theory recognized by Mill, Menger, and Neville Keynes – the fact that there can be plenty of variables, even non-economic variables, influencing economic phenomena; that the possibility and accuracy of experiments is highly limited; and that consequently, the

models can be incomplete – how can we conduct credible econometric research? How do we know that we are using the right theory and model?

    Another vision of econometrics maintains that we must let the data speak without theory. However, even though there is always a criterion behind data collection, how can we overcome the problem of underdetermination of theories by data (the same data relations can be explained by different theories)? 'Many different causal interpretations may be consistent with the same data' (Heckman, 2000: 47). Heckman analyses different econometric strategies to answer the so-called economics 'identification' problem and suggests harder work on data to overcome disagreements. From a philosophical perspective, data are relevant in contingent subjects, but the inductive problem will always remain. For a complete analysis of the methodology of econometrics, see Hoover 2005.

10 It might be added to the everyday language words expressing causal concepts listed by Elizabeth Anscombe (1993: 93).

11 Economists also use the so-called manipulative abduction. This category might include very different proceedings such as diagrams representing economic relations, laboratory experiments and natural experiments. Specific economic policies are based on economic hypotheses and theories, but their results also generate new knowledge.

12 See also the steps to find adequate models suggested by Aydinonat (2018b: 248) agreed to by Rodrik (2018: 278).

13 Rodrik, for example, states: 'the fluidity of social reality makes economic models inherently difficult, even impossible, to test' (2015: 65–66); 'despite econometricians' best efforts, convincing causal evidence is notoriously elusive' (2015: 66).

References

Alexandrova, A. (2008). 'Making Models Count'. *Philosophy of Science*, 75: 383–404.

Anscombe, G. E. M. (1993). 'Causality and Determination'. In: E. Sosa and M. Tooley (eds.), *Causation*. Oxford: Oxford University Press, pp. 88–104.

Apostel, L. (1961). 'Towards the Formal Study of Models in the Non-formal Sciences'. In: H. Freudenthal (ed.), *The Concept and the Role of the Model in Mathematics and Natural and Social Sciences*. Dordrecht: D. Reidel Publishing, pp. 1–37.

Aydinonat, N. E. (2018a). 'Philosophy of *Economics Rules*: Introduction to the Symposium'. *Journal of Economic Methodology*, 25/3: 211–217.

Aydinonat, N. E. (2018b). 'The Diversity of Models as a Means to Better Explanations in Economics'. *Journal of Economic Methodology*, 25/3: 237–251.

Barwise, J. and E. Hammer (1994). 'Diagrams and the Concept of Logical System'. In: G. Allwein and J. Barwise (eds.), *Logical Reasoning with Diagrams*. Oxford: Oxford University Press, pp. 49–78.

Berlin, I. (1953). *The Hedgehog and the Fox. An Essay on Tolstoy's View of History*. London: Weidenfeld and Nicolson.

Boland, L. (1989). *The Methodology of Economic Model Building: Method after Samuelson*. London, Routledge.

Boland, L. (2010). 'Cartwright on "Economics"'. *Philosophy of the Social Sciences*, 40/3: 530–538.

Boumans, M. J. (2015). *Science outside the Laboratory*. Oxford: Oxford University Press.

Cartwright, N. C. (2009). 'If No Capacities, No Credible Worlds. But Can Models Reveal Capacities?'. *Erkenntnis*, 70: 45–58.

Cartwright, N. C. (1999). *The Dappled World. A Study of the Boundaries of Science*. Cambridge: Cambridge University Press.

Cartwright, N. C. (2007). *Hunting Causes and Using Them*. Cambridge: Cambridge University Press.

Crespo, R. F. (2008). 'Keynes's Realisms'. *European Journal of the History of Economic Thought*, 15/4: 673–693.

Crespo, R. F. (2012). 'Models as Signs as Good Economic Models'. *Estudios Económicos*, XXIX (NS), 58: 1–12.

Cresto, Eleonora (2006). *Inferring to the Best Explanation: A Decision Theoretic Approach*, PhD thesis, Columbia University.

Davis, J. B. (2018). 'Agent-Based Modeling's Open Methodology Approach: Simulation, Reflexivity, and Abduction'. *Oeconomia*, 8/4: 1–15.

Day, T. and H. Kincaid (1994). 'Putting Inference to the Best Explanation in Its Place'. *Synthese*, 98: 271–295.

D'Orazio, P. (2017). 'Big Data and Complexity: Is Macroeconomics Heading toward a New Paradigm?'. *Journal of Economic Methodology*, 24/4: 410–429.

Dow, S. (2002). *Economic Methodology: An Inquiry*. Oxford: Oxford University Press.

Frankfurt, H. (2006). *On Truth*. New York: Alfred Knopf.

Frigg, R. (2006). 'Models in Science'. In: E. N. Zalta (ed.), *The Stanford Encyclopedia of Philosophy*, http://plato.stanford.edu/entries/models-science/. Accessed 22 September 2012.

Gabbay, D. M. and J. Woods . (2005). *The Reach of Abduction. Insight and Trial*. Amsterdam: Elsevier.

Guala, F. (2005). *The Methodology of Experimental Economics*. Cambridge: Cambridge University Press.

Haavelmo, T. M. (1944). 'The Probability Approach in Econometrics'. *Econometrica*, 12 (Supplement): i–viii, 1–118.

Hausman, D. M. (1992). *The Inexact and Separate Science of Economics*. Cambridge, New York, Melbourne: Cambridge University Press.

Heckman, J. (2000). 'Causal Parameters and Policy Analysis in Economics: A Twentieth Century Retrospective'. *Quarterly Journal of Economics*, 115: 45–97.

Hendry, D. F. (1980). 'Econometrics-Alchemy or Science?'. *Economica*, 47/188: 387–406.

Hesse, M. (1966). *Models and Analogies in Science*. Notre Dame (IN): Notre Dame University Press.

Hirschman, A. O. (1981). *Essays on Trespassing Economics to Politics and Beyond*. Cambridge: Cambridge University Press.

Hoover, K. D. (2005). 'The Methodology of Econometrics'. www.uibk.ac.at/econometrics/lit/methodology_hoover_2005.pdf. Accessed 22 June 2018.

Hoover, K.D. (2001). *Causality in Macroeconomics*. Cambridge: Cambridge University Press.

Hoover, K. D. (2004). 'Lost Causes'. *Journal of the History of Economic Thought*, 26/2: 149–164.

Hughes, R. I. G. (1997). 'Models and Representation'. *Philosophy of Science*, 64: S325–S336.

Keynes, J. M. (1973). *The General Theory and After: Part II. Defence and Development, The Collected Writings of John Maynard Keynes*, vol. 14. London: Macmillan.

Keynes, J. M. ([1921] 1973). *A Treatise on Probability, The Collected Writings of John Maynard Keynes*, vol. 8. London: Macmillan.

Kincaid, H. (2008). 'Social Sciences'. In: S. Pasillos and M. Curd (eds.), *The Routledge Companion to Philosophy of Science*. London and New York, Routledge, pp. 594–604.

Kindleberger, C. P. (1965). *Economic Development*. Second Edition. New York: McGraw-Hill.

Krantz, D., R. D. Luce, P. Suppes and A. Tversky. (1971). *Foundations of Measurement* I. New York: Academic Press.

Kuipers, A. (1961). 'Model and Insight'. In: H. Freudenthal (ed.), *The Concept and the Role of the Model in Mathematics and Natural and Social Sciences*. Dordrecht: D. Reidel Publishing, pp. 125–132.

Magnani, L. (2012). 'Scientific Models Are Not Fictions. Model-Based Science as Epistemic Warfare'. In: L. Magnani and P. Li (eds.), *Philosophy and Cognitive Science*, SAPERE 2, pp. 1–38.

Mäki, U. (2011). 'Models and the Locus of Their Truth'. *Synthese*, 180: 47–63.

Marchionni, C. (2006). 'Contrastive Explanation and Unrealistic Models: The Case of the New Economic Geography'. *Journal of Economic Methodology*, 13/4: 425–446.

McMullin, E. (1968). 'What Do Physical Models Tell Us?' In: B. van Rootselaar and J. F. Staal (eds.), *Logic, Methodology and Philosophy of Science III*. Amsterdam: North Holland, pp. 385–396.

Meier-Oeser, S. (2003). 'Medieval Semiotics'. In: E. N. Zalta (ed.), *Stanford Encyclopedia of Philosophy*, http://plato.stanford.edu/entries/semiotics-medieval/. Accessed 22 September 2015.

Morgan, M. (1999). 'Models, Stories, and the Economic World'. In: U. Mäki (ed.), *Fact and Fiction in Economics*. Cambridge: Cambridge University Press, pp. 178–201.

Morgan, M. (2012). *The World in the Model. How Economists Work and Think*. Cambridge: Cambridge University Press.

Morrison, M. and M. Morgan (1999). 'Introduction'. In: M. Morgan and M. Morrison (eds.), *Models as Mediators*. Cambridge: Cambridge University Press, pp. 1–9.

Ouliaris, S. (2011). 'What Are Economic Models?'. *Finance and Development*, 48/2, (www.imf.org/external/pubs/ft/fandd/2011/06/basics.htm). Accessed 22 June 2017.

Peirce, C. S. ([1931] 1958). *Collected Papers of Charles Sanders Peirce*. Cambridge (MA): Harvard University Press.

Peled, M. (2019). 'Multiple Models and Monetary Policy: The Role of Abduction'. Paper presented at the International Network for Economic Method 2019 Conference, Helsinki, August 2019.

Poinsot, J. ([1631–1635] 1985). *Tractatus de Signis. The Semiotic of John Poinsot*, edited by John N. Deely. Berkeley, Los Angeles and London: University of California Press.

Reiss, J. (2001). 'Natural Economic Quantities and Their Measurement'. *Journal of Economic Methodology*, 8/2: 287–311.

Reiss, J. (2013). *Philosophy of Economics. A Contemporary Introduction*. Abingdon: Routledge.

Reiss, J. (2015a). *Causation, Evidence, and Inference*. New York and Abingdon: Routledge.

Reiss, J. (2015b). 'Two Approaches to Reasoning from Evidence or What Econometrics Can Learn from Biomedical Research'. *Journal of Economic Methodology*, 22/3: 373–390.

Rescher, N. (1977). *Peirce's Philosophy of Science. Critical Studies in His Theory of Induction and Scientific Method.* Notre Dame (IN) and London: University of Notre Dame Press.

Robinson, J. (1971). *Economic Heresies.* London: Macmillan.

Rodrik, D. (2015). *Economic Rules.* Oxford: Oxford University Press.

Rodrik, D. (2018). 'Second Thoughts on Economic Rules'. *Journal of Economic Methodology*, 25/3: pp. 276–281.

Romer, P. (2016). 'The Trouble with Macroeconomics'. Delivered 5 January 2016 as the Commons Memorial Lecture of the Omicron Delta Epsilon Society. https://paulromer.net/wp-content/uploads/2016/09/WP-Trouble.pdf. Accessed 18 November 2018.

Russell, B. (1904). 'Meinong's Theory of Complexes and Assumptions (III)'. *Mind*, NS, 13/52: 509–524.

Salmon, P. (2000). 'Modèles et mécanismes en économie: essai de clarification de leurs rélations'. *Revue de Philosophie Economique*, 1/1: 105–126.

Salmon, P. (2005). 'Qu'est-ce qui représente quoi? Réflexions sur la nature et le rôle des modèles en économie', Université de Bourgogne, Document de travail July 2005, www.u-bourgogne.fr/leg/documents-de-travail/e2005-07.pdf. Accessed 30 July 2015.

Santos, A. (2010). *The Social Epistemology of Experimental Economics.* Abingdon: Routledge.

Searle, J. R. (2001). *Rationality in Action.* Cambridge (MA): MIT Press.

Sugden, R. (2000). 'Credible Worlds: The Status of Theoretical Models in Economics'. *Journal of Economic Methodology*, 7: 1–31.

Sugden, R. (2009). 'Credible Worlds, Capacities and Mechanisms'. *Erkenntnis*, 70: 3–27.

Taylor, C. (1985). *Philosophy and the Human Sciences. Philosophical Papers 2.* Cambridge: Cambridge University Press.

Teller, P. (2008). 'Representation in Science'. In: S. Psillos and M. Cud (eds.), *The Routledge Companion to Philosophy of Science.* London and New York: Routledge, pp. 435–441.

Teller, P. (2009). 'Fictions, Fictionalization, and Truth in Science'. In: M. Suárez (ed.), *Fictions in Science.* London: Routledge, pp. 235–247.

Tohmé, F. and R. F. Crespo (2013). 'Abduction in Economics: A Conceptual Framework and Its Model'. *Synthese*, 190: 4215–4237.

Veatch, H. B. (1952). *Intentional Logic.* New Haven (CT): Yale University Press and London: Oxford University Press.

7   Economic theory III
Final causes

On economic preferences

This chapter begins by looking at the notions stressed in the previous chapters that economists want to know the causes of economic phenomena, and that economic theory is that part of the economic sciences that looks for the causes of economic phenomena. In the previous chapter I dealt with positive economics, displaying how it tries to identify the *economic* causes of economic phenomena: for example, the economic causes of the last world financial crisis or of Argentinean current inflation. However, crises or inflation are not purely determined by economic causes, such as inappropriate fiscal or monetary policies, but also, for instance, by psychological or sociological characteristics of the people or nations affected by these phenomena. Overconfidence prior to the crisis and panic during it are key non-economic factors contributing to economic downturn. If economic theory is to explain adequately and predict accurately, it must take into account these non-economic causes.

Concerning individual economic agents, given that their behaviour is also likely to have multiple causes, economists – especially micro-economists – attempt to take all them into account by subsuming them under the umbrella of 'preferences'. This is not just the result of laborious work but, as Erik Angner notes, preferences are also 'a primitive' of economic theory, something economists take as given (2018: 665–666).

Preferences seem to be the motives or reasons for action, the final causes, as expounded in Chapter 5, the causes of causes. An old medieval axiom reads 'causae ad invicem sunt causae': we need to consider the final cause because without its presence the efficient cause does not move. Action is the fruit of the synergy between final and efficient cause. The economist's map of preferences determines our way of spending our money: for example, my preference for diesel cars, though demonized for their impact on the environment and probably inefficient from an economic point of view, causes me to buy a diesel car. To put it in philosophical jargon, the final cause triggers the action of the efficient cause. Given preferences, economists explain and try to predict how people act.

However, the way economists often conceive of preferences, in order to avoid omitting any cause, ironically makes them miss the real causes of economic phenomena. They fall into what Charles Taylor calls 'the formalist illusion' (1985: 233). The section on the maximizing principle in Chapter 3 is crucial for understanding this and what follows. (I suggest re-reading it; it only takes five minutes to do so.) This is not an easy topic and, as Bruce Caldwell (1991) maintains, there is a lot of confusion surrounding it.

Let us briefly recall the argument of the mentioned section (more extensively developed in Crespo 2013). There, I distinguished between an 'empirical' and a 'metaphysical' maximization principle. The former defines a specific criterion for empirically judging whether a particular conduct has been maximizing or not. The latter equates maximization with rationality and rationality with intentionality in a broad sense that includes value-driven, affective, routine, and spontaneous motives. Consequently, for the latter, given that all conduct is intentional (in a conscious or unconscious way), we always maximize or act rationally. The aim behind this definition is to evade judgements about the rationality of conduct, thus avoiding making value judgements about them. The problem with this second version of the principle is that it is uninformative. David Wiggins observes that it may be affirmed, a posteriori, through a kind of *rationalization* that conduct has been maximizing. However, he notes that this claim is nearly vacuous because 'it does not represent a falsifiable claim about the agent's springs of action' (2002: 371). The metaphysical principle is such because it is not falsifiable. Wiggins concludes that utility theory is not a sketch but a caricature of human decisions and actions (cf. 2002: 390). Geoffrey Hodgson (forthcoming; italics in the original) also distinguishes both principles. He states:

> Utility maximization is consistent with *any* data concerning the behaviour of *any* organism or machine. In other words, utility functions can be modified to fit data on any manifest behaviour. Particular utility or preference functions may be falsified because they are unable to predict some observed behaviour, but Max U in general terms is *unfalsifiable* [...] Max U offers an ex-post rationalization or 'expression' of behaviour – rather than an empirically-grounded causal explanation.

Hodgson's particular preference functions correspond to my empirical principle and his Max U to my metaphysical principle. I was very glad to read Bart Engelen's 2017 paper: he likewise realizes that,

> if every behavior can be fitted into a preference ranking or utility function, the latter is no longer doing any real explanatory work [...] The notion of preferences as all-things-considered comparisons [he is referring to Hausman's 2012 conception of preferences] lumps together all underlying motivational factors and thereby obfuscates what is of interest to whoever aims to explain human behavior.
>
> (2017: 258)

Katie Steele also holds that, thus, 'it is unclear whether maximizing expected utility has any substantial meaning' (2014: 201).

Daniel Hausman (2012: 3) distinguishes between 'total comparative evaluations' and 'overall comparative evaluations'. In the latter, some factors affect the evaluation of alternatives as competing with preferences, while in the former, all factors are included in the preferences. He states: 'This book argues that preferences in economics are rankings that express total subjective comparative evaluations and that economists are right to employ this concept of preference' (Hausman 2012: 7). Erik Angner (2018: 665) quotes from Philip Wicksteed (1933: 86):

> By a man's 'scale of preferences' or 'relative scale', then, we must henceforth understand the whole register of the terms on which (wisely or foolishly, consistently or inconsistently, deliberately, impulsively or by inertia, to his future satisfaction or to his future regret) he will, if he gets the chance, accept or reject this or that alternative.

The problem here is that we are not able to identify the specific causes of a particular behaviour.[1] Trying to encompass combined causes in only one notion of preference discards the possibility of knowing the particular causes of the considered phenomenon and hinders distinction between them. Trying to include all causes under the concept of preferences is reductive. As Amartya Sen and Bernard Williams explain, '*Reduction* is the device of regarding all interests, ideals, aspirations, and desires as on the same level, and all representable as preferences, of different degrees of intensity, perhaps, but otherwise to be treated alike' (1982: 8; italics in the original). Preferences so understood lack empirical content, thus making it difficult to detect the precise motivations lying behind the concerned behaviour (or the failure of motivations stemming from 'weakness of will' – see Slote 1989: 185).[2] We are actually abandoning the goal of discovering the ultimate causes of economic phenomena in order to explain or predict. As Mary Hirschfeld states, 'we are left with a theory that is void of any content at all' (2018: 61).[3] In addition, this concept of 'all-inclusive' preferences implies that the specific desires included in them are all commensurable and reducible to a unique unit: utility. However, not all possible motivations for actions are commensurable: either we set them away from preferences or include them in a denaturalized way.

The solution is clear: 'whatever explanatory or predictive force preference-based models have, comes from the stipulation of substantive assumptions about the content of preferences, not from stipulations about their structure' (Engelen 2017: 258). To define the content of preferences means to delimit which motivations we are going to consider in our preference functions and which not to consider. It probably presupposes making value judgements and, in this sense, economic theory is interlaced with normative economics.

Engelen proposes considering preferences as overall comparative evaluations. He suggests removing from preferences three kinds of motivations: cravings, duties, and commitments (2017: 261).[4] It is common sense to understand that actions stemming from cravings, addictions, and so on are contrary to conscious rational preferences. It is also common sense that duties and commitments may go against preferences. Likewise, in a social environment, as Karsten Stueber remarks, 'there are normative reasons whose validity is independent from one's merely subjective perspective' (2016: 98).

However, when we act contrary to our preferences, we have to internalize the reason why we do so. Could we term this a 'preference'? It all depends on how we define preferences. But, again, from a common-sense understanding, or ordinary speech, we can act against preferences: 'I would have preferred to have holidays in the beach, but my wife preferred to have them at the mountains; then, I decided to go to Mendoza instead of Mar del Plata'. Or as Brendan Hogan and Lawrence Marcelle (2017: 411) put it, 'it is near a truism in English that one can reasonably choose to do something even though one prefers not to'. Vivian Walsh actually states that the economic concept of preference is a misleading construction, because for it 'one cannot be said to have chosen what one does not prefer' (1996: 88).

Where does the all-inclusive notion of preferences have its roots? David Hume's well-known statement which reads, 'Reason is and ought only to be the slave of passions and can never pretend to any other office than to serve and obey them' ([1739–1740] 1968: 415 – II, iii, 3) entails a definition of preferences. Hume considers actions as motivated by ends determined by passions, not by reason (ibid.: 415). Given that desires are the only normative forces behind actions, actions are not rational or irrational; they are laudable or not; or, simply, they are 'non-rational'. This view of desires has had a great influence in later thinking and may also have had an effect on the economic concept of preferences.

In contrast, John Searle (2001) emphatically argues for the existence of reasons for actions independent of desires. He thoroughly analyses the assumptions made by Hume and the neo-Humean's instrumental rational model, criticizing it while defending freedom, the reality of the weakness of will, and the existence of external reasons for action. These normative reasons lie outside agents – independent of their desires – and are subsequently internalized by them (2001: 114–115). Let us recall Mill (1882: 657): 'There must be some standard by which to determine the goodness or badness, absolute or comparative, of ends, of objects of desire'.

The discussion about external or internal reasons for action is huge and I cannot deal with it here. I think Searle holds a balanced position. He states: 'Motivators can be either external or internal. Desires, for example, are internal motivators, and needs and obligations are external motivators. But, to repeat, the external motivators can function in deliberation only insofar as they are represented as internal motivators' (2001: 119). Indeed, he criticizes Bernard Williams and David Davidson for treating desires and desire-independent reasons for action as belonging to the same set as desires (such as economists do with preferences), and he maintains that a promise is a desire-independent reason that is prior to the desire and the ground of the desire, driving the performance of the corresponding action (cf. 2001: 170). We usually have reasons, which are facts, for desiring something.[5] Ends, which are final causes, are different from desires, which are efficient causes.[6] Hodgson (forthcoming) agrees with Searle. He asserts:

> Moral judgments are not simply expressions of an individual's interests, preferences, sentiments or beliefs. They are also universal claims, which are deemed to have force irrespective of the interests, preferences, sentiments or beliefs of those to whom they are supposed to apply.

Or as Hilary Putnam states, 'desires and interests are not simply givens whose satisfaction needs to be maximized (as too many economists have assumed), they need to be subjected to intelligent and informed criticism' (2016: 42).

Beyond the discussion about 'externalism' and 'internalism', it is crucial to distinguish the different kinds of motivations or reasons for action – the final causes of it – because the uniform concept of preference incorrectly amalgamates incommensurable reasons and does not enable sound explanation and, much less, prediction. Final cause is a wider concept than economic preference. As I have argued elsewhere, 'it becomes necessary to open this black box [of standard economics] in order to examine the roots and contents of preferences' (Crespo 2017: 32; cf. also 166), and these contents might not be all that motivates the specific action.

I have explained that efficient causes do not act without the influence of final causes. But, why do we need to know the final causes? Isn't it sufficient to know the direct action of the efficient cause? Habitual consumers of a product are buying more of it because its price has decreased. However, why has the price decreased? It could be a competitive pricing decision, or a response to cost reduction or a decrease in demand. Subsequently, we need to know the causes of these possible causes. Behind the first and the third causes, there are human intentions that we need to understand. We can decide to temporarily lose money in order to conquer the market or, in the case of the third cause, it may have resulted from a changing taste in the segment of consumers who usually buy this product and the incorporation of a lower segment of consumers that would buy the product at a lower cost. We are speaking of intentions, purposes, that point towards people's ends. The mere facts do not reveal preferences and underlying motivations. Mere facts do not allow us to determine if the behaviour observed is due to errors, misinformation, weakness of will, duties, and commitment, or to the specific content of the preferences. It is not the same to say that I prefer diesel cars as to state why I prefer them and buy them. The latter analysis would require a more complete and deeper explanation that could help predict my future decisions about cars. The traditional revealed preference theory equates actual choices with preferences, implicitly supposing that preferences cause choices. Modern revealed preference theory only states that preferences represent choices without implying a causal commitment.[7] However, as Hausman (2012: 33) states, preferences are different from choices. Steele (2014: 190; italics in the original) explains:

The revealed preference interpretation offers little by way of explanation and prediction of choice behavior. It does not have the resources to express what *particular* features of a prospect an agent finds (un)desirable and therefore (un)choiceworthy. There is thus no way to determine whether some current/future choice situation is relevantly similar to a past choice situation, such that one would expect an agent to behave similarly. In short, revealed preference theory has no inductive (predictive) power. Moreover, the view does not countenance an agent having irrational preferences or choosing contrary to their preferences, due to impulsiveness or weakness of will.

What I am arguing for is that actual choices can be different from preferences and that, as MacIver (1942: 8) explains, facts do not necessarily directly reveal to us human teleological causes or ends. We need to specifically ascertain them. Buchanan, in a similar comment, notes that the economic behaviour behind data may be nonexistent or swamped by non-economic considerations (1979: 49).

However, it is not easy to include ends in a model because they are often incommensurable and, in addition, they are hard to measure individually. How can I measure the impact of my preference for diesel cars on my action of buying one? Can I commensurate the hypothetical measure of my preference for diesel cars with the influence of the moral strength exerted on my decision of the damaging consequences for the environment of buying a diesel car? Can I measure this influence? In my country, the price of diesel fuel was typically less than regular gasoline, thus low-income households usually opted for the former. Today, there is almost no price difference between them. However, as a researcher, I want to identify myself with low-income people: diesel use is a sign of (low) economic status. How can I measure the impact of this sense of belonging to a low-income class on my decision? Tastes, moral motivations, and sociological characteristics are involved in this decision, and it is difficult to estimate the weight of each of them. The same complications apply to collective decisions in which the idiosyncrasy, culture, traditions, and so on of specific social groups come into play. We cannot include all these motivations in a homogeneous function corresponding to a homogeneous concept. They are all reasons for action, but of different kinds. We cannot commensurate them but only compare them by 'practical reason' and by making 'prudential' rather than technical decisions.[8]

Given all these difficulties, the economist's reaction – to adopt the notion of preferences as all-things-considered comparisons – is understandable. However, in this way, economics becomes a useless discipline. 'Houston, we have a problem'. How do we solve it?

The way in which standard economics proceeds to make the preferences logic operative is to restrict the utility function. It specifies the goods and their prices, and prescribes maximizing the consumer's income-wealth or the entrepreneur's profit. But where do the non-economic preferences remain?

In Chapter 4, I referred to the problem of incommensurability and explained the role of practical reason to overcome it. However, this role is mostly normative: we need to use practical reason in order to decide which ends we are going to emphasize and how much effort we will put into each end; this is a task of normative economics. Here, instead, we are not looking for a normative logic, but to know or understand which ends have been actually adopted.[9] I am referring to Menger's *Verständnis* or to Sidgwick trying to *understand* other motives different from economic motives and the weight of each of them. This will shed light on how we may complete economic theory adding the consideration of non-economic ends to positive economics.

Moreover, a second consideration is required. Economists apply instrumental maximizing logic to the task of achieving the all-things-considered preferences. The unity of the 'instrumental self', as Elizabeth Anderson (1993: 39) calls the 'self' involved in this economic kind of logic, hinges on the unity of its preferences. However, as she explains, it cannot account 'for the rational unity of our emotions, attitudes, internalized norms, intentions, and ways of deliberating. In unifying a person's preferences and choices around the achievement of particular consequences, the instrumental view creates discord among other aspects of the self' (1993: 40). The instrumental view includes other motivations for an instrumental reason – in order to maximize utility or preferences – and, thus, 'denaturalizes' these motivations, which do not focus on maximization.[10] In the same vein, Viktor Vanberg (2008: 605–610) notes that seeking to account for non-economic motives by including them as preferences misses the point. Instrumental motives are outcome oriented. Instead, non-instrumental motives are not guided by outcomes but by actions that are valuable in themselves, an instance of 'preferences over actions per se' instead of preferences over outcomes (Vanberg 2008: 609). Mark White (2019: 251) also notes that

> individuals do not make choices only to satisfy preferences within constraints, even if those preferences reflect other-regarding or altruistic concerns. Individuals also make choices based on principles, qualitative ideals that do not fit easily into a preference ranking, but instead often supersede the consideration of preferences entirely.

For Anderson (1993: 79), a more encompassing view of rationality 'has global authority' over all possible motivations for action, while instrumental calculations 'play various local roles within it'. Or, as Martha Nussbaum (1999: 183) puts it, cost-benefit analysis only serves as an 'acolyte'. We usually associate 'rational' with 'reasonable', thus providing a broader notion than the economic view of rationality, which is a highly restricted subset of the former.

However, the logic of this 'more encompassing view of rationality' is not a maximizing logic, because it includes incommensurable ends. It is a 'prudential logic' performed by practical reason in a non-normative but understanding role. The economist should try to present models that explain phenomena. However, models are often not enough because there are reasons behind these phenomena that cannot be included in a model empirically tested. This is because these reasons cannot be measured and made commensurate. What is the method for detecting and combining these reasons? This is the topic of the next section. However, before going into this, I want to highlight the difficulties derived from taking ends as given. Simply put, ends are not given. As Frank Knight (1956: 128–129) points out, 'given ends' are not ends in themselves; ends are redefined in the course of the action itself. In other words, not only are means adapted to their ends but also – and even more frequently – ends are adapted to their means. Ludwig Lachmann also notes that 'some of the knowledge relevant to the action will only be acquired *in agendo*' (1971: 40). For James Buchanan, choice is a process by which preferences are continuously renewing themselves.[11] He asserts that 'choice, by its nature, cannot be predetermined and remain choice' (1987: 35); 'men can choose courses of action that emerge only in the choice process itself' (1987: 78). The task of the economist is to discover what people want (1987: 16). For him, it is clear that individuals do not have given ends, and he therefore believes that this fact blurs the dividing line between positive and normative economics (1987: 15–16). In sum, means and ends mutually interact and determine each other. Malte Dold and Mario Rizzo (2019) explain how, according to Knight and Buchanan, preferences are not the input to but the result of a decision-making process: 'people often want the better but do not know exactly what that means, especially in not completely-known future situations' (2019: 3). There is a continuous redefinition of ends, which are only provisionally given. As Dold and Rizzo state (2019: 5; italics in the original), '[i]n light of uncertainty, individuals act *exploratively* (they often do not yet know what they want) and *experimentally* (they mostly learn through trial and error)'. Or as Hogan and Marcelle state, 'ends are revisable depending upon what we learn from a situation and the consequences of our values given that the environment has thrown up an obstacle to our normally smooth habitual functioning and projection of desires' (2017: 405).

The idea of ends as given implies a truncated view of action that cannot be human. It is actually a fiction. Elizabeth Anderson, commenting on John Dewey's moral philosophy, asserts (2005: 8):

> We do not first already have an end in view, with the only question how to achieve it. We lack a complete conception of our end until we have a complete grasp of the course of action that will take us there. Moreover, a judgment of the value of ends apart from the means needed to get there, and apart from the value of ends as means – as things that have consequences of their own – cannot provide the basis for rational action. Acting on such radically truncated judgments would be crazy' [...] It is irrational to take one's end as fixed before investigating the costs of the means and the consequences of achieving the end.

All practical economists and policymakers know that more than tackling the problem of allocating means to given ends, a big part of their job is to decide on ends based on existing means. As Adam Martin and Matías Petersen (2019: 208) assert, 'coping with the economic problem means adjudicating between several, heterogeneous and often incommensurable ends', and they apply this definition to poverty alleviation. This is also the case with economic agents: we are always redefining preferences. Thus, economists cannot escape decisions and investigation or ends, and economics cannot turn a blind eye to this problem. Economists cannot be mere technicians; they must be able to understand what ends people choose. Let us now address the topic of a method for knowing ends.

Explanation and understanding

For Aristotle, as explained in Chapter 5, ends or final causes are everywhere, in human and nonhuman nature: 'Nature does nothing in vain. For all things that exist by nature, exist for an end' (*On the Soul* II, 12, 434a 31–33). For him, the final cause is the primary cause, the cause of causes, impressing an order in nature. However, while this order in nonhuman nature is mostly given and, consequently, its ends are relatively easily detected, humans are free, have reasons and beliefs and, therefore, knowing their ends entails a more difficult task: a specific kind of 'interpretation' or 'understanding'.

Georg Henrik von Wright, in his classic book *Explanation and Understanding*, has distinguished the (Aristotelian) 'finalist' and the (Galilean) 'mechanistic' types of scientific explanation (1971: 2 and passim).[12] He explains that the prevalent positivistic attitude towards finalistic explanations ('to account for facts in terms of intentions, goals, purposes'; 1971: 4 – 'understanding') involves rejecting them as unscientific or reducing them to causal mechanistic explanations.

In reaction to this positivist position, as advanced in Chapter 3, German thinkers as Johann Gustav Droysen, Wilhelm Dilthey, Georg Simmel, and Max Weber distinguished a methodological dichotomy between explaining – *Erklären* – as the method of *Naturwissenschaften* and understanding – *Verstehen* – as the method of *Geisteswissenschaften*.[13] For them, understanding is connected with capturing intentionality through a form of empathy. Weber speaks about an empathic understanding that plays a role in explaining in the social sciences. According to von Wright (1971: 8), for Georg Wilhelm Friedrich Hegel, as for Aristotle, 'explanation consists in making phenomena teleologically intelligible rather than predictable from knowledge of their efficient causes'. However, the tendency to reduce teleological explanation to efficient causal explanations – 'the causalization of teleology' process, as von Wright (1971: 31) calls it – has continued throughout the twentieth century to such a degree that, at present, 'causes' are efficient causes.

Von Wright (1971: 89) claims that actions have outer and inner aspects. The phases of the outer aspect can be subsumed under the same intention, that is, intentionality brings the two aspects together. It is thanks to the teleological background that the mechanism of behaviour becomes operative (1971: 149–150). Intentionality is *in* the behaviour; it is not something behind or outside behaviour, 'as though one could discover the intentionality from a study of the movements' (1971: 115). We capture it by understanding or interpretation.[14] However, this does not mean that explanation does not have a role. For von Wright, the two activities are interconnected: 'explanation at one level often paves the way for a reinterpretation of the facts at a higher level' (1971: 134).

An ample gamut of positions on the character, role, and scope of interpretation has prevailed in the social sciences: from almost positivist perspectives, highlighting the need of empirical testing to achieve objectivity, to more subjective methods stressing the difficulties of objectification of human intentions. These different perspectives respectively tend to approach or separate the subject and methods of natural and social sciences.[15] Daniel Steel and Francesco Guala distinguish the 'theory theory' approach, proposing that 'humans interpret one another by forming and testing hypotheses', from 'simulation theory', holding that 'people have a natural tendency to put themselves in another's shoes by internally simulating what they would experience if they were in the other's position' (2011: 144). Karsten Stueber (2012: 18–19) distinguishes a psychological empathetic understanding and a non-psychological interpretive activity which proceeds holistically. In a recent article (2019), he differentiates between the 'theoretical mode of understanding' – subsuming things or events under general categories –, the 'narrative understanding' of a developmental process and 'empathic (or reenactive) understanding'.

I choose to take a conciliatory stance on this matter. Different subjects call for different methods. I think that depending on the specific subject, greater stress should be given to simulation – 'reenactive empathy', as it is called by Stueber (2012) – or to understanding particular events in the context of a larger social, cultural, historical, and institutional whole. We can apply different methods to empirically verify, albeit imperfectly, the conclusions of simulating practices. Behavioural and happiness economics are in the process of doing so. Daniel Little's following words might apply to various economic phenomena (1995: 42; italics in the original):

> It is possible to be an empiricist (that is, insisting on rigorous empirical evidence in support of a proffered interpretation). And it is possible to incorporate the perspective of *verstehen* into a broadly causal framework (maintaining, for example, that it is the meaningful self-understanding of participants in a market economy that *causes* the regularities of the price system).

Stueber (2019: 12) also holds that 'the human sciences are characterized by a complex interplay between theoretical, narrative, and empathic understanding'. In my view, this conception also applies to the explanation of economic phenomena. However, we must be cautious so as not to fall into positivist analyses that are often partial or even misleading.

References to *Verstehen* or interpretation in economics have been associated with the hermeneutic tradition, with Weber's, Alfred Schutz's and Paul Ricoeur's thought. I will briefly review these positions and some of their weak impacts on economic thought. The German tradition of *Verstehen* is closely linked with the hermeneutical tradition. Hermeneutics began as an art of historical and biblical interpretation. As time went by, awareness of the need for interpretation became widespread, expanding to literary works, other arts, language, culture, human action, and all of reality. Within this approach, interpretive understanding as well as explanatory techniques have their legitimate place as stages of what Ricoeur (1991: 164) calls the *hermeneutical arc*.[16]

Alfred Schutz has made another relevant contribution to understanding in the social sciences and economics. He takes elements from Weber, Edmund Husserl, and Henri Bergson, among others. First, in an article published in *Economica* (1943), he distinguishes two levels of analysis of social facts: the 'reasonable' pre-scientific and the 'rational' scientific. However, he links them together. In the creation of ideal types to scientifically analyse the chosen sector of the social world, we must comply with what he calls 'the principle of relevance' in relation to the specific problem analysed. To complement this, he develops the 'postulate of the subjective interpretation' – 'to ask what type of individual mind can be constructed and what typical thoughts must be attributed to it to explain the fact in question' – and the 'postulate of adequacy', formulated as follows (1943: 147):

> Each term used in a scientific system referring to human action must be so constructed that a human act performed within the life world by an individual actor in the way indicated by the typical construction would be reasonable and understandable for the actor himself, as well as for his fellow men.

This postulate requires that the typical construction be compatible with our daily life and scientific experience (1943: 148), that is, explanation and understanding. Schutz raises the question (1943: 146):

> But why form personal ideal types at all? Why not simply collect empirical facts? Or, if the technique of typological interpretation may be applied successfully, why not restrict oneself to forming types of impersonal events, or types of the behaviour of groups? Do we not have modern economics as an example of a social science which does not deal with personal ideal types, but with curves, with mathematical functions, with the movement of prices, or with such institutions as bank systems or currency? Statistics has performed the great work of collecting information about the behaviour of groups. Why go back to the scheme of social action and to the individual actor? The answer is this: It is true that a very great part of social science can be performed and has been performed at a level which legitimately abstracts from all that happens in the individual actor. But this operating with generalisations and idealisations on a high level of abstraction is in any case nothing but a kind of intellectual shorthand. Whenever the problem under inquiry makes it necessary,

the social scientist must have the possibility of shifting the level of his research to that of individual human activity, and where real scientific work is done this shift will always become possible. The real reason for this is that we cannot deal with phenomena in the social world as we do with phenomena belonging to the natural sphere. In the latter, we collect facts and regularities which are not understandable to us, but which we can refer only to certain fundamental assumptions about the world. [...] Social phenomena, on the contrary, we want to understand and we cannot understand them otherwise than within the scheme of human motives, human means and ends, human planning – in short – within the categories of human action.

Second, Schutz postulates the insertion of individuals and their actions into a specific intersubjective world of everyday life. For him, it is basic to understand and take into account this social ground of meaning to develop sciences. He states:

> The basis of meaning *(Sinnfundament)* in every science is the pre-scientific life-world *(Lebenswelt)* which is the one and unitary life-world of myself, of you, and of us all.
>
> ([1940] 1982: 120)

> Thus, every reflection finds its evidence only in the process of recurring to its originally founding experience within this life-world, and it remains the endless task of thought to make intelligible the intentional constitution of the contributive subjectivity in reference to this its basis of meaning. We, however, who live naively in this life-world, encounter it as already constituted. We are, so to speak, born into it. We live in and endure it, and the living intentionality of our stream of consciousness supports our thinking, by which we orient ourselves practically in this life-world, and our action, by which we intervene in it. Our everyday world is, from the outset, an intersubjective world of culture. It is intersubjective because we live in it as men among other men, bound to them through common influence and work, understanding others and being an object of understanding for others. It is world of culture because, from the outset, the life-world is a universe of significations to us, i.e., a framework of meaning *(Sinnzusammenhang)* which we have to interpret, and of interrelations of meaning which we institute only through our action in this life-world.
>
> ([1940] 1982: 133)

The *Verstehen* and hermeneutic methods, though not widely spread, have been applied to economics. Ricoeur himself explains how this is performed (1991: 166; 1981: 161). In Chapter 3, I recounted that prior to all these authors, but inspired in the German tradition of distinguishing *Erklären* and *Verstehen*,

Menger had stated, referring to theoretical sciences, ([1883] 1985: 43; italics in the original), that:

> The goal of scholarly research is not only the *cognition* [*Erkenntnis*], but also the *understanding* [*Verständniss* [sic]] of phenomena. We have *gained cognition* of a phenomenon when we have attained a mental image of it. We understand it when we have recognized the reason [*Grund*] for its existence and for its characteristic quality (the reason [*Grund*] for its *being* [*Seins*] and for its *being as it is* [*So-Seins*]).

This reason – *Grund* – refers to the essence and the final cause of the phenomenon. Also in Chapter 3, I noted that Sidgwick stated that 'we require for the *comprehension* of economic facts some *interpretation* of the motives of human agents' (1887: 30–31, my italics).

In his book on Weber's legacy, Ludwig Lachmann maintains that the interpretive or *Verstehen* method can be applied not only to study individual actions but also the 'classes of such actions' (1971: 22–23). It is not only a historical method but also a 'theoretical method' (1977: 47). Instead of individual purposes, we have elements common to plans such as norms, institutions, institutionalized behaviour and so on. He states:

> we are able to give an 'intelligent account' of human action by revealing the plans which guide it, a task beyond the grasp of the natural sciences. The mere fact that this possibility exists is the foundation of the method of interpretation and thus offers a vindication of the plea for the methodological autonomy of the social sciences.
>
> (1971: 30)

Lachmann reconstructs Weber's thought stating that social sciences aim to understand human action, a task which is warranted by its purposive character; and that purpose is an imagined end which becomes the cause of the action. He then holds that plans are the generalization of purposes (1971: 33). Human action is not determinate, but neither is it arbitrary; rather, it is 'oriented' (1971: 37–38), and we have to understand this. Institutions play a relevant role in this orientation (1971: 49ff.); they are 'interpersonal orientation tables' (1977: 62).

In his address to a conference on 'Interpretation, Human Agency and Economics' held at George Mason University in 1986, Lachmann stressed 'our need for conceptual schemes more congenial to the freedom of our wills and the requirements of a voluntaristic theory of action than anything we have at present' (1990: 137).[17] The following statement is clear (1990: 138–139):

> Most economic phenomena are observable, but our observations need an interpretation of their context if they are to make sense and to add to our knowledge. Only meaningful utterances of a mind lend themselves to

interpretation. Furthermore, all human action takes place within a context of 'intersubjectivity'; our common everyday world (the Schutzian 'life-world') in which the meanings we ascribe to our own acts and to those of others are typically not in doubt and taken for granted. Our empirical knowledge of economic phenomena obtained by observation must in any case be interpreted as embedded within this context [...] Hermeneutic interpretation of economic phenomena therefore has to take place within a horizon of established meanings, with one such horizon for each society. Our phenomena observed have to be placed within an order constrained by this framework.

Based on Lachmann's views, other authors outlined a 'hermeneutical' approach.[18] Concerning hermeneutics and economics, Gary Madison (1990: 39) states: 'The real object of economics is human reality, human interactions, transactions, market processes. Humans, hermeneutics insists, are not objects but subjects, purposive beings – which is to say that they are not properly understood if they are understood merely objectivistically'.

The latter seems sensible. However, certain hermeneutical approaches present a major problem; namely, that some of them hold that reality *is* just an interpretation. What is an epistemological characteristic becomes an ontological one. According to this outlook, the reality is lost in narrations or stories.[19] This position is upheld by the late Austrian school economist Don Lavoie. For him, 'the whole purpose of the theoretical social sciences (including economics and accounting research) is to equip people with the capacity to better distinguish acceptable from unacceptable historical narratives'. Then, he adds that 'the only "test" any theory can receive is in the form of a qualitative judgment of the plausibility of the sequence of events that have been strung together by narrative' (1987: 595–596). In my opinion, Lavoie has adopted an extreme and unrealistic position. However big the influence of the cultural factor might be, some general tendencies inherent in either cultural or economic conduct may be identified.[20]

Richard Ebeling is more realistic in his application of Ricoeur's arc of interpretation – explanation and understanding – and of Schutz's ideas to the analysis of prices. He recounts the standard economic analysis of price formation, reduced to a formulation of quantitative relations. He emphasizes the possibility of a deeper analysis of prices as a relation of interdependent *intentionalities*, which requires an interpretation of plans and actions (1990: 182ff.). This supposes the existence of a commonly shared world that enables individuals to understand themselves. 'The intentionalities of men as reflected in prices are what require interpretation, and not the prices themselves' (1990: 187). He states:

> The 'ideal types' that different individuals will construct in their minds, and which serve them in interpreting the market, will be products of experience with the specific markets within which they operate, the particular set

of customers with whom they normally do business, and the tangles they have had with competitors selling the same or substitute goods.

Ebeling (1990: 189) provides an example:

> A furniture manufacturer, for example, must interpret the state of the market for furniture concerning the styles, quantities and various prices for the furniture he could construct. To make his pricing and product decisions, he must draw upon his accumulated experience, knowledge, and 'feeling' for the market.

The economic logic of prices explains how prices behave but not the process by which they are formed in markets. There is a point at which the demand curve crosses the supply curve and price is determined. However, there is a complex social interaction behind this price formation that needs interpretation.[21]

Hence, explanation is complemented with understanding and the hermeneutical arc is closed. Nevertheless, somebody could claim that all this is based on an ambiguous degree of subjectivity. If we accept the previous method, one may ask what the exact task of economics would be, and how we are going to manage actual economic problems with such an unmanageable or ambiguous approach. Lachmann himself shared this concern. He claims that 'we must show the fruitfulness of the *verstehende* method in various applications' (1977: 60). He proposes to inquire into the constellation of plans that has originated a situation (1977: 154). Plans are means of interpretation. The mere action, albeit observable, does not reveal the meaning behind it. We need methods of interpretation: knowing the plans previous to actions (1977: 58); we have to 'explain human action in terms of plans conceived before action is actually taken'; 'to make events *intelligible* by explaining them in terms of the plans which guide action' (1979: 92; italics in the original).

Doubts about the 'scientific' character of this interpretive method may remain.[22] How can I prove that my interpretation is right? The answer is not easy. The researcher's beliefs and values are always present. Consequently, we must share the interpretations and find a way to test them. Harold Kincaid (1996: Chapter 6) supports an interpretive science that is good science and compatible with naturalism.[23] I agree, but I uphold (2019) another concept of naturalism that I will introduce in the next chapter: a liberal naturalism in which mind, values, and ends are part of nature and we may scientifically deal with them.

In fact, I think this is the tendency displayed by the new currents recently appearing in economics: behavioural economics, happiness economics, capabilities approaches, evolutionary economics, and institutional economics. All these currents deal with ends and make efforts to empirically verify their findings. I have shown (2017: 90) that neuroeconomics opens the black box, but it does so only to find neural mechanisms. There is more than that. The problem I still find with these new currents is that they tend to work alone. I have analysed them in my recent book (2017). I concluded it maintaining that all these currents should be integrated into a unique economic science assimilating insights from biology, neurosciences, psychology, sociology, politics, and ethics. Practical reason is a unifying faculty that can and should rule this integration.

There is still a long way to go. In effect, we face an essentially unending research program, because motivations are dynamic and always changeable. In addition, incommensurability will always remain a problem, and a prudential judgement will be needed. Good expertise is relevant for the accuracy of this kind of judgement. We need it for a good selection of models, as explained in the last chapter. We need it, even more so, for that prudential judgement. And it is imperative for the economist practicing the art of economics: it is in this transdisciplinary economic discipline that the combination of *Erklären* and *Verstehen* is most necessary and often found. In Chapter 10, I will deal with this skill and the criteria necessary to ensure the highest level of objectivity of the expert's work.

Conclusion

In this chapter, I have proposed that economic theory should deal with ends. There is no normative purpose behind this proposal, but only to stress the relevance of capturing the ends of the phenomena analysed by economic theory. 'Ends as given' does not describe a real situation, and we need to analyse real situations. However, I want to clarify that, though this chapter lacks a normative objective, standard economics' refusal to consider ends has to do with the rejection of normative considerations involved in the dichotomy of facts and values upheld by it. I will argue against this dichotomy in the following chapter.

In fact, standard economics, which adopted forms of instrumental rationality – such as the rational choice theory or the expected utility theory – takes ends (preferences) as given, only demanding their consistency, and seeks an allocation of means that maximizes preferences. Though economists know that maximizing is not the sole motivation of economic agents, they consider it sufficiently descriptive and explanatory of economic actions. In addition, this definition allows for a formal rigorous treatment of economic behaviour at the expense of its realism.

From a philosophical point of view, this is an inadequate vision that fails to take into account the characteristics of actions that are properly human – intentionality and freedom –, reducing economics to a mechanistic technique of maximization. In addition, from an empirical point of view, this approach is incorrect: real economic behaviour, as captured by empirical information and experiments, does not blindly obey the rules of standard economics. New economic currents are implicitly recognizing that if we want to carefully explain and try to predict economic phenomena, we need to take into account other non-economic motivations of economic actions. This implies opening the black box of preferences. The problem with this is that economics decreases formal rigor (though it adds realism).

The previous chapter on positive economics concludes that the economist needs to develop a special craft or expertise, good judgement to discern the most appropriate models. Abduction, the logic of formulating hypotheses, lies behind this expertise. The economist abducts a model taking into account the evidence provided by a plethora of sources and instruments: statistics, thought, natural and lab experiments, econometrics, and so on. All these are imperfect devices but provide clues to find the causes that models should help capture.

The exploration of non-economic motivations of economic phenomena further increases the need for this expertise. We need an economist able to combine explanation and understanding; we need empirical data obtained by quantitative and qualitative methods, from different sources, surveys, personal interviews, social psychology research, historical experiences, knowledge of institutions, routines, common people's reactions, and discussions with economists and other colleagues from different disciplines. This is indeed an intellectual interdisciplinary task. The economy is a complex reality and it is not easy to accurately explain and predict economic phenomena. Even more difficult is the task of the economist in charge of designing economic policy. I will discuss this in Chapter 10.

Notes

1 Hausman (2012: 71) recognizes that, as Aki Lehtinen (2013: 210) notes, models containing the total preferences evaluation option do not allow considering the complexities of human agency. He explicitly states that 'there are questions concerning, for example, agency and self-governance that the standard model does not help to answer' (2013: 220). His proposal, he confesses, relies more on usefulness than on truth (ibid.).
2 As Jane Mansbridge states, 'the notion of maximizing can itself distort reality. It does not capture the subjective experience of most individuals as they act, fail to act, choose, or fail to choose' (1990: x).
3 This has additional practical consequences. How can the economist provide an evaluation concerning decisions involving cost-benefit analyses if there is no criterion for decision-making? For example, different proposals may be submitted in response to a call for bridge construction projects. One bridge project may simply cover existing needs, while another proposal may also take into account aesthetical considerations that translate into higher costs. The economist should inform that, from a strict economic point of view, the former project is preferable to the latter.
4 I have mentioned that Pareto ([1906] 1971: 122) distinguishes utility (referring to it as an objective characteristic of goods) from *ophelimity* (its valuation or subjective aspect, today's economists' preference). He uses the example of morphine, which has *ophelimity* but not utility, given that it satisfies a morphine addict's need but it is unhealthy for him. For an addict, renouncing morphine would be inspired by a desire-independent motivation. The addict would gain utility but lose ophelimity.
5 This position, defended by Jonathan Dancy and Joseph Raz, among others, is called 'factualism'.

6 As Peter Geach (1975: 85) asserts,

> if teleology, final causation, is to be taken seriously at all, then '*p* in order that *q*' must not be reducible to the form '*p* because *a* desired, intended, willed that *q*'; in that case there would not be a special sort of causation, but only a special sort of efficient cause.

7 For a thorough analysis of revealed preference theories, see D. Wade Hands (2013) and Cyril Hédoin (2016).

8 See my article 2007.

9 Contemporary philosophical discussion about reasons for action (practical reason) distinguishes normative, motivating, and explanatory reasons. Here I am referring to the motivating reason that explains the action. See María Álvarez (2016 and 2018).

10 Slote states that considering preference maximization as rational would leave us with a view of right action that is 'philosophically aberrant' (1989: 189).

11 See Malte F. Dold (2018) for the conception of human nature underpinning Buchanan's thought on this point.

12 However, as explained in Chapter 5, though assigning priority to the final cause, Aristotle considers both types of explanation.

13 I am conscious of the controversial character of this division. However, I cannot deal with this debate here. For a survey of it, see for example Karl-Otto Apel 1982.

14 Von Wright (1971: vii) declares that he had greatly benefited from reading the work of Charles Taylor. Taylor, for example, asserts: 'I come to understand someone when I understand his emotions, his aspirations, what he finds admirable and contemptible in himself and others, what he yearns for, what he loathes, and so on' (1985: 119).

15 See Matthew David (2010) for a brief review of the history of the different positions.

16 See Hans-Georg Gadamer (1981: 88–138) for a history of hermeneutics.

17 Lachmann (1978) complains that the Chicago economists 'don't understand the difference between action and reaction. They seem unwilling to admit that there is such a thing as spontaneous action in the world'.

18 Don Lavoie states that 'his work is now the inspiration of a growing group of Austrian-oriented critics of mainstream economics who are trying to recover what might be called its interpretive dimension' (1994: 1).

19 The topic of the different versions of hermeneutics is huge and goes beyond the scope of this book. For general introductions to hermeneutics, see Richard Palmer (1969) and Jean Grondin (1994).

20 Lachmann's position is more balanced. Actually, Bruce Caldwell (1991: 143) narrates a meeting with Lachmann in which he manifested his awareness of the 'dangers' of possible 'de-constructivist' positions of the hermeneutic movement, with which he disagrees.

21 The quantitative equation of money, M.V = P.Q provides another example of explanation and understanding usefully complementing each other.

22 See Elgin (1996: 205–207) for an appraisal of the scope and limits of *Verstehen*.

23 He proposes this list of *evidential* virtues of good science: falsifiability, empirical accuracy, scope, coherence, fruitfulness, objectivity (1996: 50–51).

References

Álvarez, M. (2016). 'Reasons for Action: Justification, Motivation, Explanation'. In: E. N. Zalta (ed.), *Stanford Encyclopedia of Philosophy*, https://plato.stanford.edu/archives/win2017/entries/reasons-just-vs-expl/. Accessed 6 June 2017.

Álvarez, M. (2018). 'Reasons for Action, Acting for Reasons, and Rationality'. *Synthese*, 195: 3293–3310.

Anderson, E. (1993). *Values in Ethics and Economics*. Cambridge (MA): Harvard University Press.

Anderson, E. (2005). 'Dewey's Moral Philosophy'. In: E. N. Zalta (ed.), *Stanford Encyclopedia of Philosophy*, http://plato.Stanford.edu/entries/dewey-moral/. Accessed 23 March 2019.

Angner, E. (2018). 'What Preferences Really Are'. *Philosophy of Science*, 85: 660–681.

Apel, K-O. (1982). 'The Erklären-Verstehen Controversy in the Philosophy of the Natural and Human Sciences'. In: G. Floistad (ed.), *Contemporary Philosophy*, vol. 2: *Philosophy of Science*. Hingham and Dordrecht: Martinus Nijhoff, pp. 19–49.

Aristotle (1995). *The Complete Works of Aristotle*. Revised Oxford Translation. Ed. Jonathan Barnes. Princeton: Princeton University Press, Sixth Edition with corrections.

Buchanan, J. M. (1979). *What Should Economists Do?* Indianapolis: Liberty Fund.

Buchanan, J. M. (1987). *Economics. Between Predictive Science and Moral Philosophy*. College Station: Texas A&M University Press.

Caldwell, B. J. (1991). 'Ludwig M. Lachmann: A Reminiscence'. *Critical Review*, 5/1: 139–144.

Crespo, R. F. (2007). '"Practical Comparability" and Ends in Economics'. *Journal of Economic Methodology*, 14/3: 371–393.

Crespo, R. F. (2013). 'Two Conceptions of Economics and Maximisation'. *Cambridge Journal of Economics*, 37: 759–774.

Crespo, R. F. (2017). *Economics and Other Disciplines. Assessing New Economic Currents*. Abingdon: Routledge.

Crespo, R. F. (2019). 'Liberal Naturalism and Non-Epistemic Values'. *Foundations of Science*, 24/2: 247–273.

David, M. (2010). 'Editor's Introduction: Methods of Interpretive Sociology'. In: M. David (ed.), *Methods of Interpretive Sociology*. London: Sage, pp. xxiii–xlii.

Dold, M. F. (2018). 'Back to Buchanan? Explorations of Welfare and Subjectivism in Behavioral Economics'. *Journal of Economic Methodology*, 25/2: 160–178.

Dold, M. F. and M. J. Rizzo (2019). 'Old Chicago against Static Welfare Economics' (April 3). *Journal of Legal Studies* (forthcoming). Available at SSRN: https://ssrn.com/abstract=3411308. Accessed 20 June 2019.

Ebeling, R. M. (1990). 'What Is a Price? Explanation and Understanding'. In: D. Lavoie (ed.), *Economics and Hermeneutics*. London and New York: Routledge, pp. 177–194.

Elgin, C. Z. (1996). *Considered Judgment*. Princeton: Princeton University Press.

Engelen, B. (2017). 'A New Definition and Role for Preferences in Positive Economics'. *Journal of Economic Methodology*, 24/3: 254–273.

Gadamer, H.-G. (1981). *Reason in the Age of Science*. Cambridge (MA): MIT Press.

Geach, P. (1975). 'Teleological Explanation'. In: S. Körner (ed.), *Explanation*. Oxford: Basil Blackwell, pp. 76–95.

Grondin, J. (1994). *Introduction to Philosophical Hermeneutics*. New Haven (CT): Yale University Press.

Hands, D. W. (2013). 'Foundations of Contemporary Revealed Preference Theory'. *Erkenntnis*, 78: 1081–1108.

Hausman, D. M. (2012). *Preferences, Value, Choice, and Welfare*. Cambridge: Cambridge University Press.

Hausman, D. M. (2013). 'A Reply to Lehtinen, Teschl and Pattanaik'. *Journal of Economic Methodology*, 20/2: 219–223.

Hédoin, C. (2016). 'Sen's Criticism of Revealed Preference Theory and Its "Neo-Samuelsonian Critique": A Methodological and Theoretical Assessment'. *Journal of Economic Methodology*, 23/4: 349–373.

Hirschfeld, M. (2018). *Aquinas and the Market. Toward a Humane Economy*. Cambridge (MA): Harvard University Press.

Hodgson, G. M. (forthcoming). 'Are Rumours of the Death of Max U Exaggerated?' In: Geoffrey Hodgson, *Is There a Future for Heterodox Economics?* Cheltenham: Edward Elgar.

Hogan, B. and L. Marcelle (2017). 'The Complementary of Means and Ends. Putnam, Pragmatism, and the Critique of Economic Rationality'. *Graduate Faculty Philosophical Journal*, 38/2: 401–428.

Hume, D. ([1739–1740] 1968). *A Treatise of Human Nature*. Ed. L. A. Selby-Bigge. Oxford: Oxford University Press (reprinted).

Kincaid, H. (1996). *Philosophical Foundations of the Social Sciences*. Cambridge: Cambridge University Press.

Knight, F. H. (1956). *On the History and Method of Economics*. Chicago: University of Chicago Press.

Lachmann, L. M. (1971). *The Legacy of Max Weber*. Berkeley: Glendessary Press.

Lachmann, L. M. (1977). *Capital, Expectations, and the Market Process*, Kansas City (KS): Sheed, Andrews and McMeel.

Lachmann, L. M. (1978). 'An Interview with Ludwig Lachmann'. *Austrian Economic Newsletter*, 1/3, https://mises.org/library/interview-ludwig-lachmann. Accessed 4 March 2019.

Lachmann, L. M. (1979). 'Methodological Individualism and the Market Economy'. In: E. Streissler et al. (eds.), *Roads to Freedom*. New York: A. M. Kelley, pp. 89–103.

Lachmann, L. M. (1990). 'Austrian Economics. A Hermeneutic Approach'. In: D. Lavoie (ed.), *Economics and Hermeneutics*. London and New York: Routledge, pp. 133–146.

Lavoie, D. (1987). 'The Accounting of Interpretations and the Interpretation of Accounts: The Communicative Function of "the Language of Business"'. *Accounting, Organizations and Society*, 12/6: 579–604.

Lavoie, D. (1994) (ed.). *Expectations and the Meaning of Institutions. Essays in Economics by Ludwig Lachmann*. London and New York: Routledge.

Lehtinen, A. (2013). 'Preferences as Total Subjective Comparative Evaluations'. *Journal of Economic Methodology*, 20/2: 206–210.

Little, D. (1995). 'Objectivity, Truth, and Method. A Philosopher's Perspective on the Social Sciences. Commentary'. *Anthropology Newsletter*, 36/8: 42–43.

MacIver, R. M. (1942). *Social Causation*. Boston: Ginn and Co.

Madison, G. B. (1990). 'Getting beyond Objectivism. The Philosophical Hermeneutics of Gadamer and Ricoeur'. In: D. Lavoie (ed.), *Economics and Hermeneutics*. London and New York: Routledge, pp. 34–58.

Mansbridge, J. J. (1990). 'Preface'. In: J. J. Mansbridge (ed.), *Beyond Self-Interest*. Chicago and London: University of Chicago Press, pp. ix–xiii.

Martin, A. and M. Petersen (2019). 'Poverty Alleviation as an Economic Problem'. *Cambridge Journal of Economics*, 43: 205–221.

Menger, C. ([1883] 1985). *Investigations into the Method of the Social Sciences with Special Reference to Economics*. Ed. Louis Schneider, Transl. Francis J. Nock. New York and London: New York University Press (*Untersuchungen über die Methode der Socialwissenschaften und der Politischen Oekonomie insbesondere*, Leipzig: Ducker & Humblot).

Mill, J. S. (1882). *A System of Logic, Ratiocinative and Inductive*, Eighth Edition. New York: Harper & Brothers.

Nussbaum, M. C. (1999). 'Virtue Ethics: A Misleading Category?'. *Journal of Ethics*, 3: 163–201.

Palmer, R. E. (1969). *Hermeneutics*. Evanston (IL): Northwestern University Press.

Pareto, W. ([1906] 1971). *Manual of Political Economy*. New York: A. M. Kelley.

Putnam, H. (2016). *Naturalism, Realism, and Normativity*. Ed. Mario De Caro. Cambridge: Cambridge University Press.

Ricoeur, P. (1981). *Hermeneutics and the Human Sciences*. Cambridge: Cambridge University Press.

Ricoeur, P. (1991). *From Text to Action. Essays in Hermeneutics II*. Evanston (IL): Northwestern University Press.

Schutz, A. ([1940] 1982). 'Phenomenology and the Social Sciences'. In: A. Schutz and M. Natanson (eds.), *The Problem of Social Reality*. The Hague: Martinus Nijhoff, pp. 118–139. Original in: *Philosophical Essays in Memory of Edmund Husserl* (edited by Marvin Farber), Harvard University Press, Cambridge, 1940.

Schutz, A. (1943). 'The Problem of Rationality in the Social World'. *Economica*, NS, 10/38: 130–149.

Searle, J.R. (2001). *Rationality in Action*. Cambridge (MA) and London: MIT Press.

Sen, A. and B. Williams (1982). 'Introduction: Utilitarianism and Beyond'. In: A. Sen and B. Williams (eds.), *Utilitarianism and Beyond*. Cambridge: Cambridge University Press, pp. 1–21.

Sidgwick, H. (1887). *The Principles of Political Economy*. Second Edition. London: Macmillan.

Slote, M. (1989). *Beyond Optimizing. A Study of Rational Choice*. Cambridge (MA): Harvard University Press.

Steel, D. and F. Guala (2011). 'Interpretation'. In: D. Steel and F. Guala (eds.), *The Philosophy of Social Science Reader*. Abingdon: Routledge, pp. 143–147.

Steele, K. (2014). 'Choice Models'. In: N. Cartwright and E. Monstuschi (eds.), *Philosophy of Social Science. A New Introduction*. Oxford: Oxford University Press, pp. 185–207.

Stueber, K. (2012). 'Understanding Versus Explanation? How to Think about the Distinction between the Human and the Natural Sciences'. *Inquiry*, 55/1: 17–32.

Stueber, K. (2016). 'Agents, Reasons, and the Nature of Normativity'. In M. Risjord (ed.), *Normativity and Naturalism in the Philosophy of the Social Sciences*. London: Routledge, pp. 96–113.

Stueber, K. (2019). 'The Ubiquity of Understanding: Dimensions of Understanding in the Social and Natural Sciences'. *Philosophy of the Social Sciences*. https://doi.org/10.1177/0048393119847103.

Taylor, C. (1985). *Philosophy and the Human Sciences. Philosophical Papers 2*. Cambridge: Cambridge University Press.

Vanberg, V. (2008). 'On the Economics of Moral Preferences'. *American Journal of Economics and Sociology*, 67/4: 606–628.

Von Wright, G. H. (1971). *Explanation and Understanding*. Ithaca (NY): Cornell University Press.

Walsh, V. (1996). *Rationality, Allocation, and Reproduction*. Oxford: Clarendon Press.

White, M. D. (2019). 'Nudging Merit Goods: Conceptual, Normative, and Practical Connections'. *Forum for Social Economics*, 48/3: 248–263.

Wicksteed, P. H. (1933). *The Common Sense of Political Economy and Selected Papers and Reviews on Economic Theory*, vol. 1. London: Routledge.

Wiggins, D. 2002. *Needs, Values, Truth*. Third Edition. Amended. Oxford and New York: Oxford University Press.

8   Ethical values and economic sciences

At the end of the last chapter, I stated that the refusal to consider ends in economic theory has to do with maintaining the value-free thesis in science. Ends often entail values, and if values are outside science, defining or deliberating about ends is not a task of economics. This chapter will present diverse arguments against the value-free thesis. In this way, it will not only contribute to validating the argument put forth in the previous chapter, but it will also prepare the ground for the next chapter on normative economics.

The history of normative economics goes back a long way. I recall that John Stuart Mill affirmed that there is an art that defines and proposes an end to itself (1882: 653). I also recalled in the previous chapter Mill's (1882: 657) statement about the nature of this 'art': 'There must be some standard by which to determine the goodness or badness, absolute or comparative, of ends, of objects of desire'. Neville Keynes treats normative economics as a part of Political Economy, 'a *normative or regulative science* as a body of systematized knowledge relating to criteria of what ought to be, and concerned therefore with the ideal as distinguished from the actual' ([1890] 1955: 34–35, italics in the original). He wonders whether or not we should place under Political Economy 'a branch of ethics which may be called the *ethics of political economy*, and which seeks to determine *economic ideals*' ([1890] 1955: 36), or the ideals with which normative economics is concerned.

Mill's vision of the art of defining ends and Keynes' normative economics are closely related to ethics. However, normativity is broader than ethical normativity. Normativity is not necessarily ethical (see Hands 2012a, 2012b). Ethical judgements constitute a subset of normative judgements and values, which, in turn, are also a subset of normativity. There is a technical normativity – if you want to achieve a result you must put in specific means – that is only indirectly linked with ethics. The art of economics deals with this technical normativity. For Keynes, however, the art of economics cannot be isolated from ethics, 'for no solution of a practical problem, related to human conduct, can be regarded as complete, until its ethical aspects have been considered' ([1890] 1955: 60). That is, the two kinds of normativity operate together in the art of economics.

Values can be aesthetical, cultural, epistemic or theoretical, and ethical.[1] When analysing normative economics, we can be interested in ascertaining its relation to ethical values: should economics be value neutral according to the so-called value-free ideal, or should it consider ethical values? According to Philippe Mongin (2006: 258–261), there are four possible positions or theses in this regard:

1   A strong neutrality position claims that economists qua economists should always refrain from making value judgements. Robbins, for example, distinguishes economics, the economic value-free science, and 'political economy', a 'branch of intellectual activity' that includes value judgements (1981: 9).[2] For him (1981), welfare economics (a twentieth-century form of normative economics) includes value judgements and, consequently, he dismisses it as a science. Robbins holds that ethics has no place in economics. Maynard Keynes disagrees with him: 'As against Robbins, Economics is essentially a moral science and not a natural science. That is to say, it employs introspection and judgment of value' (Letter to Roy Harrod, 4 July 1938, 1973: 297).

In accordance with this strong neutrality position, if welfare economics is a part of science, it should be neutral. This is the position endorsed by G. C. Archibald (1959), for example. However, John Davis (2016) shows how the first fundamental theorem of welfare economics, that is, every Walrasian equilibrium is Pareto efficient, involves at least four value judgements: first, Pareto judgements assume that all individuals' preferences have the same weight; second, this implies that distributional issues are not relevant; third, Pareto efficiency ignores preference contents; and, finally, the Pareto principle defines well-being as preference satisfaction, which is just one possible interpretation (see also Kenneth Boulding 1969: 5). Davis concludes, 'Economists consequently promote one ethical vision of the world, while claiming that economics is a positive value-neutral subject, and extol the positive-normative distinction while systematically violating it' (2016: 213).

As Tony Atkinson shows, since the 1970s, 'welfare economics was sidelined' (2009: 792, and see 2001). Faruk Gull and Wolfgang Pesendorfer state that 'standard welfare economics functions as a part of positive economics' (2008: 5): it consists in an uncommitted 'external' appraisal of the efficiency of institutions or lack thereof. However, Atkinson notes, 'economists have not ceased to make welfare statements' (2009: 793). These often include value judgements which are not scrutinized – for example, to consider efficiency as a goal is a value judgement in itself. Indeed, there are goods that are not efficient (for example, goods motivated by Sen's 1977 and 2002 concept of commitment), and not all efficiencies are good.

2   A second weaker neutrality position holds that there are specific, well-defined value judgements that economists might or even should make; for example, Pareto optimality and Pareto superiority. Pursuant to this thesis, positive economics would be value neutral, while normative economics

would entail some specific value judgements. Mongin (2006: 260) regards Samuelson (1947) as an example of the latter. Samuelson asserts that 'it is a legitimate exercise of economic analysis to examine the consequences of various value judgments, whether or not they are shared by the theorist' (1947: 220).

3   Third, a strong non-neutrality thesis denies that economists should refrain from making value judgements and maintains that they should be made as openly as possible. Gunnar Myrdal (1958) and some philosophers of economics are good representatives of this position. Mongin (2006: 274) interprets Myrdal as holding that all economic predicates are evaluative.

4   Last, a weak non-neutrality thesis defended by Mongin asserts that we must distinguish between a value statement and a judgement. We should first ask whether a statement is evaluative, and if this is the case, whether the econo-mist is responsible for the judgement associated with the statement: 'the economist makes a judgment of value if the statement [for example, "X is a good policy"] is logically evaluative and the economist sincerely asserts it' (2006: 263). I will come back to Mongin's arguments for this thesis in the last section of this chapter.

From theses 3 and 4, it can be deduced that ethical values can be present not only in normative economics but also in positive economics. Depending on which thesis you uphold, ethical values are or are not present in every eco-nomic discipline. I will advance what I defend as an *ethical normative economics* against the so-called value-free ideal of science and more pragmatic visions of the positive-normative division. I will also seek to discern whether ethical value judgements can properly be involved not only in normative but also in positive economics. This task requires explaining why ethical values can legitimately intervene in science: that is, rejecting the so-called value-free ideal. This will be the topic of the next section.[3] In the last section, I will come back to the rela-tion between economics and ethics.

In the next chapter, having shown the relevance of ethics to economics, I will develop a proposal regarding the ends or ethical values, the 'ideals' that normative economics should define, and I will concisely assess the new norma-tive current in economics called 'libertarian paternalism'.

Values in science

In this section, I will proceed in the following way. First, I will review the main arguments against the value-free ideal. Then, I will briefly propose an alterna-tive argument.

As Reiss and Sprenger (2014, 7) explain, what they call contextual values – personal, moral, or political values – may bear an impact on science at four points:

i) the choice of a scientific research problem; ii) the gathering of informa-tion; iii) the acceptance of a scientific hypothesis or theory as an adequate answer to the problem based on the evidence and iv) the proliferation and application of scientific research results.

Most philosophers of science – and economists – concur on the influence of contextual values in i) and iv). Accordingly, Reiss and Sprenger define the value-free ideal as follows (2014, 9), 'Scientists should strive to minimize the influence of contextual values on scientific reasoning, e.g., in gathering evidence and assessing/accepting scientific theories' – that is, in steps ii) and iii). Reiss and Sprenger also distinguish the 'value-neutrality thesis', which asserts that the value-free ideal is attainable, as well as its counterpart, the 'value-laden thesis', which argues that it is not possible to evade values in those steps. These last two theses are descriptive, while the first – the value-free ideal – is normative.[4] What are the main arguments against the value-free ideal?

Mapping key arguments

Kincaid, Dupré, and Wylie (2007: 14; henceforth, 'Kincaid et al.') describe three types of arguments for the value-laden thesis (thus, against the value-free ideal): 1) arguments that deny the distinction between fact and value, 2) arguments based on underdetermination, and 3) arguments drawing from the social processes of science. My argument falls within the first category: basically, I will argue that values are natural facts within a broad concept of nature. Consequently, science cannot be accused of dealing with metaphysically absurd properties, as John Mackie (1977: 38ff.) does.

Arguments that deny the distinction between fact and value

To explain these arguments, first, we have to understand where this distinction comes from. The value-free ideal is connected with the idea that values are not facts and that science deals only with facts, leading to a 'fact-value dichotomy' that dates back to Hume's dichotomy between 'is' and 'ought' judgements (Kincaid et al. 2007: 5). As Hilary Putnam (2002: 14ff.) explains, this dichotomy stems from Hume's division between 'matters of facts' and 'relations of ideas', stating that 'Hume's metaphysics of "matters of facts" constitutes the whole ground of the underivability of "oughts" from "ises"' (2002: 15). This 'metaphysics' is conditioned by what Putnam calls a 'pictorial semantics': ideas are pictorial. There are no matters of facts about virtue or vice because these cannot be envisioned like an apple, and, therefore, they are sentiments. Thus, values are not facts but something subjective that escapes science.

Putnam (2002: 2 and passim) argues that the fact-value dichotomy depends on the separation between analytic and synthetic propositions and relies on Willard van Orman Quine's (1951) challenge to this distinction. Facts provide not only verifiable propositions but also theoretical terms in the context of a scientific theory where values also matter.

Simultaneously, Putnam revisits classical pragmatists' ideas regarding the links between facts and values; for them, value and normativity permeate all experience. Putnam (2017) refers to John Dewey's position regarding facts and values and looks at the notions presented by Ruth Anna Putnam (2017) with William James and C. S. Peirce on the same subject, returning to Dewey once again. In short, these authors regard fact and value statements as intertwined, and we can apply reason to values.

For Putnam, facts and values become entangled as a result of the use in science of notions dubbed as 'thick' ethical concepts in the meta-ethical literature, that is, terms with both descriptive and normative content.[5] He illustrates his point with the example of the word 'cruel'. Dupré (2007), for his part, provides other examples, such as the concepts of rape in evolutionary psychology and inflation in economics, arguing that, in topics that especially concern us, the use of both normative and factual notions combined together proves unavoidable and necessary. The human or social relevance of some topics necessarily forces on us the consideration of values. For Dupré (2007), value-free situations appear in uninteresting cases, whereas hypotheses and conclusions that matter to us are not value free and include 'thick' ethical terms.

Anna Alexandrova's (2017: Chapter 4) proposal for legitimately considering 'mixed claims' in sciences (though she tries to avoid meta-ethical discussions such as those surrounding thick ethical concepts) could also be grouped here: they are causal or correlational claims with normative presuppositions. She argues that these value-laden claims do not go against objectivity. She proposes three rules to guarantee it: unearthing the value presuppositions in constructs and measures, checking if they are controversial and, in this case, consulting the relevant parties (2017: 99–105).

While I regard Richard Rudner (1953) – probably the most cited author when it comes to values in science – as part of the second category of arguments, his views on the presence of values in science also hinges on the importance of the subject under analysis. Also heeding the relevance of research topics, Carla Bagnoli's (2017) recent 'constructivist' position revolves around the idea that emotions and reason shape facts, bringing what matters into view. She states that '[t]o some important extent, then, the facts are not fully separable from the concerns of the agents in their perspective' (2017: 137).

Elizabeth Anderson can also be considered to partake in this category of arguments. Her 'pragmatic account of how we can objectively justify our value judgments' (1993: 91) is achieved by appealing to reasons – that is, there is no room for scepticism or subjectivism. What is valuable is not merely liking something (take Facebook or Instagram) but the object of a rational argument. For Anderson, this does not mean that values can be everywhere in science, as 'a bias in relation to the object of inquiry is inevitable' (2004: 19). However, 'a bias in relation to hypotheses is illegitimate. If a hypothesis is to be tested, the research design must leave open a fair possibility that evidence will disconfirm it' (2004: 19). Values are thus facts and can be known, but they do not replace empirical evidence.

Constructivist approaches such as Christine Korsgaard's can also be included in this group. While a Kantian, she also draws from Aristotle, Wittgenstein, and

Rawls. Human beings' reflexive nature drives their personal identity, which provides reasons for acting appropriately. She states:

> A human being is an animal who needs a practical conception of her own identity, a conception of who she is that is normative for her. Otherwise she could have no reasons to act, and since she is reflective she needs reasons to act.
>
> (1992: 92)

Human nature is a value in itself, and it is 'open' to different possible identities: 'a human being is an animal whose nature it is to construct a practical identity that is normative for her' (1992: 105). Practical identity, Korsgaard argues, 'is better understood as a description under which you value yourself, a description under which you find your life worth living and your actions to be worth undertaking' (1992: 83). Practical identity bears strong ties to other human beings and animals, because, she states, 'human beings are social animals in a deep way' (1992: 101).

Summing up, most authors in this category refute the value-free ideal by arguing that values are facts that can be rationally known and, therefore, have a legitimate role in science, which does not replace but, rather, complements data and theoretical reasoning.

Arguments from underdetermination

Kincaid et al. (2007: 15) take into account both data-based theory underdetermination (multiple hypotheses can be compatible with data) and theory choice underdetermination based on epistemic values (different scientists may weigh the various epistemic values differently and, as result, choose different hypotheses).

While Rudner's (1953) argument does not come from underdetermination as defined above but from the impossibility of complete empirical induction, his above-mentioned paper proves useful here as well.[6] For Rudner, accepting or rejecting a hypothesis always incurs a risk of error, since it will never be completely verified, due to the intrinsic imperfection of inductive inferences. Hence, scientists must consider whether there is enough evidence to accept or reject a hypothesis, and this depends on how ethically serious the potential consequences of error are, which entails a value judgement (1953: 2–3); thus, the acceptance or rejection of a hypothesis involves an ethical decision, because it always carries the risk of error.

Heather Douglas (2009) also highlights the role of inductive risk in the context of the current authority of science in our culture (2000: 563). She notes that values are recognized as relevant in these steps: problem selection, knowledge utilization, and methodology limitations. Yet, she also points out, 'where the weighing of inductive risk requires the consideration of non-epistemic consequences, non-epistemic values have a legitimate role to play in the internal stages of science' (2000: 565). She holds that this role is indirect, as it involves considering the consequences of a possible error. With low uncertainty, it is not necessary to consider these potential outcomes (2000: 577).

Douglas (2016) discusses three challenges to the value-free ideal. First, she considers the descriptive challenge, which was originally raised by feminist critics, who noted the presence of value-laden presuppositions even in the gathering of empirical evidence. Douglas' argument rests on underdetermination: the evidence available allows for all plausible theories and assumptions. There is a gap between theory and evidence that should be filled by value judgements. Second, the 'boundary challenge' stems from the lack of a clear distinction between epistemic and contextual values (an argument explored by Helen Longino, 1990, see the following subsection). Third, comes the normative challenge. Uncertainty brings about inductive gaps and risks, and establishing sufficient evidence proves necessary. Longino makes a distinction between the direct (choice of topic, method and application) and indirect roles of values in science (evidence sufficiency). Epistemic values reveal the degree of uncertainty at play, while non-epistemic values indirectly appraise whether the evidence suffices or not. However, she also points out that epistemic values, such as simplicity or elegance, sometimes do not apply to or suit our complex social world.

In addition, Douglas notes, values are embedded in the language we use in science, in the construction and testing of some models and in the use and dissemination of science. All these considerations highlight the need to take into account the impact of science on society (see also Douglas 2009). She states: 'With values openly on the table as part of the scientific process, scientists and policy-makers can include both evidence and values, in their legitimate roles, as part of the public discussion' (2014: 181). These considerations take Douglas' arguments into the next category.

Mary Hesse (1980) carefully develops the underdetermination of theories via the factual argument. In the case of the social sciences, she speaks about a second type of value judgement that does not apply to the natural sciences (where the 'pragmatic criterion' – predictability – can filter out a first type of 'basic' value judgements), and that establishes *value goals* as the criterion to overcome underdetermination (1980: 195).

Longino also upholds the underdetermination argument, positing a gap:

> This gap, created by the difference in descriptive terms used in the description of data and in the expression of hypotheses, means that evidential relations cannot be formally specified and that data cannot support one theory or hypothesis to the exclusion of all alternatives. Instead, such relations are mediated by background assumptions [...] the only check against the arbitrary dominance of subjective (metaphysical, political aesthetic) preference in such cases is critical interaction among the members of the scientific community or among members of different communities.
> (2015: 11)

Indeed, this makes Longino a suitable participant for the next category as well.

Arguments from the social processes of science

Several arguments stem from the social processes of science. Longino questioned the division between epistemic and non-epistemic values because, as she sees it, epistemic values are embedded in social and political perspectives. In turn, these outlooks, also ingrained in scientific research, claim that no distinction can be made between cognitive and non-cognitive elements in science (2004: 128). Nonetheless, Longino argues that this embeddedness does not imply denying objectivity but understanding it as built into a social context. Longino views objectivity as 'a characteristic of a community's practice of science' (1990: 179). She states,

> [S]cientific knowledge is, therefore, social knowledge. It is produced by processes that are intrinsically social, and once a theory, hypothesis, or set of data has been accepted by a community, it becomes a public resource. It is available to use in support of other theories and hypotheses and as a basis of action. Scientific knowledge is social both in the ways it is created and in the uses it serves.
>
> (1990: 180)

Thus, individual values are sifted out, and values become good for science (2004: 127). Moreover, Longino stresses, 'the objectives of the value-free ideal are better achieved if the constructive role of values is appreciated and the community structured to permit their critical examination' (2004: 140). In a nutshell, she thinks that values do not prevent objectivity but secure it when they are socially discussed and set.

While holding that values do not affect the acceptance of data, hypotheses, and theories, Hugh Lacey identifies a moment in the scientific process in which they 'often play indispensable roles' (2003: 209): the 'adoption of strategy'. He adds that most modern sciences adopt 'materialist strategies' that cast other possible strategies aside: for example, 'agroecological strategies' include ecological and social categories typically neglected by ordinary materialist strategies. He states, 'the value judgments that are part of the grounds for adopting a strategy play a causal role in enabling the conditions under which factual judgments can be made, but they are not part of the evidence' (2003: 217). He suggests relying on multiple strategies according to different values and researching them empirically (2002).

Philip Kitcher's reflections on values and science are deeply associated with the need to link scientific topics and their development with social requirements and values established via public discussion. He introduces 'an ideal of "well-ordered science", intended to capture what inquiry is to aim at if it is to serve the collective good' (2001: xii; also see Chapter 10). For Kitcher, the categories used to characterize reality are 'consequential', that is, they play a causal role. Science cannot turn a blind eye to its consequences; 'because I believe no such conception can be found, I take moral and social values to be intrinsic to the practice of the science' (2001: 65). The major issues facing society should be taken into account when designing the categories used: 'the aim of the sciences', he states, 'is to address the issues that are significant for people at a particular stage in the evolution of human culture' (2001: 59). Hence, moral and social values are intrinsic to the practice of science (2001: 65). However, Kitcher also believes that the presence of values in science does not challenge the objectivity of reality (2001: 53 and 66). He argues that 'value-judgments are deeply embedded in the practice of science' (2011: 34), while he 'resist[s] the suspicion that the incursion of values inevitably undermines scientific authority' (2011: 40).

Values in the context of 'liberal naturalism'

Now I will concisely present another argument I have developed at length in Crespo (2019). Current predominant naturalistic thinking tends to 'naturalize' values by seeking physicalist explanations for them – an attempt resisted by defenders of normativism in the social sciences. At the same time, a contending 'liberal naturalist' stream has emerged, claiming that not all natural entities can be explained by the methods and concepts of the physical sciences, and favouring a non-materialist naturalism which includes mind, consciousness, meaning, and value as fundamental parts of nature that cannot be reduced to matter. Hence, in this context, it may be posited that ethical values could be 'naturally' included in the field of human sciences.

John McDowell (2004, originally 1999) coined the term 'liberal naturalism', and other scholars have used this or other expressions to refer to the idea that there are human realities that, while ontologically belonging to the realm of nature, do not fall under the materialistic version of naturalism and cannot be addressed and explained by the natural science methods.[7] These realities include – in a somewhat rough classification – the mind, thinking, knowing, reasons, and meaning, followed by the realm of values, practical reason and normativity, and, finally, the so-called first-person perspective or agency, self-subjectivity, common-sense psychology, and free will.

McDowell's liberal naturalism deals with the first two reality types: mind and normativity. For him (2002, 2004: 92), modern natural science has evolved as a mechanistic approach to natural processes – 'a disenchanted conception of the natural world' (2002: 174) – in which the knowing subject (the human being) threatens to withdraw from the natural world. It is tempting to identify nature with the subject matter of modern natural sciences (2004: 92), but McDowell thinks it is wrong to do so. He makes a distinction between a 'restrictive naturalism' – or 'bald naturalism' (1996: 73ff.) – that intends 'to naturalize the concepts of thinking and knowing by forcing the conceptual structure in which they belong into the framework of the realm of law [as opposed to the realm of reason, expressions taken from Sellars (1956)]' (2004: 95), and a 'liberal naturalism' that does not integrate our capacities of thinking into this narrow scientific framework – 'our capacities to acquire knowledge are natural powers' (2004: 95).

McDowell also refers to it as 'relaxed naturalism' (1996: 89). For him, 'knowledge and intentions can be in view only in the framework of the space of reasons' (2004: 93). Hence, 'we can bring practical reason back into nature' (2002: 184). In other words, nature provides for more than what natural sciences consider: it leaves room for practical reason – the human ability to rationally choose ends. McDowell also calls liberal naturalism 'a naturalism of second nature' (1996: 86). He takes the expression from Aristotle's account of the 'construction' (my term; McDowell uses the German word *Bildung*) of an ethical character. An ethical upbringing creates thinking and action habits – that is, practical wisdom – which are 'second nature' (see McDowell 1996: 84; 2002: 184): 'one's formed practical intellect [...] just is an aspect of one's nature as it has become' (2002: 185). For McDowell, this internal state has a normative force (see McGinn 2014: 68). Scientific or 'restrictive naturalism', as it is often called,

> interprets the natural strictly in terms of the scientific image of the world, narrowly or broadly conceived, whereas Liberal Naturalism – or some versions of it – offers a broader, more expansive conception of nature that makes room for a class of nonscientific, but nonetheless non-supernatural, entities.
> (De Caro and Macarthur 2010: 3–4)

Thomas Nagel (2012: 8) favours 'a pervasive conception of natural order', in which the mind has its place. He states (2012: 8):

> The great advances in the physical and biological sciences were made possible by excluding the mind from the physical world. This has permitted a quantitative understanding of that world, expressed in timeless, mathematically formulated physical laws. But at some point, it will be necessary to make a new start on a more comprehensive understanding that includes the mind.

As mentioned earlier and as construed by McDowell, practical reason is a topic that needs a liberal naturalist approach. From a reductive materialist naturalism standpoint – that is, what McDowell calls 'restrictive or scientific naturalism' – the adequate rationality needed to explain human action is instrumental rationality because it is a rationality that specifically fits with the supposedly deterministic work of the physical world. Actions come as a result of a chain of physical efficient causes. 'Liberal naturalism', instead, makes use of both instrumental and practical rationality, considering reasons or ends – including values – as final causes. With this approach, this 'liberal' non-materialist naturalism, teleology, practical reason and freedom are intrinsically linked.[8]

Similarly, the 'first-person perspective' cannot be grasped by a restricted naturalism, and justifies the use of a liberal naturalist standpoint. Typically, liberal naturalism upholds that some things are evidently shown by our everyday experience,[9] from a first-person or 'common sense' perspective, and cannot be reached by the methods of natural sciences, a 'third-person' perspective.[10] As Wilfried Sellars (1963: 6ff.) puts it, the conception of human beings underlying liberal naturalism is the 'manifest image' of ourselves as rational, sentient persons, accountable to norms, different but probably not incompatible with the 'scientific image' – that is, a scientific representation of our nature. Reasons for action, which are not considered by the third-person perspective, actually explain them at a level that is different from causal efficient physical explanations. We act for specific reasons. The neurochemical reactions that supposedly underlie these reasons and actions provide at most a partial explanation of them. Reductivist non-normativists claim that reasons can be reduced to non-normative objects or relations, while liberal naturalists believe that there are 'mundane, ordinary facts, essential to our self-understanding as agents who can perform actions on the basis of reasons within the natural world' (Christias 2015: 149) which are irreducible to 'scientific naturalist' explanations.[11] These facts amount to our *ordinary* concept of 'nature' (see Christias 2015: 147). Some authors (for example, Alasdair MacIntyre, Philippa Foot, and Mark Bedau) regard this common-sense knowledge as a rebirth of classical metaphysics.

It should finally be noted that the defence of a liberal naturalism does not necessarily imply a rejection of a 'hard' scientific study of human behaviour. I think that Johannes Brandl (2007: 256) elaborates on this quite effectively:

> Modest naturalism, as I understand it, is a pluralistic doctrine according to which knowledge can arise from many different sources. There are the sources that can be explained in terms of chemical or biological processes, but there are other sources as well that are therefore no less 'natural'. The first task for a modest naturalist, therefore, is to introduce a broader notion of what it means to be 'natural' that is not tied to the perspective of the natural sciences.

However, the natural sciences fail to grasp some essential features of human beings and their actions – such as mind, thinking, knowing, intentionality, agency, freedom, practical reason, normativity, and values. In a nutshell, the thesis supported here and standing at the core of this section is that the distinction between a scientific or restrictive naturalism and a liberal naturalism leaves room, within the latter, for freedom and practical reason at a methodological level, while implying the ontological existence of ethical values and their legitimate place in social sciences.

Yet, the question posed in the introduction to this chapter remains unanswered: do values play a legitimate role in the economic sciences and, if so, in which steps of economic reasoning? What is the more adequate non-neutrality thesis, the weak or the strong version? In the next section I will first present some economists' positions on these topics and then I will try to answer these questions.

Coming back to economics

First, it is worth mentioning that in addition to the ethics-based approach to normative economics, there is a vision of normative economics with a pragmatic purpose. David Colander and Huei-Chun Su (2015) argue that the positive-normative distinction in economics only served practical purposes: avoiding illegitimate applications of economic theory to practical affairs. There is another pragmatic motivation to uphold value neutrality in economics. Relatedly, as Terence W. Hutchison (1964: 17) asserts, 'the dichotomy between normative and positive statements is not simply a matter of philosophy or logic. It has a considerable political significance'. Indeed, regardless of the unavoidable influence of values in the selection of problems and the application of theory, theoretical biases produced by personal, political, or ideological influences have played a role in the history of social sciences – including economic thinking and practice – and should be avoided.

However, this mistake could be avoided with rational argumentation or an open discussion of values (see McMullin 1983: 22–23). In fact, Amartya Sen has heavily based his capability approach on practical reason (see 2002). Daniel Hausman and Michael McPherson, specifically referring to economics and its adoption of a theory of rationality – rational choice theory – show that rationality is normative and that endorsing this theory unavoidably commits it to moral principles (1996: 7, 25, 45ff.).[12] In the case of economics, as Hausman and McPherson show, its normative theory of rationality underlies specific moral principles. They state that 'rationality can function as a Trojan horse, smuggling ethical commitments into the theoretical citadel of positive economics' (1996: 45). Actually, new currents – such as the capability approach, happiness economics, civil economy, and behavioural economics – implicitly or explicitly consider values. Values can be brought to the table to achieve a desirable objectivity (see Douglas 2007: 136).

However, in which part of the economic process and to what extent do values play a legitimate role? As discussed in the introduction to this chapter, Mongin favours the weak non-neutrality thesis. He connects it with Williams' distinction, taken up by Putnam, between thick and thin ethical concepts and by a reconsideration of Weber's ideal types. Where there is an evaluative statement, including in positive economics, we can say that the economist should make value judgements. The weak neutrality thesis affirms that (Mongin 2006: 282):

> (i) economics needs relatively few value judgments; (ii) the value judgments it needs are easy to identify; and (iii) these judgments can be separated not just logically, but practically, from the judgments of fact also made.

Against it, Mongin (2006: 282) asserts:

> I have argued to the contrary [for the weak non-neutrality thesis] that economists make, and are justified in making, a large number of value judgments; that some of these are easy to pinpoint, but others are not; and that judgments of fact and of value often turn out to be inseparable from each other. This threefold denial of the containment claim was warranted by my examination of thick predicates and ideal-typical reconstructions of evaluative positions.

Reiss (2017) has also recently argued for the fact–value entanglement in positive economics. He has pointed out that facts and values are entangled in economic theory's development, economic concepts formation, economic models and in hypothesis testing and acceptance. Concerning economic theory, he points at the value ladenness of rational choice theories. In respect to concept formation, he agrees with Putnam's on the evaluative aspects of thick ethical concepts. He also notes the value-based character of the decisions involved in building economic indicators such as indexes. For him, the selection of models is also influenced by value considerations. The methodology chosen for hypothesis testing makes implicit value judgements about the relevant questions to be answered. Finally, concerning hypotheses acceptance, he considers the arguments of Rudner and Douglas (inductive risk). He concludes: 'making value judgments is a core task of positive economist qua positive economist' (2017: 147). He had previously argued that 'economics, even in areas that would traditionally be counted as "positive" rather than "normative" economics, is an enormously value-laden endeavour' (2008: 13).

Hands (2012b) likewise develops three arguments for the 'entanglement of Positive and ethically normative'. First, from a consequentialist perspective, the fact that some actions have certain consequences implies whether they have to be performed or not; second, he considers the fact that social values cause and explain behaviours; and third, inversely, he notes that what one ought to do depends on what it is possible to do. That is, ethical value judgements would also be present in positive economics.

Boumans and Davis (2010) also explain the presence of value judgements in the different steps of economics. They note the value ladenness of some economic concepts: 'it depends on the concept and the uses to which it is put' (2010: 176). They also pinpoint the ethical commitments of rational choice explanations. In addition, they emphasize that economic explanations take into account ethical dimensions that influence economic behaviour. Finally, they point at the usefulness of economics for people's lives: this point is intrinsically linked with the aim of normative economics, which is the topic of the next chapter.

In an interesting chapter of his *Essays on Trespassing* (1981), after describing the history of the relationship between economics and ethics, Hirschman expresses his 'ambitious project':

> a moral-social science where moral considerations are not repressed or kept apart, but are systematically commingled with analytic argument, without guilt feelings over any lack of integration; where the transition from preaching to proving and back again is performed frequently and with ease; and where moral considerations need no longer be smuggled in surreptitiously, nor expressed unconsciously, but are displayed openly and disarmingly.
>
> (1981: 305–306)

Having offered the previous arguments, I will synthesize and express my position in the conclusion.

Conclusion

The aim of this chapter was to ascertain the role of ethical values in economic sciences. I started by showing that Mill and Neville Keynes' views of what we would currently call normative economics is linked with ethical values. However, when analysing different positions on the relation between value neutrality and non-neutrality with normative economics (Mongin 2006), I found that two of these positions hold that ethical values not only bear on normative economics but also on positive economics.

Next, following Reiss and Sprenger (2014), I took as a given that values are present in the selection of the problems to be investigated and in the application of economic theories, that is, in applied economics and economic policy, as even Robbins recognizes (1935: 149–150; 1981: 8). In addition, as I explained in Chapter 4, decisions about index dimensions and measurands also imply a commitment to values. I provided the Human Development Index as an example, while Reiss uses the US Consumer Price Index (2008: Chapters 2 and 3, and 2013: Chapter 8), which is 'replete with value judgments' (2008: 14) to illustrate the point.

As for economic theory, I have proposed to consider two parts of it: positive economics and the investigation of the ends or final causes of economic phenomena, which are liable to ethical appraisal. My vision of ethical values as natural facts of the human and social realms legitimizes their presence in social science such as the economic sciences, specifically in positive economics. This perspective agrees with Putnam's position regarding the descriptive and evaluative double role of ethically thick concepts.

In an article I co-authored with Irene van Staveren about the 2007 financial crisis, we detected the following ethically thick concepts – the ethical dimension in italics – in the list of causes of the crisis (Crespo and van Staveren 2011: 243; italics in the original): '*hiding* risky situations', '*excessive* liberalization', '*extremely* high bonuses', '*irresponsible* loans', '*failing* control', '*wrong* incentives', 'moral hazard', '*too rosy* assessments', and '*consumerism*'. We also noted that, in addition to numerous wanton instances of fraud and greed, laziness was also a significant factor behind the 2007 crisis, in the sense that many financial institutions turned a blind eye to excessive risk-taking and moved on irresponsibly despite the warning signs. It is clear that too much mediocrity, badly done work, disregard for others and complicity with egoistic or short-run pragmatic concerns largely contributed to the widespread financial meltdown. Economists who resign themselves to oversimplified models may also be labelled as lazy and irresponsible. To sum up, explaining the 2007 crisis, a function of positive economics, certainly includes a lot of ethically thick concepts.[13] Catherine Herfeld and Charles Djordjevic (2019), taking Gary Becker's Theory of Rational

Addiction as an example, show that theories containing thick concepts often commit the economist to making value judgements. Thick concepts cannot be 'purified' from their evaluative aspect, because this aspect is essential for our understanding of the phenomena involved.

However, not all the propositions and concepts of social sciences are ethical values. As Mongin (2006: 274) remarks, 'not everything in economics can be evaluative, simply because not every predicate of economics is evaluative'. However, whenever values are present, as in the ethically thick concepts of Williams and Putnam, we need both a descriptive and an evaluative analysis to achieve a complete scientific consideration of the economic phenomenon analysed. I agree. Yet, sometimes it will not be clear whether a concept is ethically thick: we will need an ethical theory and reasoning to ascertain it.

Having defined this relevant topic, the following chapter will explore the adequate ends of normative economics. The main conclusion that can be drawn from this chapter is that ethical values have a place in economics. The next chapter will try to ascertain which values have this place. In addition, it will seek to determine to which ethical theory they pertain. As Mark White (2009) remarks, economists have started to speak of ethics, but they do it imprecisely, without basing their concepts on adequate philosophical foundations. Atkinson (2009: 791) maintains that economics has to analyse different ethical positions. This is a gap to be filled if it aims to firmly ground the values it adopts.

Notes

1 For an updated description and classification of epistemic values, see Michael N. Keas (2018).
2 See Andrea Scarantino (2009: 460ff) and my 1998 paper for a more thorough elaboration on this notion according to Robbins.
3 I will draw material from my 2019 paper.
4 This is a bit of a paradox, since, given that the source of normativity is value, the value-free ideal is in itself a value – albeit an epistemic one. For Ruth Chang (2013: 2) and 'value-centrist' advocates, values are the direct 'key' to normativity. In the editor's introduction to his book on normativity and naturalism, Mark Risjord notes, 'contributors to this volume do not distinguish systematically between norms and values. Henceforth, the qualifier "… and values" will be dropped' (2016b: 7). For Joseph Raz, values recognized by people are reasons and become normative (Raz 2010: 22) – that is, Raz regards values as indirect sources of normativity. He asserts:

> Values whose existence does not depend on the culture of rational creatures are values and have instances, whether or not people are able to perceive and respond to them as values. Our rational capacities enable us to recognize and respond to reason-constituting facts; as reflective powers, they enable us to improve our understanding of what makes those facts what they are, and how best to identify them for what they are.
>
> (2010: 22)

5 A classification coined by Bernard Williams ([1985] 1993: 129, 140, 143–145). See Catherine Z. Elgin (1996 and 2007) for a similar argument. John Davis (2016) has proposed slight changes to Putnam's arguments in order to apply them to economics. Specifically, given that economists could argue that their concepts are technical and free of value resonances, he translates the analysis from concepts to theories: we cannot understand the explanations these theories provide unless we understand the value judgements we make in these theories. However, I think that some economic concepts such as inflation, devaluation, disequilibrium, unemployment, and welfare have value resonances.

6 Elizabeth Anderson (2004) also refers to the incompleteness of induction when she states,

> Even if we grant that no substantive value judgment logically follows from any conjunction of factual statements, this merely puts value judgments on a logical par with scientific hypotheses. For it is equally true that there is no deductively valid inference from statements of evidence alone to theoretical statements. Theories always logically go beyond the evidence adduced in support of them. The question of neutrality is not whether factual judgments logically entail value judgments, but whether they can stand in evidentiary relations to them.
>
> (2004: 5)

7 Jennifer Hornsby (who calls it 'naïve naturalism', 1997); Barry Stroud ('a more open-minded or expansive naturalism', 1996: 54); Peter Strawson ('liberal', 'Catholic' or 'soft' naturalism, 1985: 1 and 42); Johannes Brandl ('a modest form of naturalism', 2007: 256); and James Griffin ('an expansive naturalism', 1988: 51).

8 On teleology and practical reason in social sciences, see my 2016 paper. Here I drew on some material from my 2017 book.

9 Though her argument follows a different path, I think that the following passage by Christine Korsgaard conveys this attitude quite eloquently: 'For it is the most familiar fact of human life that the world contains entities that can tell us what to do and make us do it' (1992: 108).

10 Lynne Rudder Baker (2014) argues that a 'robust first person perspective' ('the ability to refer to oneself as oneself') cannot be described by natural sciences, which are entirely formulated in third-personal terms.

11 There is a debate between normativists and non-normativists. It is not my intention here to automatically identify normativists with liberal naturalists, because, as described by Stephen Turner (2010), for most non-normativists, normativists are anti-naturalists (referring to scientific naturalists). 'Normativity', Turner (2010, 5) asserts, 'is the name for the non-natural'. Risjord (2016b: 9, my italics) explains: 'Normativists – or at least some of them – claim to have a *non-natural* motivator that actually accounts for action'. Liberal naturalists, instead, follow another 'strategy', broadening the scope of naturalism. I believe this is a more adequate strategy because it does not leave values in a mysterious limbo. A non-normativist, Turner argues that, for normativists, '[values] exist, if they exist, in a special nether world' (2010: 191). However, normativists and liberal naturalists share their opposition to scientific naturalism as an exclusive means to explain human reality and as the belief that the physical realm encompasses all of reality. Yet, when normativist Joseph Rouse speaks about 'practices' – 'in which human organisms and discursively articulated environments are formed together

through an ongoing, mutually interactive reconfiguration' (2016: 38) – as 'ends' or 'energeia' in the context of a naturalist position, he is in a certain way enlarging the scope of naturalism, going beyond what is merely physical. For Karsten Stueber, facts are not intrinsically normative but become normatively relevant in social contexts. Associating his proposal with Adam Smith's notion of the 'impartial spectator', he asserts that 'normative reasons are not queer facts or queer properties. Rather, they are rather ordinary facts and properties [...] that are grasped from within the impartial spectator perspective as considerations that speak for adopting certain attitudes' (2016: 109). This view may be linked to McDowell's notion of 'second nature'. Most normativists tend to consider that normativity stems from social relations (see for example Mark Okrent 2016, Risjord 2016a). However, some norms could also stem from human nature itself.

12 As Jaroslav Peregrin asserts, 'The concept of reason is normative in that it cites a fact or a belief that *should* be compelling for a *rational* being' (2016: 69; italics in the original).

13 Catherine Herfeld and Charles Djordjevic (2019), taking Gary Becker's Theory of Rational Addiction as an example, show that theories containing thick concepts often commit the economist to making value judgements.

References

Alexandrova, A. (2017). *A Philosophy for the Science of Well-Being*. Oxford: Oxford University Press.

Anderson, E. (1993). *Value in Ethics and Economics*. Cambridge (MA): Harvard University Press.

Anderson, E. (2004). 'Uses of Value Judgments in Science: A General Argument, with Lessons from a Case Study of Feminist Research on Divorce'. *Hypathia*, 19/1: 1–24.

Archibald, G. C. (1959). 'Welfare Economics, Ethics and Essentialism'. *Economica*, New Series 26: 316–327.

Atkinson, T. (2001). 'The Strange Disappearance of Welfare Economics'. *Kyklos*, 54: 193–206.

Atkinson, T. (2009). 'Economics as a Moral Science'. *Economica*, 76: 791–804.

Bagnoli, C. (2017). 'Change in View. Sensitivity to Facts and Prospective Rationality'. In: G. Marchetti and S. Marchetti (eds.), *Facts and Values: The Ethics and Metaphysics of Normativity*. London: Routledge, pp. 137–157.

Baker, L.R. (2014). 'The First-Person Perspective and Its Relation to Natural Science'. In: M. C. Haug (ed.), *The Armchair or the Laboratory?* London and New York: Routledge, pp. 318–333.

Boulding, K. (1969). 'Economics as a Moral Science'. *American Economic Review*, 59/1: 1–12.

Boumans, M. J. and J. B. Davis (2010). *Economic Methodology: Understanding Economics as a Science*. New York: Palgrave Macmillan.

Brandl, J. L. (2007). 'The Unmysteriousness of Consciousness: A Case Study in Naturalistic Philosophy'. In G. Gasser (ed.), *How Successful Is Naturalism?* Publications of the Austrian Ludwig Wittgenstein Society. NS/4. Frankfurt: Ontos Verlag, pp. 203–226.

Chang, R. (2013). 'Raz on Reasons, Reason, and Rationality: On Raz's *From Normativity to Responsibility*'. *Jerusalem Review of Legal Studies*, 8/1: 1–21.

Christias, D. (2015). 'A Sellarsian Approach to the Normativism-Antinormativism Controversy'. *Philosophy of the Social Sciences*, 45/2: 143–175.

Colander, D. and H.-Ch. Su. (2015). 'Making Sense of Economists' Positive-Normative Distinction'. *Journal of Economic Methodology*, 22/2: 157–170.

Crespo, R. F. (1998). 'The Rebirth of Political Economy and Its Concept According to Lionel Robbins'. *Jahrbuch des Forschungsinstituts für Philosophie Hannover*, 9: 233–248.

Crespo, R. F. (2016). 'Causality, Teleology and Explanation in Social Sciences', *CHESS Working Paper No. 2016–02 Durham University*, February, ISSN 2053–2660, www.dur.ac.uk/resources/chess/CHESS_WP_2016_2.pdf. Accessed 8 June 2019.

Crespo, R. F. (2017). *Economics and Other Disciplines: Assessing New Economic Currents*. Abingdon and New York: Routledge.

Crespo, R. F. (2019). 'Liberal Naturalism and Non-Epistemic Values'. *Foundations of Science*, 24/2: 247–273.

Crespo, R. F. and I. Van Staveren (2011). 'Would We Have Had This Crisis If Women Had Been Running the Financial Sector?'. *Journal of Sustainable Finance and Investment*, 1/2011: 241–250.

Davis, J. B. (2016). 'Economists' Odd Stand on the Positive-Normative Distinction: A Behavioral Economics View'. In: G. DeMartino and D. McCloskey (eds.), *Oxford University Press Handbook on Professional Economic Ethics: Views from the Economics Profession and Beyond*. Oxford: Oxford University Press, pp. 200–218.

De Caro, M. and D. Macarthur (2010). 'Introduction. Science, Naturalism, and the Problem of Normativity'. In: M. De Caro and D. Macarthur (eds.), *Naturalism and Normativity*. New York: Columbia University Press, pp. 1–19.

Douglas, H. (2000). 'Inductive Risk and Values in Science'. *Philosophy of Science*, 67: 559–579.

Douglas, H. (2007). 'Rejecting the Ideal of Value-Free Science'. In: H. Kincaid, J. Dupré and A. Wylie (eds.), *Value-Free Science? Ideals and Illusions*. Oxford: Oxford University Press, pp. 120–139.

Douglas, H. (2009). *Science, Policy, and the Value-Free Ideal*. Pittsburgh: University of Pittsburgh Press.

Douglas, H. (2014). 'Values in Social Science'. In: N. Cartwright and E. Montuschi (eds.), *Philosophy of Social Science. A New Introduction*. Oxford: Oxford University Press, pp. 162–182.

Douglas, H. (2016). 'Values in Science'. In: P. Humphreys (ed.), *Oxford Handbook of the Philosophy of Science*. Oxford: Oxford University Press, pp. 609–630.

Dupré, J. (2007). 'Fact and Value'. In: H. Kincaid, J. Dupré and A. Wylie (eds.), *Value-Free Science? Ideals and Illusions*. Oxford: Oxford University Press, pp. 27–41.

Elgin, C. Z. (1996). 'The Relativity of Fact and the Objectivity of Value'. *Harvard Review of Philosophy*, Spring: 4–15.

Elgin, C. Z. (2007). 'La fusione di fatto e valore', *Iride* XX/50: 83–104. English version, 'The Fusion of Fact and Value', online, http://elgin.harvard.edu/misc/ffv.pdf. Accessed 12 December 2018.

Griffin, J. (1988). *Value Judgement*. Oxford: Oxford University Press.

Gull, F. and W. Pesendorfer (2008). 'The Case for Mindless Economics'. In: A. Caplin and A. Schotter (eds.), *The Foundations of Positive and Normative Economics: A Handbook.* Oxford: Oxford University Press, pp. 3–69.

Hands, D. W. (2012a). 'Normative Rational Choice Theory: Past, Present, and Future'. Available at SSRN: https://ssrn.com/abstract=1738671. Accessed 14 December 2019.

Hands, D. W. (2012b). 'The Positive-Normative Dichotomy and Economics'. In: U. Mäki (ed.), *Philosophy of Economics*, vol. 13 of D. Gabbay, P. Thagard and J. Woods (eds.), *Handbook of the Philosophy of Science.* Amsterdam: Elsevier, pp. 219–239.

Hausman, D. M. and M. S. McPherson (1996). *Economic Analysis and Moral Philosophy.* Cambridge: Cambridge University Press.

Herfeld, C. and C. Djordjevic. (2019). 'The Evaluative Aspect of the Concept of Addiction in Economics: The Case of Gary Becker's Theory of Rational Addiction', paper presented at the International Network for Economic Method 2019 Conference, Helsinki.

Hesse, M. (1980). 'Theory and Value in the Social Sciences'. In: Mary Hesse, *Revolutions and Reconstructions in the Philosophy of Science.* Brighton (Sussex): The Harvester Press, pp. 187–205.

Hirschman, A. O. (1981). *Essays on Trespassing Economics to Politics and Beyond.* Cambridge: Cambridge University Press.

Hornsby, J. (1997). *Simple Mindedness: In Defense of Naïve Naturalism in the Philosophy of Mind.* Cambridge (MA): Harvard University Press.

Hutchison, T. W. (1964) *'Positive' Economics and Political Objectives.* Cambridge (MA): Harvard University Press.

Keas, M. N. (2018). 'Systematizing the Theoretical Virtues'. *Synthese*, 195: 2761–2793.

Keynes, J. M. (1973). *The General Theory and After: Part II. Defence and Development, The Collected Writings of John Maynard Keynes*, vol. 14. London: Macmillan.

Keynes, J. N. ([1890] 1955). *The Scope and Method of Political Economy.* Fourth Edition. New York: Kelley and Millman.

Kincaid, H., J. Dupré and A. Wylie (2007). 'Introduction'. In: H. Kincaid, J. Dupré and A. Wylie (eds.), *Value-Free Science? Ideals and Illusions.* Oxford: Oxford University Press, pp. 1–15.

Kitcher, P. (2001). *Science, Truth, and Democracy.* Oxford: Oxford University Press.

Kitcher, P (2011). *Science in a Democratic Society.* New York: Prometheus.

Korsgaard, C. M. (1992). The Sources of Normativity'. The Tanner Lectures on Human Values. Delivered at Clare Hall, Cambridge University, 16 and 17 November, http://tannerlectures.utah.edu/_documents/a-to-z/k/korsgaard94.pdf. Accessed 25 June 2017.

Lacey, H. (2002). 'The Way in Which the Sciences Are and Are Not Value Free'. In: P. Gradenfors, K. Kijania-Placek and J. Wolenski (eds.), *Proceedings of the 11th International Congress of Logic, Methodology and Philosophy of Science.* Dordrecht: Kluwer, pp. 191–202.

Lacey, H. (2003). 'The Behavioral Scientist *qua* Scientist Makes Value Judgments'. *Behavior and Philosophy*, 31: 209–223.

Longino, H. E. (1990). *Science as Social Knowledge: Values and Objectivity in Scientific Inquiry.* Princeton: Princeton University Press.

Longino, H. E. (2004). 'How Values Can Be Good for Science. In: Peter K. Machamer and Gereon Wolters (eds.), *Science, Values, and Objectivity*. Pittsburgh: University of Pittsburgh Press, pp. 127–142.

Longino, H. E. (2015). 'The Social Dimensions of Scientific Knowledge'. In: E. N. Zalta (ed.), *The Stanford Encyclopedia of Philosophy*, https://plato.stanford.edu/entries/scientific-knowledge-social/. Accessed 14 November 2017.

Mackie, J. L. (1977). *Ethics. Inventing Right and Wrong*. New York: Penguin Books.

McDowell, J. (1996). *Mind and World*. Cambridge (MA): Harvard University Press.

McDowell, J. (2002). 'Two Sorts of Naturalism'. In: John McDowell (ed.), *Reason, Value, and Reality*. Cambridge (MA): Harvard University Press, pp. 167–197.

McDowell, J. (2004). 'Naturalism in the Philosophy of Mind'. In: M. De Caro and D. MacArthur (eds.), *Naturalism in Question*. Cambridge (MA): Harvard University Press, pp. 91–105.

McGinn, M. (2014). 'Liberal Naturalism: Wittgenstein and McDowell'. In: M. C. Haug (ed.), *The Armchair or the Laboratory?* London and New York: Routledge, pp. 62–85.

McMullin, E. (1983). 'Values in Science'. *PSA* 1982 2: 3–28. East Lansing: Philosophy of Science Association.

Mill, J. S. (1882). *A System of Logic, Ratiocinative and Inductive*, Eighth Edition. New York: Harper & Brothers.

Mongin, P. (2006). 'Value Judgments and Value Neutrality in Economics'. *Economica*, 73: 257–286.

Myrdal, G. (1958). *Value in Social Science*. London. Routledge.

Nagel, T. (2012). *Mind and Cosmos*. Oxford and New York: Oxford University Press.

Okrent, M. (2016). 'Responsiveness to Norms'. In: M. Risjord (ed.), *Normativity and Naturalism in the Philosophy of the Social Sciences*. London: Routledge, pp. 135–151.

Peregrin, J. (2016). 'Social Normativism'. In: M. Risjord (ed.), *Normativity and Naturalism in the Philosophy of the Social Sciences*. London: Routledge, pp. 60–77.

Putnam, H. (2002). *The Collapse of the Fact/Value Dichotomy and Other Essays*. Cambridge (MA) and London: MIT Press.

Putnam, H. (2017). 'The Fact/Value Dichotomy and the Future of Philosophy'. In: Giancarlo Marchetti and Sarin Marchetti (eds.), *Facts and Values. The Ethics and Metaphysics of Normativity*. London: Routledge, pp. 27–41.

Putnam, R. A. (2017). 'Reflections Concerning Moral Objectivity'. In: G. Marchetti and S. Marchetti (eds.), *Facts and Values: The Ethics and Metaphysics of Normativity*. London: Routledge, pp. 105–118.

Quine, W.v.O. (1951). 'Two Dogmas of Empiricism', *Philosophical Review*, 60/1: 20–43.

Raz, J. (2010). 'Reason, Reasons and Normativity'. In: R. Shafer-Landau (ed.), *Oxford Studies in Metaethics*, vol. 5. Oxford: Oxford University Press, pp. 5–23.

Reiss, J. (2008). *Error in Economics*. New York and London: Routledge.

Reiss, J. (2013). *Philosophy of Economics. A Contemporary Introduction*. New York and London: Routledge.

Reiss, J. (2017). 'Fact-Value Entanglement in Positive Economics'. *Journal of Economic Methodology*, 24/2: 134–149.

Reiss, J. and J. Sprenger (2014). 'Scientific Objectivity'. In: E. N. Zalta (ed.), *The Stanford Encyclopedia of Philosophy*, https://plato.stanford.edu/entries/scientific-objectivity/. Accessed 23 June 2018.

Risjord, M. (2016a). 'Ecological Attunement and the Normativity of Practice'. In: M. Risjord (ed.), *Normativity and Naturalism in the Philosophy of the Social Sciences*. London: Routledge, pp. 175–193.

Risjord, M. (2016b). 'Introduction'. In: M. Risjord (ed.), *Normativity and Naturalism in the Philosophy of the Social Sciences*. London: Routledge, pp. 1–8.

Robbins, L. C. (1935). *Essay on the Nature and Significance of Economic Science*. Second Edition. London: Macmillan.

Robbins, L. C. (1981). 'Economics and Political Economy'. *American Economic Review*, 71/2: 1–10.

Rouse, J. (2016). 'Toward a New Naturalism. Niche Construction, Conceptual Normativity, and Scientific Practice'. In: M. Risjord (ed.), *Normativity and Naturalism in the Philosophy of the Social Sciences*. London: Routledge, pp. 28–42.

Rudner, R. (1953). 'The Scientist *qua* Scientist Makes Value Judgments'. *Philosophy of Science*, 20: 1–6.

Samuelson, P.A. (1947). *The Foundations of Economic Analysis*. Cambridge (MA): Harvard University Press.

Scarantino, A. (2009). 'On the Role of Values in Economic Science: Robbins and His Critics'. *Journal of the History of Economic Thought*, 31: 449–473.

Sellars, W. (1956). 'Empiricism and the Philosophy of Mind'. In: H. Feigl and M. Scriven (eds.), *Minnesota Studies in the Philosophy of Science*, vol. 1: *The Foundations of Science and the Concepts of Psychology and Psychoanalysis*. Minneapolis: University of Minnesota Press, pp. 127–196.

Sellars, W. (1963). 'Philosophy and the Scientific Image of Man'. In: Wilfrid Sellars, *Science, Perception, and Reality*. London: Routledge, pp. 1–40.

Sen, A. (1977). 'Rational Fools: A Critique of the Behavioral Foundations of Economic Theory'. *Philosophy and Public Affairs*, 6: 317–344.

Sen, A. (2002). *Rationality and Freedom*. Cambridge (MA): Belknap Press of Harvard University Press.

Strawson, P. F. (1985). *Skepticism and Naturalis: Some Varieties*, London: Methuen.

Stroud, B. (1996). 'The Charm of Naturalism'. *Proceedings and Addresses of the American Philosophical Association*, 70/2: 43–55.

Stueber, K. (2016). 'Agents, Reasons, and the Nature of Normativity'. In: M. Risjord (ed.), *Normativity and Naturalism in the Philosophy of the Social Sciences*. London: Routledge, pp. 96–112.

Turner, S. P. (2010). *Explaining the Normative*. Cambridge: Polity Press.

White, M. D. (2009). 'Introduction to Ethics and Economics'. *Review of Social Economy*, 67/1: 1–2.

Williams, B. ([1985] 1993). *Ethics and the Limits of Philosophy*. London: Fontana Press.

9 Normative economics and the common good

In the previous chapter, following the ideas of John Stuart Mill and Neville Keynes, I established a relation between normative economics and ethical values. That led to considering the role of values in economic sciences and defining a position about this role. Now, I come back to normative economics, which, according to Neville Keynes, has the mission of defining 'economic ideals' ([1890] 1955: 34–35).

In this chapter, I will argue that normative economics should ideally define the way in which it will contribute to the common good of people. I could have used the term 'well-being' of people, but I prefer the more classical expression 'common good' because I believe that it carries a more complete connotation than the former. Following are some definitions of well-being:

Cambridge Dictionary: 'the state of feeling healthy and happy'.
Merriam-Webster: 'the state of being happy, healthy, or prosperous: welfare'.

In my view, this 'feeling' or 'state' falls short of the ideal that normative economics should seek. Additionally, on philosophical grounds, well-being is closely related to hedonism and utilitarianism (see Atkinson 2009: 798). According to this latter ethical theory, the criterion for moral conduct is the maximization of well-being (see Crisp 2017). Although Crisp also favours 'objective list theories' of well-being and Anna Alexandrova (2017) proposes a rich concept of well-being with which I am mostly in agreement, the expression is usually associated with the notions of pleasure and utility. As the Merriam-Webster definition indicates, well-being is often identified with welfare, and welfare with economic prosperity, which is, at best, only one element of the common good.

Actually, a quick review of the literature on happiness economics and survey questions designed to measure subjective well-being (SWB) reveals that the words associated with happiness and well-being have hedonic and utilitarian connotations – 'tastes', 'feelings', 'desires', 'satisfaction', 'pleasure and displeasure'. A European survey of 'flourishing' – a more comprehensive notion than SWB inspired by Aristotle's ideas and including positive emotions, engagement, interest, meaning, purpose, self-esteem, optimism, resilience, vitality, self-determination, and positive relationships) – revealed SWB's shortcomings (Huppert and So 2009, p. 6; and Huppert and So 2013).

Indeed, I think that some facts about the world today, such as the consequences of the vertiginous progress of techniques and sciences or globalization call for an Aristotelian notion of flourishing (*eudaimonia*). We live in a superfast world in which technological advances should be monitored to make sure that they contribute to human enhancement. C. W. M. Naastepad and Jesse M. Mulder (2018), for example, have warned about the adverse effects of the information and communication technology (ICT) revolution to achieve an inclusive and sustainable society. They stress and consistently argue about the need for replacing utilitarian normative economic principles with an Aristotelian ethical conception, based on the development of human virtues. An economy guided by utilitarian ethics will not prove a good guide to follow. In the paper I co-authored with Irene van Staveren – mentioned in the previous chapter – (Crespo and van Staveren 2011) on the causes of the 2007 world financial crisis, we showed how a utilitarian position, far from promoting conduct that would restrain it, actually favoured the conduct that drove us to it. In contrast, a feminist ethics – which we considered a form of Aristotelian virtue ethics – would be against that conduct.

For Aristotle, the content of flourishing is regulated by practical reason and, in people's actual behaviours, by the exercise of virtue, particularly by practical wisdom (prudence), which is a 'recta ratio agibilium', that is, the reasonable way of acting on any occasion, given the particularities and the aims or plans of life of each person, and by justice, given the 'political' character of human beings. It does not exclude pleasure, which Aristotle considers one of the ends of life, or self-interest, but for him, these are not the greatest and most important goods. For Aristotle, people do not flourish when isolated, but are together with others. The common good rectifies the individual good in a way that the latter becomes coincident with the former. These are the reasons why I prefer to speak of common good instead of well-being.

Unfortunately, however, 'common good' has also become a buzzword, used in so many different contexts, and, consequently, far from univocal, its meaning proves baffling at best.[1] Yet, even considering the difficulties involved in the expression 'common good', I prefer it to 'well-being', and, more specifically, I adopt the 'classical notion of the common good', which is clearly not utilitarian. Conceived by Aristotle and further developed by Thomas Aquinas, it has been widely used for centuries. Waheed Hussain, in his entry on the common good in the *Stanford Encyclopedia of Philosophy* (2018), points out the differences between the notion of the common good and utilitarian notions.

'Common good' is a political concept. For Aristotle, it is the aim or final cause of the political community. To conceive of its fostering as the ideal of normative economics is to conceive that normative economics should be subordinated to the ends of politics. In effect, according to the Aristotelian view, if we do not orient Political Economy towards a certain end – the common good of the polis – we cannot judge if economics is fulfilling its mission – that is, if it is just – nor can we judge if individual economic behaviours are just. For him, markets are part of society, and their proper functioning depends on their orientation towards the common good (*Politics* VII, 1, 1324a 1). In this line of reasoning, it is a conceptual error to think of economics independently of politics. This provides a sound argument for preserving the original name 'Political Economy' to refer to economics.

There are more recent antecedents of this view. Indeed, Adam Smith, for example, claims that '[t]he wise and virtuous man is at all times willing that his own private interest should be sacrificed to the public interest of his own particular order or society' (1976: 235 – VI, iii). For Mill, a fair government must look after citizens' common good (see Brink 2014). Luigino Bruni has written extensively on eighteenth-century Neapolitan philosopher and economist Antonio Genovesi, who revisits the classical tradition of the polis based on *philia* to posit that the market is built on *philia*. For Genovesi, reciprocity, mutual assistance and fraternity are typical elements of human sociability, while the market is part of civil society and, as such, requires individuals' love for the common good and public faith to operate properly (see Bruni 2012: Chapters 8 and 9).

As Andrew Yuengert states in his essay 'The Common Good for Economists' (2000: 1):

> economics has always been oriented towards discussion of the public welfare; arguments for free markets and free trade, and analytical concepts like public goods, Pareto optimality, externalities, and game theory have all been developed with the public welfare and public policy in mind.

However, 'public interest' and 'common good' do not have the same meaning for Smith, Mill, and Genovesi, or for contemporary public welfare and welfare state supporters. Moreover, at present, an atomistic view of utility-oriented individuals with very limited room for the idea of a common good seems to prevail. As a result, the privatized individual good is dissociated from the public goods supported by a welfare state.

This is why my approach is Aristotelian. It is not something new. There has recently been a reconsideration of Aristotelian arguments in economics. Books by Irene van Staveren (2001), Andrew Yuengert (2004 and 2012), and James Halteman and Edd Noell (2012) contain an Aristotelian approach to economics. In their book, *How Much Is Enough?* (2012), Robert and Edward Skidelsky put forward a proposal largely based on Aristotle's notion of the good life. Arjo Klamer (2017) also makes references to Aristotelian values. These authors and others propose a virtue ethics approach to the relationship between ethics and economics (see, for example, the review by Bruni and Sugden 2013).

The next section introduces Aristotle's view on the meaning of the common good. The third section addresses the different meanings of the common good in the twentieth century. Given that the classical concept of the common good implies an anthropological position and a Theory of the Good, the fourth section extracts them both from Aristotle's works, while the following section deduces policy implications from the previous definitions.

The sixth section analyses two current economic theories from the point of view of their relation with the common good: the economics of happiness and the capability approach. Why these two theories? Because, given that they particularly deal with individuals' ends – happiness and capabilities – they may have close ties with the common good or may benefit from considering it. I believe that these theories could positively contribute to building a human-centred economics if their definitions of happiness and capabilities are consistent with and oriented towards the search for the common good. Finally, in the last section, I will analyse the nudge proposal. A brief conclusion will follow.

On the common good[2]

The Aristotelian roots of the concept of the Common Good

In *Politics* I, 1–2, Aristotle presents two strong metaphysical theses: first, the natural character of the polis – the community – and, second, the political nature of the human being (*Politics*, I, 2 1253a 2–3). From a metaphysical point of view, it seems obvious that the human being takes precedence over the city, which is an association of human beings. However, Aristotle asserts that 'the *polis* is prior by nature to the house and to each one of us' (1253a 19). He recognizes the temporal priority of the parts of the polis when he explains how a house stems from the union of a man and a woman, a clan stems from the union of many houses, and a polis stems from a group of clans. But he adds 'for it [the polis] is the end of the [former] and the nature is the end' (1252b 31–32). Thus, individuals, houses and clans have the polis as their final end and, in Aristotle's system, the final end ('the reason for the sake of which') is the first cause of every reality.

For Aristotle, this end, albeit last in terms of time, is the first from an onto-logical perspective. If we incorporate the notion that the highest end of the human being is *eudaimonia* or *eu zên* (*happiness* as personal fulfilment or flourishing as a result of a good life) into the thesis that the human being is pol-itical, then it follows that human beings can only achieve their end within the end of the polis. The polis exists 'for the sake of a good life' (*eu zên*, 1252b 30); for him, the polis is and 'includes' (*Nicomachean Ethics* – *NE* – I, 2, 1094b 7) the end of human beings. The happiness of the polis (*eudaimonia*) is the same as the happiness of the individual (*Politics* VII, 2, 1324a 5–8), which explains why 'for even if the good is the same for a city as for an individual, still the good of the city is apparently a greater and more complete good to acquire and preserve' (*NE* I, 2, 1094b 8–9; see also *NE* VIII, 9, 1160a 9–30).

This good of both the polis and individuals is to achieve a good life that leads to happiness: 'the best way of life, for individuals severally as well as for states collectively, is the life of goodness' (*Politics* VII, 1, 1323b 40–41). When this good is complete (*teleion*), it is self-sufficient (*autarkes*). However, Aristotle notes, what we count as self-sufficient is not what suffices for a solitary person by himself, living an isolated life, but what suffices also for parents, children, wife, and, in general, for friends and fellow citizens, since a human being is a naturally political animal.

(*NE* I, 7, 1097b 9–12)

Aristotle repeats these ideas in *Politics* and in his books on ethics – for example:

> The end [*télos*] and purpose of a *polis* is the good life, and the institutions of social life are means to that end. A *polis* is constituted by the association of families and villages in a perfect and self-sufficing existence; and such an existence, on our definition, consists in a life of true felicity and goodness [*tò zên eudaimónos kaì kalôs*]. It is therefore for the sake of good actions [*kalôn práxeon*], and not for the sake of social life, that political associations [*politikèn koinonían*] must be considered to exist.
>
> (*Politics* III, 9, 1280b 29–35 and 1280b 39–1281a 4)

Thus, 'the *polis* which is morally the best is the *polis* which is happy and does well [*práttousan kalôs*]' (*Politics* VII, 1, 1323b 30–31).

Consequently, the task of the political community and its related science – politics –, the political organization, and society's authorities is to drive and support the good actions that enable all citizens to live this life of true happiness and goodness – that is, a life of virtues: 'the political philosopher is the architect of the end that we refer to in calling something bad or good' (*NE* VII, 11, 1052b3–4). Three additional quotations on this topic are worth mentioning:

1   Political science spends most of its pains on making the citizens to be of a certain character, viz. good and capable of noble acts (*NE* I, 9, 1099b 30–31). To have a good character that enables noble acts is to be virtuous.

2   There is one thing clear about the best constitution: it must be a political organization which will enable all sorts of men [e.g. the 'contemplative' as well as the 'practical'] to be at their best and live happily [*árista práttoi kaì zóe makaríos*] (*Politics* VII, 2, 1324a 23–25; also quoted by Nussbaum 1987: 2).

3   The true end which good law-givers should keep in view, for any state or stock or society with which they may be concerned, is the enjoyment of partnership in a good life and the felicity [*zoês agathês* [...] *kaì* [...] *eudaimonías*] thereby attainable (*Politics* VII, 2, 1325a 7–10; also quoted by Nussbaum 1987: 3).

The idea of the common good underlies each of these notions. Indeed, in *Politics* III, 6 and 7, Aristotle refers to the 'common interest' (*koine sympheron*), noting, for example, that 'governments which have a regard for the common interest are constituted in accordance with strict principles of justice [general or legal]' (1279a 17–18).

As a result, Mary Keys (2006: 3) calls him 'the founder' of 'common good-centred political theory'. In a nutshell, Aristotle views the common good (or end) as *eudaimonia* for all citizens, who are political animals and, thus, only achievable within the polis; for him, the common good is the end of a just polis. It is individual and common at the same time. Leo Elders explains the classical common good doctrine as follows (1996: 50–51):

> In a just society there is no opposition between the good of the whole and that of the individual members: by promoting one's own well-being within the framework of the society one promotes the common good. On the other hand, by working for the common good one serves best one's own authentic interests. One cannot act against the common good without at the same time causing damage to one's own well-being.

Aristotle thus views the common good as rooted in the legitimacy of a theory of the good. This theory indicates what the specific content of a happy or eudaimonic life is. I will come back to this content.

The Common Good in the twentieth century

The classical theory of the common good was revisited in the twentieth century, mainly by Catholic thinkers, and was incorporated into the Catholic Church's social teachings. This doctrine's renaissance included a debate about the relation between particular goods and the common good to determine which takes precedence over the other, especially according to Aquinas.

Aristotle holds that there is no opposition between these goods: true personal good is a common good. As already noted, for him, ontologically speaking, the individual person takes priority; however, concerning the individual's end, given that he/she is a political being by nature, his/her end is a common end, specified in each person in a particular way through practical reason. The political common good is, then, a justice-centred coordination of individual actions and society's institutions – good for both society and every citizen. Indeed, far from being opposites, common and particular (true) goods are complementary or correlative. The fact that the specific content of the common good is determined by practical reason does not imply a sort of relativism, because practical reason is capable of discovering the universal requirements of the common good.

Aristotle criticized two alternative theories of society and the common good. In *Politics* III, 3, he asserts that a city is more than its place, using Babylon to illustrate his point, as this city 'had been taken for three days before some part of the inhabitants became aware of the fact' (1276a 29–30). This case evokes the ethos of modern liberal societies in which individuals mostly care about themselves. For Aristotle, the polis is more than a mere plurality of individuals (see, e.g. II, 2, 1261a 23).

He also considers the antecedents of current totalitarianisms, where the individual good is subsumed into the 'common good'. In fact, in this version, the common good becomes a generalized private good. As Aristotle notes,

> the nature of a polis is to be a plurality, and in tending to greater unity, from being a polis, it becomes a family, and from being a family, an individual [...] So that we ought not to attain this greatest unity even if we could, for it would be the destruction of the polis.
>
> (1261a 18–23)

Let us take a quick glance at these two alternative views of the common good.

John Rawls developed a theory of a 'thick common good' but, while it concerns the common good, this theory has serious problems. For Rawls, his theory of a well-ordered society, based on his famous two principles of justice, makes it possible for individuals to pursue their individual conceptions of the good. Yet, his view of rationality, reducing it to instrumental rationality and neglecting reasoned evaluation of the content of people's desires or preferences, precludes a shared view of the good by definition (see 1971: Chapter 7). Rawls' theory is procedural: for him, 'right' is universal, while 'good' is individual. The role of the state is instrumental: it should guarantee this combination of right and good by means of procedural regulations. This common good notion hinges solely on citizens' assumed ability to realize their own individual conceptions of the good. Rawls' attempts to match a thick theory of the 'common good' with a thin theory of the 'good' illustrates a liberal theory of privatization of the good. Changing the meaning of the words, this may be dubbed a theory of the common good, but it strays far from the classical theory. For this liberal view, the human being is not a political animal in the classical sense, because being a political animal means sharing a theory of the good. Instead, from the classical standpoint, the individual good is not different from the common good. As Alasdair MacIntyre (1990: 344–345) notes, all substantively Aristotelian views rely on a rational agreement on the content of the human good.

The liberal position is beset by severe issues. First, as MacIntyre also states, many incompatible theoretical positions coexist within the liberal view – 'a range of types of Kantianism, a similar range of types of utilitarianism, and of intuitionism, contractarianism and various blends of these [as in Rawls]' (1990: 348) – with no specific meta-criteria to choose among them. Second, a theory of rights or rules without a theory of the good does not help us find consensual solutions for deep moral questions. For example, MacIntyre raises the issues of abortion and old age, noting that a procedural approach to these matters automatically implies adopting a theory of the good without discussing it. Here is MacIntyre once again: 'without some determinate conception of the good and the best, it would be impossible to provide adequate answers to these questions' (1990: 353) and, 'a necessary prerequisite for a political community's possession of adequately determinate, shared, rationally founded moral rules is the shared possession of a rationally justifiable conception of human good' (1990: 351). Like Robert Gallagher writes about Rawls' theory in his book on Aristotle's political economy, 'why should people who have very different beliefs, priorities and values help others who don't share them? No reason is given' (2018: 43). It is for this reason that Leszek Kolakowski (1993) contends that a perfectly neutral liberal society is actually unviable.

Regarding the second alternative in Aristotle's classical doctrine of the common good, it has become widely rejected today, because it implies the dissolution of individuality within the whole of society. However, the twentieth century has witnessed strong totalitarian regimes that, paradoxically as it may sound, have vowed to uphold citizens' 'common good'. Clearly, these regimes conceived the common good in utilitarian terms, defending their abusive behaviour in the name of the 'greatest good for the greatest number'. 'Gemeinnutz geht vor Eigennutz' – 'the common good before the good of the individual' – was a Nazi slogan. Rudolf Jung popularized it in his book *Der Nationale Sozialismus*.[3] Communists also claimed to work for the common good. Cuba, Venezuela, and China currently illustrate this regime type.

Though 'softer' than these regimes, current 'communitarian' thinkers, as some defenders of the common good are termed, sometimes lean towards this wing, as they react against liberals. Roughly, for them, the common good is more common than good. A strong intersubjective 'anthropological' conception builds on the idea that specific communities shape personal character. As Mary Keys (2006: 46) points out, 'it is difficult to see where these communities and their members are to look beyond (or beneath) their own bounds for insight into the nature and content of the manifold human good'. Consequently, regardless of appearances, communitarians stand closer to liberals than to 'monists', as, in fact, the communitarian proposition often comes down to a liberal union of many communities (rather than individuals). After reviewing the failed communitarian critique of liberalism, Amy Gutmann explains why she sees both positions as complementary: 'communitarianism has the potential for helping us discover a politics that combines community with a commitment to basic liberal values' (1985: 320).

Given the shortcomings of liberal, 'totalitarian', and communitarian views on the common good described earlier, I think it worthwhile to explore the implications of the classical common good notion, which requires a theory of the good based on an anthropological inquiry that aims to discover the characteristics of human nature and rationally argues for them. This basis will prove essential to building a social and economic policy leading to the Aristotelian version of the common good.

The Aristotelian conception of human nature and the consequent Theory of the Good

In the chapter on the Human Development Index in my book (2012), I presented a list of Aristotelian 'anthropological constants' that included (with slight changes) the following:

1 Reason: 'Man alone of the animals is furnished with the faculty of language' (*Politics* I 2, 1253a 9–10). The word used by Aristotle to express language is *logos*, also meaning reason, which is the source of language. Reason has a threefold use: theoretical, technical, and practical. Relying on practical reason, human beings are able to discriminate between good and evil.
2 Sociability (a political animal): 'there is therefore an immanent impulse in all men towards an association of this order' (*Politics* I 2, 1253a 29–30). For Aristotle, social interaction proves crucial for life and the development of rationality. Individuals have a natural impulse towards association: they do not need a contract to become social – they are born social.
3 Language: the human being is the only animal furnished with this capacity. Language does not develop independently from society (*Politics* I 2).
4 Communication: this is enabled by rationality, sociability, and language.
5 Moral sense: Aristotle asserts that 'it is the peculiarity of man […] that he alone possesses a perception of good and evil, of the just and the unjust, and of other similar qualities' (*Politics* I 2, 1253a 14–18).
6 The ability to look for common aims: this is a clarification of the deep meaning of sociability. For Aristotle, these aims are shared by a family or polis: they are not mere aggregations (*Politics* I 2, 1253a 18–20).
7 Freedom.

A few more can be added:

8 Fulfilment or *eudaimonia*: the individual and common end of all human beings (*NE* I, 4 and 7).
9 Virtue: the way of achieving *eudaimonia* (*NE* I, 7).
10 Striving for the common good: given that man is a political animal, individuals must look for the common good, which is their true good. This makes them flourish (*eudaimonia NE* I, 2).

Given the previous traits of human nature, which are the anthropological bases of the common good, what is good for man?

1 *Life* is the cornerstone without which human beings cannot develop their capabilities. Furthermore, in contemporary times, life is the highest value.
2 *Virtue*, that is mainly necessary for achieving *eudaimonia*.

3   *Sociability* and all the virtues that foster it – including justice, friendship, and magnanimity – are also good for the human being. The main bond that brings people together is sharing the knowledge of the common good. A lot of activities and forms of association depend on sociability and fulfilment.

4   *Theoretical and practical knowledge* are basic goods. According to the famous Aristotelian *ergon* argument, contemplation is the final end of human beings: 'the human good proves to be activity of the soul in accord with virtue, and indeed with the best and most complete virtue [...] Moreover in a complete life' (*NE* I, 7, 1098a 17–19). In the final chapter of *NE* (X, 7, 1177a 13–23), he goes on to specify this virtue:

> If happiness is activity in accordance with virtue, it is reasonable that it should be in accordance with the highest virtue; and this will be that of the best thing in us. Whether it be reason (*noûs*) or something else that is this element which is thought to be our natural ruler and guide and to take thought of things noble and divine, whether it be itself also divine or only the most divine element in us, the activity of this in accordance with its proper virtue will be perfect happiness. That this activity is contemplative (*theoretikê*) we have already said.

Theoretical knowledge implies receiving education, having the freedom to investigate, and devoting time to learning and studying. Practical knowledge requires education, both formal (ethics) and informal (*paideia*, aimed at shaping a good character).

5   *Freedom* to act in the pursuit of the goals contributing to personal fulfilment is a relevant good.
6   *Communication and participation* foster the good for men.
7   *Work* is also a significant means to achieve other goods, becoming, in and by itself, another good.

The mentioned goods contribute to human fulfilment, the ultimate end of the human being, his individual and common good. However, these considerations might prove too general to design specific policies, as Aristotle himself would probably note. In *Politics* II, 6, he complains about the vague character of Plato's criterion for determining the ideal amount of property in cities, an amount 'sufficient for a good life: this is too general' [*kathóloumallon*]. Thus, Aristotle wonders 'whether it is not better to determine it in a different – that is to say, a more definite – way than Plato' (*Politics* II 6 1265a 28–32). In *NE* I, 7, Aristotle introduces the '*ergon* argument', also complaining: 'Presumably, however, to say that happiness is the chief good seems a platitude, and a clearer account of what it is, is still desired' (1097b 22–24). Indeed, Aristotle is aware of the need for a more specific definition of the goods that are to be sought to attain happiness. In my 2016 article, I identified some of the more concrete goals that Aristotle mentions throughout his works on politics and ethics. I summarize them here.

As previously mentioned, Aristotle believes that happiness needs a basis upon which it can be built; it needs 'external goods' (*NE* I, 8, 1099a 31–32). He affirms in *Politics* that 'it is impossible to live well or indeed to live at all, unless the necessary [property] conditions are present' (*Politics* I, 4, 1253b 24–25). 'We have to remember', he also affirms, 'that a certain amount of equipment is necessary for the good life' (*Politics* VII, 8, 1331b 39–40). These external goods have to be in accord with the goods of the body and the goods of the soul: 'all of these different goods should belong to the happy man' (VII, 1, 1323a 26–27).

What 'external goods' do members of a city need? What 'external goods' must a city provide?

> The first thing to be provided is food. The next is arts and crafts; for life is a business which needs many tools. The third is arms: the members of a state must bear arms in person, partly in order to maintain authority and repress disobedience, and partly in order to meet any thread of external aggression. The fourth thing which has to be provided is a certain supply of property, alike for domestic use and for military purposes. The fifth (but in order of merit, the first) is an establishment for the service of the gods, or as it is called, public worship. The sixth thing, and the most vitally necessary, is a method of deciding what is demanded by the public interest and what is just in men's private dealings. These are the services which every state may be said to need.
>
> (*Politics* VII, 8, 1328b 5–16)

Food is essential to Aristotle: 'none of the citizens should go in need of subsistence' [*trophês*: food] (*Politics* VII, 10, 1130a 2). He proposes a system of common meals funded by individual contributions, depending on the wealth level of citizens. He also emphasizes the relevance of water:

> this [provision of good water] is a matter which ought not to be treated lightly. The elements we use the most and oftenest for the support of our bodies contribute most to their health; and water and air have both an effect of this nature.
>
> (*Politics* VII, 11, 1330b 10–14).

For Aristotle, the best form of a political regime 'is one where power is vested in the middle class' (*Politics* IV, 11, 1295b 34–35). Thus, 'it is therefore the greatest of blessings for a state that its members should possess a moderate and adequate property' (id., 1295b 39–40). However, he is against an 'over-assistance' of people:

> the policy nowadays followed by demagogues should be avoided. It is their habit to distribute any surplus among the people; and the people, in the

act of taking, ask for the same again. To help the poor in this way is to fill a leaky jar [...] Yet it is the duty of a genuine democrat to see to it that the masses are not excessively poor. Poverty is the cause of the defects of democracy. That is the reason why measures should be taken to ensure a permanent level of prosperity. This is in the interest of all the classes, including the prosperous themselves [...] The ideal method of distribution, if a sufficient fund can be accumulated, is to make such grants sufficient for the purchase of a plot of land: failing that, they should be large enough to start men in commerce or agriculture. Notables who are men of feeling and good sense may also undertake the duty of helping the poor to find occupations – each taking charge of a group, and each giving a grant to enable the members of his group to make a start.

(Politics VI, 5, 1320a 30–1320b 9)

According to Aristotle, external goods are necessary to achieve happiness, but they do not in themselves constitute happiness: 'Success or failure in life does not depend on these [fortunes], but human life, as we said, needs these as mere additions, while virtuous activities or their opposites are what determine happiness or their reverse' (*NE* I, 10, 1100b 9–10).

What are, according to Aristotle, the facts and virtues that contribute to a happy life? In *Nicomachean Ethics* he mentions honour, wisdom, and pleasure (I, 6, 1096b), and then he adds reason (*noûn*) and every virtue (I, 7, 1097b 2). In *Rhetoric* he lists 'good birth, plenty of friends, good friends, wealth, good children, plenty of children, a happy old age, also such bodily excellences as health, beauty, strength, large stature, athletic powers, together with fame, honor, good luck, and virtue' (*Rhetoric* I, 5, 1360b 19 ff). Does this mean that a person, for example, of short stature, cannot be happy? No, this list includes some of the things that may contribute to happiness, not its necessary constituents. Virtue determines happiness. The virtuous man, that is, the man who rightly exercises his practical reason, knows how to combine the elements at hand, even when something is lacking, in order to be happy. From a *eudaimonist* perspective, happiness is not a matter of what you own but a matter of how you live your life, whatever your circumstances: 'healthy or unhealthy, rich or poor, educated or uneducated, we should think about our lives and try to live them well' (Annas 2011: 129). To live our lives well is to develop our capacities in the pursuit of worthwhile or useful objectives (see Annas 2011, p. 140). Therefore, practical reason and virtue are the keys to happiness.

Lawgivers must foster the development of virtue in their citizens (*NE* II, 1, 1103b 3–6). Aristotle states that lawgivers can promote virtues through two indirect ways: education and law (cf. *NE* V, 2, 1130b 23–27 and X, 9, 1179b 20–1180a. 22; *Politics* V, 9, 1310a 12–18). Friendship and unanimity (concord – *omónoia*) also hold cities together (*NE* VIII, 1, 1155a 22–26; IX, 6, 1167b 2).

Summing up, law and education foster the development of virtues, and a life of virtues brings about fulfilment, which is the end or the common good of the political community. In line with these notions:

1   The best political system is an egalitarian regime, 'a general system of liberty based on equality' (*Politics* VI, 2, 1317b 16–17); thus, government should concern itself with maintaining a certain equality, but not through confiscatory measures; 'the magistrate […] is the guardian of justice, and, if of justice, then of equality also' (*NEV*, 6, 1134b 1). People must participate in politics.

2   Specifically, an Aristotelian policy would not distribute funds directly to people except for funds targeted at creating jobs.

3   The government should actively seek to avoid unemployment and promote business and exchange.

4   In extreme cases, it should provide food.

5   The government should also concern itself with the health of individuals, ensuring the necessary conditions for adequate healthcare (safe drinking water and clean air).

6   Another topic of great concern should be education. The government should create adequate educational institutions and offer necessary funding, whether education be public or private.

7   It should also focus largely on creating and enforcing good laws and courts, and providing legal institutions and their corresponding funding.

8   The government should encourage all kinds of intermediate organizations that freely promote family, education, friendship, children and elderly care, job creation, sports, arts, religion, charity, and, especially, virtues of all kinds.

9   In the absence of institutions to protect children and the elderly, it should step up and undertake this social activity.

These are more specific means to achieving the general end of *eudaimonia*. Governments should identify the best specific means to enable its citizens to achieve the happiest ('eudaimoniest') possible life. However, citizens must also play their part, promoting and exploiting these means in order to carry out the activities that make them *eudaimon*. Clearly, the pursuit of the common good is a task which not only the government but also every citizen must undertake. At this point, someone may object to this proposal with the following argument: 'The Aristotelian political program is an interesting addition, though one might ask whether a program intended for a small, homogeneous Greek city-state can be so easily applied to the present'. This is a usual objection to Aristotelian political theory. It has been suggested that smaller societies in current states may be recognized as embodying a theory of the good. Aristotle also recognizes the limits to the size of cities, and he is also aware that his ideal city did not exist in his time. However, we should not forget that Aristotle's proposal is ethical: it explains what can be done, a normative ideal, a paradigm. In fact, I think that we, citizens of different states, aspire to more than a mere conglomeration of people.

In my opinion, these ideals are sensible and might serve as guidelines for developing specific policies. In fact, W. Hussain (2018: 1) offers the following examples of the content of the common good that are very similar to the Aristotelian:

Some canonical examples of the common good in a modern liberal democracy include: the road system; public parks; police protection and public safety; courts and the judicial system; public schools; museums and cultural institutions; public transportation; civil liberties, such as the freedom of speech and the freedom of association; the system of property; clean air and clean water; and national defense.

A more detailed specification of these lists is highly dependent on the society or social group we are analysing. Furthermore, we can concentrate our thinking not only on the whole of society but also on particular groups or contexts: there is a common good for the whole of society, but there are also common goods for specific social groups, or for people in diverse contexts. Alexandrova (2017) specifically stresses this point when referring to well-being. In some way, I would say her approach is 'pragmatic'. She tries to ascertain the particular goods adequate for particular social groups or contexts, for example, child well-being (2017: Chapter 3). She calls these analyses 'mid-level' theories of well-being. Mid-level theories define characteristics of well-being inspired in the philosophical theories that best adapt to the kind of group or context. Alexandrova complains that philosophical theories alone should, but actually may not, help us select constructs and measures (2017: xxxiv). She believes these theories can provide a toolbox of concepts to help us build such constructs (2017: xxxix) and that the task of discovering the content of the specific kinds of well-being is a joint undertaking: we need 'practicing science and philosophy in a joined up manner' (2017: xxxiv). In my view, as I have shown in Chapter 4, practical reason and practical discussion can help define particular characteristics of well-being for particular groups of people in particular contexts. A theory of good would leave a lot of details unspecified. Practical reason and public discussion would fill this gap.

In summary, in this section, based on Aristotle's anthropological conception of the nature of human beings, I have extracted a set of contents of the common good of people. Given that, first, we need further specification, constructs, and measures of those contents and, second, since these contents are often specific to particular groups, contexts, or positions that are not necessarily linked to human nature, science has to work with philosophy, practical reason, and public discussion to discover or define those contents.

In the next section, I will deal with two new economic currents concerned with human ends from the perspective of the common good.

The Economics of Happiness and the Capability Approach in light of the classical doctrine of the Common Good

At present, we are witnessing an increasing acknowledgement of the need to take into account the ends of individual behaviour in economics. According to the classical doctrine of the common good, people's individual ends should match the common good. Examples of this tendency to consider ends in economics include the Economics of Happiness (EH) and the Capability Approach (CA).

The Economics of Happiness

First and foremost, it should be emphasized that the fact that the EH focuses on happiness makes for a good starting point since the theory of common good also features happiness as the ultimate good. However, the concept of happiness adopted can make a significant difference. The concept of *eudaimonia* differs largely from our modern notion of happiness, which carries utilitarian and hedonistic resonances. Both Annas (2011: 127) and Pierluigi Barrotta (2008: 149) critically quote the same passage in Richard Layard's *Happiness. Lessons from a New Science* (2005: 4): 'Happiness is feeling good, and misery is feeling bad'. Following Bentham, Layard believes that happiness is a hedonic quality that can be measured. At the same time, he rejects Mill's qualitative dimension of happiness. Additionally, Layard (2007: 162) asserts that 'good tastes are those which increase happiness, and vice versa'. Wijngaards (2012: 103) summarizes his analysis of Layard's concept of happiness by stating that 'it is to be understood in a hedonic sense, based upon a pleasure/pain duality'. The problem with this concept of happiness is that it is too rudimentary. Undergoing difficulties is part of true happiness. As Annas asserts, 'a life of having all your desires fulfilled without the problems created by human neediness leaves humans with nothing to live *for*, nothing to propel them onwards' (2011: 137; italics in the original). True happiness goes beyond life satisfaction. Aristotle strongly rejects the hedonic view: 'the generality of mankind then shows themselves to be utterly slavish, by preferring what is only a life for cattle' (*NE* I, 4, 1095b 18–20). He states that *eudaimonia* is an ultimate end, not a good for the sake of another end, as is the case of enjoyment.

Nick Begley (2010) has reviewed the literature surveying subjective well-being and physiological (objective) studies of happiness. He concluded that there is general agreement that these two psychological approaches to happiness are mainly hedonic and that truly *eudaimonic* dimensions would complete the assessment of happiness. Flavio Comim (2005: 163) remarks that the EH is a basically descriptive approach, 'without a clear link with established ethical paradigms that discuss not only what people do, but what they should do to live well as human beings'. More sophisticated psychological constructs include *eudaimonic* elements such as positive relations with others, personal growth, and purpose or meaning in life. However, Begley notes, they make no references to virtue. Luigino Bruni and Pier-Luigi Porta (2007: xx–xxiv) add that economic theories that indirectly attempt to understand the logic of happiness do not consider the role of sociality-as-relationality. A quick review of the literature on methods and questionnaires for measuring subjective well-being reveals that the words usually associated with happiness include 'tastes', 'feelings', 'desires', 'satisfaction', 'pleasure and displeasure'. As regards objective happiness, as Bruno

Frey and Aloys Stutzer (2002: 5; italics in the original) assert, 'this approach comes close to the idea of a *hedometer*'.

I conclude that in order to effectively focus on and address happiness, the EH should pay attention to and adopt the Aristotelian concept of *eudaimonia*. More than an economics of happiness we need an economics of *eudaimonia* or flourishing. This means a radically different conception from current happiness economics. The very resonance of the word 'happiness' advises us to reformulate and rename happiness economics as maybe 'economics of flourishing' (see Crespo and Mesurado 2015) or, better, 'economics of the common good' in its classical version.

The Capability Approach

Compared to happiness economics, first, it should be noted that Sen's CA comes closer to being a theory of common good. However, I argue that it fails to do so in the classical way. Amartya Sen's CA concentrates on well-being, capabilities, and functionings, on achievement and commitment, and gives priority to ends. This concern with ends leads Sen to realize the narrowness of the current leading conception of economic rationality. He notes: 'Indeed, at the risk of sounding unduly "grand", it can be argued that it is important to reclaim for humanity the ground that has been taken from it by various arbitrarily narrow formulations of the demands of rationality' (2002: 51). He stresses the need to use practical reason to scrutinize and decide upon ends.

The problem with Sen's approach is his deliberate underdetermination of the contents of ends. Martha Nussbaum has criticized Sen in this respect, giving rise to a huge debate on the 'list of capabilities'. Nussbaum argues in favour of a particular list of capabilities that all individuals ought to have, while Sen prefers to leave the matter open (see, e.g. Sen 1993, Sen 2004, Nussbaum 2003). Nussbaum's list comprises as 'central human capabilities' (2003: 41–42): 1) life, 2) bodily health, 3) bodily integrity, 4) being able to use senses, imagination and thought, 5) being able to have emotions, 6) practical reason, 7) affiliation or identity, 8) concern for other species, 9) play, and 10) control over one's environment. I consider it a convincing list.[4]

However, from my perspective, the issue is the following: should there be a list of specific capabilities to guide public policy or would a formal framework to be filled in later according to the occasion be enough? Sen's answer favours the latter, and he is concerned that a unique list may be tremendously overspecified (1993: 47).

From the viewpoint of the classical theory of the common good, although an overspecification is undesirable, Sen's proposal for an open list is not enough. His conception is ultimately liberal, in the sense used here. This means that in Sen's view, the CA is consistent with diverse individual theories of the good, and this implies that common good is not understood in classical terms. Now, I argue that this results from the lack of a conception of human nature. Sen devotes a whole section of his book *Reason Before Identity* to the question 'Discovery or

Choice?' (1999: 15–19). He concludes that individual identity is constructed and not simply discovered. People have the power of self-definition. Thus, we cannot prescribe a set of goals without falling into a paternalistic or authoritarian stance.

Sen explicitly asserts (1993: 48) that 'quite different specific theories of value may be consistent with the capability approach', and that 'the capability approach is consistent and combinable with several different substantive theories'. The fact is that, in the end, Sen is a liberal à la Rawls (despite his critique of him). This criticism of Sen is consistent with others' disapproval of Sen for his 'under-elaborated and overextended notion of freedom' (see, e.g. Des Gasper and Irene van Staveren 2003; Nussbaum 2003). Deneulin clearly expresses the central idea underlying this criticism: 'Freedom is not the only good to promote, but one among others' (2002: 506).

Nussbaum, Gasper, and van Staveren view Sen's recent emphasis on freedom with suspicion, particularly in *Development as Freedom*. In their opinion, Sen has always concerned himself with poverty and inequality and, now, they complain, he has abandoned his first concern to defend freedom. Their rationale is not unfounded. Freedom may include both good and bad dimensions. Freedom leading to bad actions is not a desirable value. The very language of freedom may be misleading: 'since freedom does not have this overarching meaning in everyday parlance [...] Sen has, in some sense, downsized his notion of capability in giving so much importance to the language of freedom, ignoring the baggage that comes with the term' (Agarwal, Humphries and Robeyns 2003: 8). Gasper and van Staveren recommend, among other things, the use of the term 'capabilities' over 'freedom' (2003: 138) when stressing the values of democracy, respect, and friendship (2003: 146), and they emphasize that freedom is just one value, and that there are two other spheres of value in life, namely, justice and caring (2003: 152). Similar to the EH, the CA needs to embrace a theory of the good to fulfil its aims. As Deneulin states, 'the capability approach hides unavowed positions about the good, positions that it can no longer hide when the theoretical framework becomes practice' (2002: 502). She argues that, upon implementation, the CA ends up being perfectionist and paternalist (Deneulin 2002: 502). Deneulin carried out a field study in El Salvador on the effect of migrations and remittances on poor families. She concludes that a freedom-centred approach to development such as Sen's is not enough to improve the living conditions of deprived people. She asserts (2006: 13): 'what matters is not as much the expansion of individual freedoms, by whatever human actions, but the expansion of the common good which cannot be reduced to the freedoms of individual agents'.

I conclude that the CA would benefit from the adoption of the classical theory of the common good to effectively enhance the living conditions of individuals.

Libertarian paternalism

In the introduction to this chapter, I said I would analyse the libertarian paternalist or 'nudge' proposal, which derives from Modern (or New) Behavioral

Economics (MBE) and proves relevant due to its possible practical effects on social and economic policies of many countries.[5] In 2003, Richard Thaler and Cass Sunstein published 'Libertarian Paternalism' (2003a), an article presented at the Annual Meeting of the American Economic Society. Soon after, they published 'Libertarian Paternalism Is Not an Oxymoron' (2003b), a paper addressed to lawyers. These articles rapidly triggered many comments and criticism. The main assumption in their papers stems from MBE: people often unintentionally make bad choices, that is, against their best interest. Without coercing them, they argue, we may help people make right choices: 'if no coercion is involved, we think that some types of paternalism should be acceptable to even the most ardent libertarian. We call such actions *libertarian paternalism*' (2003a: 175; italics in the original). The following passage taken from the second article clearly explains their proposal:

> The idea of libertarian paternalism might seem to be an oxymoron, but it is both possible and desirable for private and public institutions to influence behavior while also respecting freedom of choice. Often people's preferences are unclear and ill-formed, and their choices will inevitably be influenced by default rules, framing effects, and starting points. In these circumstances, a form of paternalism cannot be avoided. Equipped with an understanding of behavioral findings of bounded rationality and bounded self-control, libertarian paternalists should attempt to steer people's choices in welfare-promoting directions without eliminating freedom of choice.
>
> (2003b: 1159)

In 2008 they published *Nudge: Improving Decisions about Health, Wealth and Happiness*, in which they extensively developed their program. It was and still is a bestseller, widely commented upon and criticized. A 'sensible planner' designs a 'choice architecture' to make people 'better off', allowing them to decide in the way they would have chosen had they not been subject to any bias (2008: 5). The 'objective' way for the planner to define the best choices is to apply a cost-benefit analysis, and when this is not possible, to use some indirect methods to ascertain what is better for people.

'Nudging' has both critics and defenders. Besides that, its different specificities originate diverse combinations of situations – more paternalistic or more libertarian – and differences between nudge and libertarian paternalism. As in any field where philosophers become involved, it quickly becomes complex (sometimes too complex).[6] I will mention only a few criticisms and defences. Hausman and Brynn Welch (2010) argue that paternalist policies may threaten liberty. In the same line of thought, José Edwards (2016) even suggests that nudge shares the controlling ethos of Watson and Skinner's behaviourism. Sugden (2009) seriously doubts and warns about the possibility of respecting the presumed will of *nudgees* when liberated from their biases. He also makes a point, related to the previous point, which he shares with others: 'Thaler and Sunstein seem to be assuming that inside every Human there is an Econ – that, deep down, each of us has coherent preferences, of the kind that economic theory has traditionally assumed' (2009: 370). If Rational Choice Theory or Expected Utility Theory is considered 'the' rational model, as in MBE, it is right. But this cannot be assumed. Gilles Saint-Paul is also against the utilitarian model behind the cost-benefit tool for defining the content of people's presumed goals: 'there is no outside system of values' (2001: 91). Or the values are utilitarian. Adrien Barton and Grüne-Yanoff (2015) note that though Sunstein (2015a) claims that libertarian paternalism is not a form of ends paternalism but of means paternalism, it actually judges people's preferences which are their ends (2015: 346). By nudging, Davis holds (2013 and forthcoming) that RCT becomes not only normative but also performative. He argues (forthcoming: 3):

> Contrary to the view that these programs [mechanism design and nudge theory] are a departure from rational choice theory, I take them to be intrinsic to the evolution of neoclassicism from a science claiming rational choice is descriptive of the world to a performative science intent on securing the practice of rational choice behavior in the world.

Thomas C. Leonard identifies a paradox about behavioural economics and nudging: 'The irony is that behavioral economics, having attacked *Homo Economicus* as an empirically false description of human choice, now proposes, in the name of paternalism, to enshrine the very fellow as the image of what people should want to be' (2008: 359).

On the other hand, Gerd Gigerenzer (2010: 542) defends nudging on the grounds that 'changing environments may be more efficient than changing minds, and creating environments that facilitate moral virtue is as important as improving moral values'. However, he distinguishes nudging from libertarian paternalism, defending the former and criticizing the latter for its adherence to a narrow view of rationality (RCT and EUT), its consequent disapproval of other forms of rationality, its scepticism about educating people and for omitting mentioning the responsibility of firms that invest great budgets to nudge people into unhealthy behaviour. He proposes investing in teaching people to become 'risk savvy' (2015). Based on Gigerenzer's 'simple heuristic' research program, Till Grüne-Yanoff and Ralph Hertwig (2016) and Hertwig and Grüne-Yanoff (2017) have distinguished 'boosting' from nudge. While nudge seeks behavioural change, boosts are interventions that target competences, 'preserving personal agency and enabling individuals to exercise that agency' (2017: 5).

Sunstein (2015a) has used different arguments to defend nudging, drawing on ten different critical papers trying to show its compatibility with human agency and freedom. Analysing specific cases helps discern when nudges are 'appropriate' (Sunstein 2015b). He has noted that sometimes people choose not to decide: they choose not to choose with sensible arguments (2014 and 2017). The 'Nudge Theory' assumes that there is always a better choice. The individual may or may not opt for it, for several reasons.

From an Aristotelian point of view, practical reason tries to succeed in discovering what is good for people to aim at and to do, thus creating a theory of the good. First, practical reason should discover the content of a list of basic human goods. Second, it has to deliberate upon specific ways of realizing alternative means to achieve those goods. Then, it has to discriminate between decisions that should be imposed for 'political reasons' from a 'genuine paternalism', not using welfare-based criteria (see Guala and Mittone 2015), and decisions that can fall under the umbrella of nudging. Concerning the latter kind of decisions, from this viewpoint, nudging can be considered legitimate provided that:

- it clearly leaves room for alternative decisions;
- it adequately defines the target of 'better off' decisions.

Mark White (2019) has shown, and criticized, that, in practice, nudges are based on community preferences or objective theories of the good regarding people's subjective preferences. Earlier in this chapter, I drew from Aristotle's ethical and political writings a list of goods: good health, good nutrition, work, freedom, political participation, provision of justice, education, and fostering intermediate organizations that promote family, education, friendship, child and elder care, job creation, sports, arts, religion, charity, and, specially, virtues of all kinds. Aristotle provides reasonable arguments for all these objectives, with which most people would generally agree. The argument about incommensurability of ends previously advanced in Chapter 7 also applies to using cost-benefit analysis to decide actions concerning these kinds of objectives: it is not a matter of instrumental rationality, but of practical reason. Practical reason must wisely harmonize the attainment of heterogeneous ends.

In this context, then, I defend a different type of nudging. It is a way of helping people who are not able to soundly analyse their choices at all times and under all circumstances surrounding their decisions, uninformed people or poor people facing difficult trade-off decisions (see Reiss 2013: 296–297). However, I do not defend the 'neoclassical' method for ascertaining the content of welfare and the means to achieving it which is advocated by libertarian paternalists. This vision would render society an uncomfortable environment to live in, because we would be forced by psychological pressure to make decisions in an economically reductive way.

Conclusion

In this chapter, I have dealt with the 'ideals' that normative economics should identify. I have proposed that they be based upon the common good of people, and I have investigated and suggested its possible content. Having explained different versions of the common good, I have decided to use the classical Aristotelian conception. This classical concept implies an anthropological position and a Theory of the Good. I have borrowed from Aristotle's works the specific goods composing it and I have proceeded to use this perspective to analyse happiness economics, the capability approach, and libertarian paternalism in order to ascertain how they could support this vision. My conclusion is that incorporating the Aristotelian frame into these theories can strongly contribute to develop an economic setting not only compatible with a flourishing life but also leading to it. This conclusion confirms that, as advanced in the introduction to this book, normative economics has a strong relation with ethics and should actually be a *transdisciplinary* discipline.

In the next chapter I will address the most transdisciplinary economic discipline, the art of Political Economy, which combines the elements of all previously analysed economic disciplines to implement economic policies in real life.

Notes

1 On the history and different conceptions of the 'common good', see Keys and Godfrey (2010), Mansbridge (2013), Jaede (2017), Hussain (2018).
2 This section and the two following ones draw material from my 2016 article.
3 1922, second edition, information excerpted from http://en.wikipedia.org/wiki/Glossary_of_Nazi_Germany.
4 John Finnis (1980: 59) proposes seven basic goods: life, knowledge, play, aesthetic experience, sociability of friendship, practical reasonableness, and religion.
5 In this section I drew material from Crespo (2017: Chapter 3, last section).
6 See Barton and Grüne-Yanoff (2015) for a classification.

References

Agarwal, B., J. Humphries and I. Robeyns (2003). 'Exploring the Challenges of Amartya Sen's Work and Ideas: An Introduction'. *Feminist Economics*, 9/2–3: 3–12.
Alexandrova, A. (2017). *A Philosophy for the Science of Well-Being*. Oxford: Oxford University Press.
Annas, J. (2011). *Intelligent Virtue*. Oxford: Oxford University Press.
Aristotle (1954). *Nicomachean Ethics*. Translated and Introduced by Sir David Ross. Oxford: Oxford University Press.
Aristotle (1958). *Politics*. Edited and Translated by Ernest Barker. Oxford: Oxford University Press.
Aristotle (1995). *The Complete Works of Aristotle. The Revised Oxford Translation*, J. Barnes (ed.), Princeton: Princeton University Press, sixth printing with corrections.
Atkinson, T. (2009). 'Economics as a Moral Science'. *Economic Journal*, 76: 791–804.
Barrotta, P. (2008). 'Why Economists Should Be Unhappy with the Economics of Happiness'. *Economics and Philosophy*, 24: 145–165.
Barton, A. and T. Grüne-Yanoff (2015). 'From Libertarian Paternalism to Nudging –and Beyond'. *Review of Philosophy and Psychology*, 6/3: 341–359.
Begley, N. (2010). 'Psychological Adoption and Adaption of Eudaimonia'. http://positivepsychology.org.uk/pp-theory/eudaimonia/140-the-psychological-adoption-and-adaptation-of-eudaimoni.html. Accessed 1 March 2012.
Brink, D. (2014). 'Mill's Moral and Political Philosophy'. In: E. N. Zalta (ed.), *The Stanford Encyclopedia of Philosophy*, http://plato.stanford.edu/entries/mill-moral-political/. Accessed 30 August 2015.
Bruni, L. (2012). *The Genesis and the Ethos of the Market*. London: Palgrave Macmillan.

Bruni, L. and P.-L. Porta (2007). 'Introduction'. In: Luigino Bruni and Pier-Luigi Porta (eds.), *Handbook on the Economics of Happiness*. Cheltenham: Edward Elgar.

Bruni, L., and R. Sugden (2013). 'Reclaiming Virtue Ethics for Economics'. *Journal of Economic Perspectives*, 27/4: 141–164.

Comim, F. (2005). 'Capabilities and Happiness: Potential Synergies'. *Review of Social Economy*, 63/2: 161–176.

Crespo, R. F. (2012). 'Practical Reasoning in Economic Affairs: The HD Index as a Case Study'. In: J. Castro Caldas and V. Neves (eds.), *Facts, Values and Objectivity in Economics*. Abingdon and New York: Routledge, pp. 158–179.

Crespo, R. F. (2016). 'The Common Good and Economics'. *Cuadernos de Economía*, 39: 23–33. http://dx.doi.org/10.1016/j.cesjef.2015.09.001.

Crespo, R. F. (2017). *Economics and Other Disciplines. Assessing New Economic Currents*. London: Routledge.

Crespo, R. F. and B. Mesurado (2015). 'Happiness Economics, Eudaimonia and Positive Psychology: From Happiness Economics to Flourishing Economics'. *Journal of Happiness Studies*, 16: 931–946.

Crespo, R. F. and I. van Staveren (2011). 'Would We Have Had This Crisis If Women Had Been Running the Financial Sector?'. *Journal of Sustainable Finance and Investment*, 1/2011: 241–250.

Crisp, R. (2017). 'Well-Being'. In: E. N. Zalta (ed.), *The Stanford Encyclopedia of Philosophy*, https://plato.stanford.edu/entries/well-being/. Accessed 22 December 2018.

Davis, J. B. (2013). 'Economics Imperialism under the Impact of Psychology: The Case of Behavioral Development Economics'. *Oeconomia*, 3/1, https://oeconomia.revues.org/638. Accessed 29 February 2016.

Davis, J. B. (forthcoming). 'Economics Imperialism versus Multidisciplinarity'. *History of Economic Ideas*.

Deneulin, S. (2002). 'Perfectionism, Paternalism and Liberalism in Sen and Nussbaum's Capability Approach'. *Review of Political Economy*, 14/4: 497–518.

Deneulin, S. (2006). 'Amartya Sen's Capability Approach to Development and *Gaudium et Spes*'. *Journal of Catholic Social Thought*, 3/2. http://www.stthomas.edu/cathstudies/cst/conferences/gaudium/papers/Deneulin.pdf. Accessed 25 April 2013.

Edwards, J. (2016). 'Behaviorism and Control in the History of Economics and Psychology'. *History of Political Economy*, 48 Supplement 1: 170–197.

Elders, L. J. (1996). 'The Actuality of St. Thomas Aquinas' Teachings on the Common Good'. *Doctor Communis*, 49: 44–58.

Finnis, J. M. (1980). *Natural Law and Natural Rights*. Oxford: Clarendon Press.

Frey, B. S. and A. Stutzer (2002). *Happiness and Economics: How the Economy and Institutions Affects Human Well-Being*. Princeton: Princeton University Press.

Gallagher, R. (2018). *Aristotle's Critique of Political Economy. With a Contemporary Application*. London: Routledge.

Gasper, D. and I. van Staveren (2003). 'Development as Freedom – and as What Else?0'. *Feminist Economics*, 9/2–3: 137–161.

Gigerenzer, G. (2010). 'Moral Satisficing: Rethinking Moral Behavior as Bounded Rationality'. *Topics in Cognitive Science*, 2: 528–554.

Gigerenzer, G. (2015). 'On the Supposed Evidence for Libertarian Paternalism'. *Review of Philosophy and Psychology*, 6/3: 361–383.

Grüne-Yanoff, T. and R. Hertwig (2016). 'Nudge versus Boost: How Coherent Are Policy and Theory?'. *Minds and Machines*, 26: 149–183.

Guala, F. and L. Mittone (2015). 'A Political Justification of Nudging'. *Review of Philosophy and Psychology*, 6/3: 385–395.

Gutmann, A. (1985). 'Communitarian Critics of Liberalism'. *Philosophy and Public Affairs*, 14/3: 309–322.

Halteman, J. and E. Noell, 2012. *Reckoning with Markets. Moral Reflection in Economics*. Oxford and New York: Oxford University Press.

Hausman, D. M. and B. Welch (2010). 'Debate: To Nudge Or Not to Nudge'. *Journal of Political Philosophy*, 18/1: 123–136.

Hertwig, R. and T. Grüne-Yanoff (2017). 'Nudging and Boosting: Steering or Empowering Good Decisions'. *Perspectives on Psychological Science*: 12/6: 973–986.

Huppert, F. A. and T. T. C. So (2009). *What Percentage of People in Europe Are Flourishing and What Characterises Them?* Cambridge: Well-Being Institute, University of Cambridge, Prepared for the OECD/ISQOLS meeting 'Measuring Subjective Well-Being: An Opportunity for NSOs?' Florence, 23 and 24 July 2009, http://www.isqols2009.istitutodeglinnocenti.it/Content_en/Huppert.pdf. Accessed 1 May 2013.

Huppert, F. A. and T. T. C. So (2013). 'Flourishing across Europe: Application of a New Conceptual Framework for Defining Well-Being'. *Social Indicators Research*, 110: 837–861. http://link.springer.com/content/pdf/10.1007%2Fs11205-011-9966-7.pdf, Accessed 1 May 2013.

Hussain, W. (2018). 'The Common Good'. In: E. N. Zalta (ed.), *The Stanford Encyclopedia of Philosophy*, https://plato.stanford.edu/entries/common-good/. Accessed 22 December 2018.

Jaede, M. (2017). *The Concept of the Common Good* (PSRP Working Paper No. 8). Edinburgh: Global Justice Academy, University of Edinburgh.

Keynes, J. N. ([1890] 1955). *The Scope and Method of Political Economy*. Fourth Edition. New York: Kelley and Millman.

Keys, M. M. (2006). *Aquinas, Aristotle, and the Promise of the Common Good*. Cambridge: Cambridge University Press.

Keys, M. M. and C. Godfrey (2010). 'Common Good'. In: M. Bevir (ed.) *Encyclopedia of Political Theory*. Los Angeles: Sage, pp. 239–242.

Klamer, A. (2017). *Doing the Right Thing. A Value Based Economy*. London: Ubiquity Press.

Kolakowski, L. (1993). 'On the Practicability of Liberalism: What About the Children?'. *Critical Review*, 7/1: 1–13.

Layard, R. (2005). *Happiness. Lessons from a New Science*. New York: Penguin.

Layard, R. (2007). 'Happiness and Public Policy: A Challenge to the Profession'. In: B. Frey and A. Stutzer (eds.), *Economics and Psychology. A Promising New Cross-Disciplinary Field*. Cambridge (MA): MIT Press, pp. 155–168.

Leonard, T. C. (2008). 'Review of Richard Thaler and Cass Sunstein, Nudge: Improving Decisions about Health, Wealth and Happiness'. *Constitutional Political Economy*, 19/4: 356–360.

MacIntyre, A. (1990). 'The Privatization of Good'. *Review of Politics*, 52/3: 344–361.

Mansbridge, J. (2013). 'Common Good'. In: H. LaFollette (ed.), *International Encyclopedia of Ethics*, vol. 2. Malden (MA): Wiley-Blackwell.

Naastepad, C.W. M. and J. M. Mulder (2018). 'Robots and Us: Towards an Economics of the "Good Life"'. *Review of Social Economy*, 76/3: 302–334.

Nussbaum, M. C. (1987). 'Nature, Function, and Capability: Aristotle on Political Distribution'. *WIDER Working Paper* 31, Helsinki.

Nussbaum, M. C. (2003). 'Capabilities as Fundamental Entitlements: Sen and Social Justice'. *Feminist Economics*, 9/2–3: 33–59.

Rawls, J. (1971). *A Theory of Justice*. Cambridge (MA): Harvard University Press.

Reiss, J. (2013). *Philosophy of Economics. A Contemporary Introduction*. Abingdon: Routledge.

Saint-Paul, G. (2001). *The Tyranny of Utility: Behavioral Social Science and the Rise of Paternalism*. Princeton: Princeton University Press.

Sen, A. (1993). 'Capability and Well-Being'. In: M. Nussbaum and A. Sen (eds.), *The Quality of Life*. Oxford: Oxford University Press and The United Nations University, pp. 30–53.

Sen, A. (1999). *Reason Before Identity*. Oxford: Oxford University Press.

Sen, A. (2002). *Rationality and Freedom*. Cambridge (MA): Belknap Press of Harvard University Press.

Sen, A. (2004). 'Dialogue. Capabilities, Lists, and Public Reason: Continuing the Conversation'. *Feminist Economics*, 10/3: 77–80.

Skidelsky, R. and E. Skidelsky (2012). *How Much Is Enough*. New York: Other Press.

Smith, A. (1976). *The Theory of Moral Sentiments*, Glasgow Edition. Oxford: Oxford University Press.

Sugden, R. (2009). 'On Nudging: A Review of Nudge: Improving Decisions about Health, Wealth and Happiness by Richard H. Thaler and Cass R. Sunstein'. *International Journal of the Economics of Business*, 16/3: 365–373.

Sunstein, C. (2014). *Why Nudge? The Politics of Libertarian Paternalism*. New York: Palgrave Macmillan.

Sunstein, C. (2015a). 'Nudges, Agency, and Abstraction: A Reply to Critics'. *Review of Philosophy and Psychology*, 6: 511–529.

Sunstein, C. (2015b). 'Nudges Do Not Undermine Human Agency: A Note'. *Journal of Consumer Policy*, 38: 207–210.

Sunstein, C. (2017). *Human Agency and Behavioral Economics: Nudging Fast and Slow*. New York: Palgrave Macmillan.

Thaler, R. H. and C. Sunstein (2003a). 'Libertarian Paternalism'. *American Economic Review*, 93/2: 175–179.

Thaler, R. H. and C. Sunstein (2003b). 'Libertarian Paternalism Is Not an Oxymoron'. *University of Chicago Law Review*, 70/4: 1159–1202.

Thaler, R. H. and C. Sunstein (2008). *Nudge: Improving Decisions about Health, Wealth and Happiness*. New Haven (CT): Yale University Press.

Van Staveren, I. (2001). *The Values of Economics: An Aristotelian Perspective*. London: Routledge.

White, M. D. (2019). 'Nudging Merit Goods: Conceptual, Normative, and Practical Connections'. *Forum for Social Economics*, 48/3: 248–263.

Wijngaards, A. (2012). *Worldly Theology. On Connecting Public Theology and Economics*. PhD thesis, Radboud Universiteit Nijmegen, The Netherlands. http://hdl.handle.net/2066/93624. Accessed 23 November 2013.

Yuengert, A. (2000). 'The Common Good for Economists'. Working paper, Pepperdine University. www.gordon.edu/ace/pdf/Yuengert_CommonGood.pdf. Accessed 29 August 2015.

Yuengert, A. (2004). *The Boundaries of Technique. Ordering Positive and Normative Concerns in Economic Research.* Lanham (MD): Lexington Books.

Yuengert, A. (2012). *Approximating Prudence: Aristotelian Practical Wisdom and Economic Models of Choice.* London: Palgrave Macmillan.

10 The art of economics

Lionel Robbins maintained that 'few become economists for mere curiosity' (1963: 9). Most economists are concerned with performing actions that impact real life. Or, as Philip Wicksteed has asserted (1888: viii),

> Be it known, then, that there are certain things, in no degree subject to our power, which we can make the objects of speculation, but not of action. Such are mathematics, physics and theology. But there are some which are subject to our power, and to which we can direct not only our speculations but our action. And in the case of these, action does not exist for the sake of speculation, but we speculate with a view to action; for in such matters action is the goal.

In Chapter 3 on economic sciences, I drew on the classical economists to consider 'the art of economics' as the 'last' economic science. The task of this last science is to produce a synthesis of the contents of the previous sciences in order to make them operational. In effect, economic theory looks for the causes – efficient and final, economic and non-economic – of economic phenomena so as to explain and predict them. Normative economics determines the desirable ends of economic policy. The art of economics combines all the previous input in order to design and implement an effective economic policy. The aim of this policy is *to achieve the defined ends*, taking into account all the means that may cause the desired effects and, consequently, all the motives influencing economic phenomena.

The first author that I mentioned in Chapter 3 was John Stuart Mill. He holds that there are two kinds of arts: the art of defining ends (which is morality) and the art of performing the actions directed to these ends, enlightened by science. The previous chapter dealt with the art of defining ends. This chapter will deal with the latter art. Let me quote once again the corresponding passage of Mill in the *System of Logic* (1882: 653;VI, XXI, 2):

> The relation in which rules of art stand to doctrines of science may be thus characterized. The art proposes to itself an end to be attained, defines the end, and hands it over to the science. The science receives it, considers it

as a phenomenon or effect to be studied, and having investigated its causes and conditions, sends it back to art with a theorem of the combination of circumstances by which it could be produced. Art then examines these combination [sic] of circumstances, and according as any of them are or are not in human power, pronounces the end attainable or not.

Menger also regards *practical or applied economics* as an economic science with a specific method (1960: 16, 21–22), including economic policy and the science of finance ([1883] 1985: 97). Adolf Wagner proposes we distinguish five steps of economic work (1886: 128). The fifth is the search for the way to effectively attain the ends set by the fourth step (normative economics). Henry Sidgwick also considers the art of political economy (1887: 28).

Finally, Neville Keynes suggests a threefold distinction between 'positive science', 'normative or regulative science', and 'an art' ([1890] 1955: 34–35), respectively dealing with '*economic uniformities, economic ideals and economic precepts*' ([1890] 1955: 31, 35). He asserts that Adam Smith and his contemporaries use the term 'science' to refer to a systematic body of knowledge of theoretical propositions or practical rules ([1890] 1955: 35, nt 2 and 40, nt). For Neville Keynes, the art should have its own place within the science ([1890] 1955: 118 and 145).

Economists from the twentieth century have generally witnessed the main division between positive and normative economics. At the same time, how-ever, the art of economics has been almost completely forgotten or subsumed under positive or normative economics. This last fact has been noted by David Colander (1992, 1994 and 2001). It has also been the subject of Luis Mireles Flores' dissertation (2016). Colander believes that both positive economics and the art of economics fall under the rubric of economic science (1994: 35), but he emphatically states that the methodology of the art of economics is funda-mentally different from the methodology of positive economics (1994: 36). Let us examine this point.

A different methodology

My country, Argentina, holds the shameful world record for the largest number of financial crises over the last 100 years (Atkinson and Morelli 2011). The economic history of Argentina is a history of systematic failures of economic policies. Although an economy is a highly complex reality and it is very difficult to identify the causes of crises, many argue that the crises that I have lived through in my country were to a large extent the result of implementing theoretical positive economics recipes without taking into account the specific characteristics of our people's idiosyncrasies and history, or doing so only as a second step. Economic theories' recipes are too simple to manage such a complex reality. I will now get back to Mill, Menger, and Neville Keynes and their teachings about the method of the art of eco-nomics. Mill warns:

No one who attempts to lay down propositions for the guidance of mankind, however perfect his scientific acquirements, can dispense with a practical knowledge of the actual modes in which the affairs of the world are carried on, and an extensive personal experience of the actual ideas, feelings, and intellectual and moral tendencies of his own country and of his own age. The true practical statesman is he who combines this experience with a profound knowledge of abstract political philosophy.

(Mill [1844] 2006: 333)

Mill applies these ideas to the art of economics. Menger distinguishes the practical economic sciences (economic policy and finance) from the even more concrete, practical application of these sciences, 'according to the particularity of the conditions of individual countries and nations' ([1883] 1985: Appendix III). He also states that 'not considering the variety of conditions is a crude error in any type of research in the realm of the practical sciences' ([1883] 1985: 101). He explicitly affirms that the different formal approaches used by theoretical and practical sciences call for different methods ([1883] 1985: xii and 73).

Furthermore, Neville Keynes was certainly correct when he asserted:

[F]ew practical problems admit of complete solution on economic grounds alone ([1890] 1955: 56) [...] Account must also be taken of ethical, social, and political considerations that lie outside the sphere of political economy regarded as a science [...] If, on the other hand, the art attempts a complete solution of practical problems, it must of necessity be to a large extent non-economic in its character, and its scope becomes vague and ill-defined.

([1890] 1955): 57)

This vagueness leads Neville Keynes even to suggest treating the art of economics as 'the economic side of political philosophy' ([1890] 1955): 58 and see 83). Other statements by him stress the context-dependence of adequate economic policy and the specific method for it:

It is even possible that what is excellent for a given nation at a given time may be actively mischievous and injurious for another nation, or for the same nation at a different period of its economic history. It follows, similarly, that the value of the economic institutions of the past cannot adequately be judged by reference to existing conditions alone ([1890] 1955: 64–65). [...] Even where the forces in operation are the same, the relative strength that should be assigned to each may vary indefinitely.

([1890] 1955: 300)

This is why 'concrete economic doctrines', as he terms the art of political economy in another part of the book, are 'contingent and indeterminate', though still part of science ([1890] 1955: 145). By definition, positive economics seeks to select, through the use of models, the causal variables deemed essential for the phenomenon to be explained and puts aside the rest. Instead, the art of economics should try to evaluate the impact of all causes simultaneously. This has consequences, for example, for the evidence needed by the art of economics. As Mireles Flores (2016: 135; italics in the original) explains:

> research that aims at supporting policy recommendations requires the use of evidential methods to generate results not only about causal relations in isolation, but also about potential sources of error (from all the known and unknown factors Z) are present and active in the intended concrete context of policy application. Thus, the assessment of a policy hypothesis 'is effective to generate Y in a concrete context' requires *valid* evidence that X *tends to cause* Y, plus *valid* evidence about whether all the relevant factors Z (pertaining to the relevant causal structure) are or are not active in the concrete intended context of application.

The introduction of the historical, sociological, and psychological dimensions in the analysis should be consistent with strict economic analysis. As Colander maintains, 'the art of economics is contextual and as much dependent on non-economic political, social, institutional, and historical judgments as it is on economics' (1992: 197); there are qualitative variables that cannot be precisely measured but that also have to be considered (1994: 41).

Colander (2013) adopts what Billy Vaughn Koen (2003) calls the 'engineering method', a method oriented at solving problems that allows a variety of sources: historical and intuitive knowledge, guestimates, economic and non-economic dimensions, case studies, and interviews with specialists.

The case for an engineering approach was also previously made by Alvin Roth, though mainly considering economic factors. His paper abstract proves telling, and concerns methodology (2002: 1341):

> Economists have lately been called upon not only to analyze markets, but to design them. Market design involves a responsibility for detail, a need to deal with all of a market's complications, not just its principle features. Designers therefore cannot work only with the simple conceptual models used for theoretical insights into the general working of markets. Instead, market design calls for an engineering approach.

He started working on 'matching markets' in 1982. In his Biographical on the Nobel Prize website, he explains that in matching markets

> price adjustment alone doesn't clear the market. Loosely speaking, these are markets that have application procedures, or selection criteria or other institutions, in which you cannot simply choose what you want (even if you can afford it), but also have to be chosen.
>
> (www.nobelprize.org/prizes/economic-sciences/
> 2012/roth/auto-biography/)

'The new economics of matchmaking and market design', as the subtitle of his 2015 book reads, assumes that this kind of detailed work occurs beyond abstract economics. Roth has worked on a variety of mechanisms, for example, to assign medical residents and students to schools, or to exchange of kidneys.

Abhijit V. Banerjee holds that 'positive economics, as the one clear methodological stance that one finds among economists, [...] at best applies only to a quite limited domain within economics' (2002: 3). He thinks of economic decision-making as a craft that cannot be acquired through learning but only through experience (2002: 5). Esther Duflo claims that the economist should be like a plumber. She explains (2017: 5):

> The plumber goes one step further than the engineer: she installs the machine in the real world, carefully watches what happens, and then tinkers as needed. At the time she inherits the machine, the broad goals are clear, but many details still need to be worked out. The fundamental difference between an engineer and a plumber is that the engineer knows (or assumes she knows) what the important features of the environment are, and can design the machine to address these features – in the abstract, at least. [...] When the plumber fits the machine, there are many gears and joints, and many parameters of the world that are difficult to anticipate and will only become known once the machine grinds into motion. The plumber will use a number of things – the engineering design, his understanding of the context, prior experience, and the science to date – to tune every feature of the policy as well as possible, keeping an eye on all the relevant details as best he can. But with respect to some details, there will remain genuine uncertainty about the best way to proceed, because the solution depends on a host of factors she cannot easily quantify, or sometimes even identify, in the abstract. (These are the 'unknown unknowns': all the issues we can't predict but will arise anyways).

That is, Duflo is asking the economist for more than just the designing of economic policies. She is asking him/her to implement such policies and, in the process, to deal with unforeseen events that may require corrective actions. Let us recall Chapter 6 where Knight (1956) and Buchanan (1987) characterize the economic process and economic ends as changing and as being defined by that very process. Duflo states:

> There is no general theory of how to design policy under this kind of model uncertainty [concerning what the true model is], however, and in many cases, even the best-educated guess will still be just that, a guess. The economist-plumber will use all they know (including model uncertainty), to come up with the best guess possible, and then pay careful attention to what happens in reality. The uncertainty in the environment creates a highly stochastic world.
>
> (2017: 6)

In her paper, Duflo considers a lot of 'ad-hoc' details of a sociological, psychological, technical, or practical character to be taken into account in order to succeed in the implementation of – often very local – economic policies. This does not mean, however, as Banerjee and Duflo sometimes seem to maintain, that theory is less relevant.[1] As I have held in Chapter 6, the work of the economist consists in an interplay between theory and evidence, which cannot be disconnected from a theoretical point of view.

Coming back to some philosophical concepts explained in Chapter 3, we can conceive of the art of economics as a practical science with a practical aim. Its 'material object' – its subject matter – is the same as that of other economic sciences – economic phenomena – but its 'formal object' – the perspective or approach to them – is different: it aims at producing economic results. 'It is actually ordered to perform something', in Aquinas' words (*De Veritate*, q. 3, a. 3). This specificity of the formal object conditions the method.

What is the incidence of values in this discipline? The art of economics conforms to a means–ends logic, given the ends determined by normative economics. It would consequently seem that values are not related to this instrumental task. However, they are implied in various ways. First, the designer of an economic policy considers values among the causes of or influences exerted on economic phenomena. Second, not all means are ethically acceptable. Third, as Neville Keynes points out, 'no solution of a practical problem, relating to human conduct, can be regarded as complete, until its ethical aspects have been considered' ([1890] 1955: 60). He additionally thinks that the 'art of political economy' does not aim at fulfilling the desires of an individual but of what is desirable for the whole of society ([1890] 1955: 75). He even adds that

> accepting as its function a high moral task, it may seek in various ways to influence the economic activity of individuals so as to bring them into harmony with sound economic morality and secure the supremacy of right habits and customs in industrial life.
>
> ([1890] 1955: 76, nt)

The aforementioned may lead us to conclude that the work of the economist in charge of designing and implementing economic policy, that is the economist who practices the 'art of political economy', is extremely difficult. The well-known description of the economist by John Maynard Keynes in his obituary essay for Marshall seems particularly relevant here. Let us recall it:

> The study of economics does not seem to require any specialised gifts of an unusually high order. Is it not, intellectually regarded, a very easy subject compared with the higher branches of philosophy and pure science? Yet good, or even competent, economists are the rarest of birds. An easy subject, at which very few excel! The paradox finds its explanation, perhaps, in that the master-economist must possess a rare combination of gifts. He must reach a high standard in several different directions and must combine

talents not often found together. He must be mathematician, historian, statesman, philosopher – in some degree. He must understand symbols and speak in words. He must contemplate the particular in terms of the general, and touch abstract and concrete in the same flight of thought. He must study the present in the light of the past for the purposes of the future. No part of man's nature or his institutions must lie entirely outside his regard. He must be purposeful and disinterested in a simultaneous mood; as aloof and incorruptible as an artist, yet sometimes as near the earth as a politician. Much, but not all, of this ideal many-sidedness Marshall possessed. But chiefly his mixed training and divided nature furnished him with the most essential and fundamental of the economist's necessary gifts – he was conspicuously historian and mathematician, a dealer in the particular and the general, the temporal and the eternal, at the same time.

(1924: 321–322)

The economist requires a very sophisticated expertise. In the next section, I will analyse its nature and conditions for acquiring it.

On economic expertise

Let's get back to my Argentinian experience. I finished my undergraduate studies at the end of 1978 and soon after I started working in the finance area. During the 1975–1990 period, the annual inflation rate exceeded 100 per cent. For example, in 1979, my first year in the workforce as an economist, the inflation rate stood at 139.7 per cent. This led to hyperinflation, with inflation peaking at 200 per cent in July 1989 and reaching an annual rate of 3079 per cent. These high and consistent inflation rates often eroded the real value of the local currency, triggering abrupt devaluations, significant distortions in relative prices and salaries, and changes in the balance of trade and in external capital flows. Asset protection was a hard task. People in the financial sector watched the market closely and made changes in the composition of portfolios almost daily.

During this period, I worked with two colleagues managing family funds. We used to start the day at the coffee shop reading the economic newspaper and trying to guess and infer the reactions of the financial market to the latest economic, social, and political breaking news. One of my fellow workers used to walk the city to visit other colleagues and gather information and opinions. We made financial decisions on a day-to-day basis.

We finally acquired an almost instinctive knowledge of the best actions to carry out each day. This knowledge consisted in a combination of data analysis, estimates of price distortions (in order to buy cheap assets and sell expensive ones), people's response to the crisis, inside information about future policy measures, political and international news (for example, nothing less than a war against Great Britain [...] once 'Las Malvinas' – the Falkland Islands – had been temporarily recovered), and so on.

We only experienced one financial loss. The circumstances were as follows: Forecasts for the presidential election of 30 October 1983 predicted that Peronists ('Partido Justicialista') would win by a small margin. Peronists have always upheld demagogic policies. Thus, we expected the exchange rate to depreciate and, consequently, we bought US dollars in the futures market at a high price, anticipating that its price would rise significantly by the end of the month, enabling us to sell the dollars at a higher price and make a profit. However, an unpredictable incident changed the outcome of the election. Herminio Iglesias was the Peronist candidate for governor of the Buenos Aires Province. At the closing act of the Peronist campaign, his followers approached him with a coffin with the inscription 'UCR' (representing their main opposition), which he set on fire. Given the small expected difference between the two parties, this brutal episode led undecided voters to shift their preference towards the opposition party. As a result, the UCR won the election and Ricardo Alfonsín was elected president. This outcome brought tranquillity to people and, consequently, the price of the dollar remained unchanged. Thus, instead of making some money on the currency exchange, we had to pay for the difference. However, this was only an early market reaction. The UCR party could not tame the economy, which exhibited a rather erratic course, culminating in the above-mentioned hyperinflation. Simultaneously, we went on taking advantage of these disparate economic phenomena and winning money for our clients with our financial deals.

What were the key factors of our good performance? On reflection, we boasted a lot of economic theory, calculation skills, empirical information, experience with previous people's reactions to economic and political measures, inside information, and exchange of opinions, all in the back of our minds. We combined all these elements; we discussed things and decided what to do during our coffee meetings, and then we put them into action. It was a real transdisciplinary effort.

This was relatively simple. Managing the whole economy was clearly more difficult. There are very good economists in Argentina, many of them with PhDs from American or European universities. I know quite a lot of them, and I am sure they are clever people, highly educated, academically outstanding professionals. However, they probably needed (and need) more life experience. The economy is a very complex reality, and Argentina's economy is still more complex:

> The economic history of Argentina is one of the most studied, owing to the '*Argentine paradox*', its unique condition as a country that achieved advanced development in the early 20th century but experienced a reversal, which inspired an enormous wealth of literature and diverse analysis on the causes of this decline.[2]

The following abstract of a paper by Alan M. Taylor titled 'The Argentina Paradox: Microexplanations and Macropuzzles', states (2018):[3]

The economic history of Argentina presents one of the most dramatic examples of divergence in the modern era. What happened and why? This paper reviews the wide range of competing explanations in the literature and argues that, setting aside deeper social and political determinants, the various economic mechanisms in play defy the idea of a monocausal explanation.

Certainly, the economic explanation of the 'paradox' is not only not mono-causal but, moreover, we cannot set apart political and social determinants, including ethical determinants such as generalized corruption or serious deficiencies in the rule of law: 'for every law there is a loophole', especially in my country. There are also a lot of ingrained habits: for example, automatically raising domestic prices whenever the dollar rate goes up, but never lowering them when the opposite occurs. Argentina has, in fact, a bi-monetary economic system resting on strong psychosociological attitudes. It exhibits endemic distrust in the domestic currency due to its frequent devaluations. This is why my former professor Ricardo Arriazu, who at the end of the seventies fervently defended the floating exchange rate system when he taught monetary economics, today he defends interventions in the foreign currency market to avoid inflationary spirals.

The recessionary effects of multiple devaluations in Argentina, a topic that has been extensively studied by many scholars, beginning with Carlos F. Díaz Alejandro (1965: Chapter 2; 1970: Chapter 7), have also responded to the very idiosyncratic economic and social characteristics of the country. Inter alia, devaluations produce a redistribution of income to the agricultural export sectors that have a lower marginal propensity to consume domestic goods. Another cause of the recessionary effects of multiple devaluations is the link between the increase in the foreign exchange rate and price inflation that leads to stabilization policies. All these phenomena are very idiosyncratic.

In addition, Domingo F. Cavallo (1977) has studied the circumstances under which using a restrictive monetary policy to fight inflation has brought about a fall in real output and acceleration of inflation in Argentina, Brazil, Chile, and Uruguay: a 'stagflationary' effect. Rudiger Dornbusch and Sebastián Edwards (1991) have explained the catastrophic and economically irrational 'macroeconomics of populism' into which Latin America countries often fall. Demagogic and often corrupt politicians regularly take advantage of the cultural shortcomings of people. Martín Lagos and Juan José Llach (2011) mention 38 different hypotheses proposed to explain the causes of the Argentine decline, including sociological, cultural, institutional, historical, political, and also many economic hypotheses – sometimes contradictory: the phenomenon is highly complex. In a subsequent book, Llach and Lagos (2014) review the previous theses and contribute their own, comparing Argentina with Brazil, Chile, Uruguay, and New Zealand. They postulate historical (strong path-dependency), economic, structural, institutional, sociological, ethical, and cultural interacting causes which, albeit also present in the other countries under study, seem to prevail extensively in Argentina.

The combination of the previous results makes management of economic affairs in my country very difficult. We need a positive current account balance to avoid default. To this end, we need a devaluated domestic currency. Consequently, foreign currency is overvalued, thus affecting the weight of the external debt relative to GDP. Additionally, devaluation of the domestic currency produces inflation, thus sterilizing its effect and generating a recession. Implementing a stabilization plan – a restrictive monetary policy and tax increases to eliminate government deficit – deepens recession and reinforces stagflation. However, it is also necessary to reach fiscal equilibrium to mitigate inflation and to avoid increasing external public debt that injects foreign currency into the economy appreciating the domestic currency. Recession and debt increase lead to default. Real wages continuously decrease, spurring strong social discontent. A populist irresponsible policy is eventually implemented, relaxing the stabilization policy and leading to higher inflation that may end up in hyperinflation.[4] This is the 'Argentina dilemma' (in Harvard economist Carmen Reinhart's words): devaluation and stabilization policies are a necessary evil.

Ultimately, the problem is not economic but cultural. Nobody would choose to be worse off and engage in conduct – pressures on increasing salaries and prices – that paradoxically drives the economy to increased general impoverishment. The lesson is that there is an intricate relation between politics, institutions, social psychology, social movements, and economic performance.[5] All in all, the problem is essentially not with positive economics. The problem is to find economic theories that can help overcome the dilemma – which cannot be overcome only with economic theory. We also need politicians convinced of the need to maintain unpopular measures, something that seems unfeasible in a democratic regime with an uncultured and individualistic society. However, Argentina's experience with undemocratic regimes, in which, ironically, people have seen some hope of change, has proven equally poor. Consequently, the feeling is one of impotence. We are destined for failure. Fortunately, happiness and intelligence can also emerge from these muddy waters.

However, my intention here is not to play a plaintive Argentine tango. I give these examples in order to make clear that we need expert plumbers to practice the art of the economy. I hold that two concepts that have frequently appeared in this book have a close relation with the role of the expert: abduction and practical reason. In fact, his/her role and expertise is to reach successful abductions in terms of the truth of the hypotheses. The expert discovers and proposes previously unknown reasonable answers to problems. Practical reason does not only discover and decide on ends, but it also plays a role of synthesizing diverse dimensions that affect a situation, offering reasonable solutions.

Contemporary literature on experts is huge.[6] I will not try to review it all here but only mention that which is more relevant for the aim of this book. There is a seminal paper by Olaf Helmer and Nicholas Rescher (1958–1960), titled 'On the Epistemology of the Inexact Sciences', that it is often quoted.[7] They state that inexact sciences call for particular methodological innovations, including 'the systematic employment of expert judgment' (1960: iii). The starting point of their paper is a passage by Alfred Marshall referring to the variable and uncertain character of human actions (1960: vi). They distinguish two steps in which the experts take part, 'the intuitive spark that may be the origin of a new discovery', and the confirmation by the intersubjective findings that provides objectivity (1960: 3). Their main focus is on prediction in the inexact sciences, which, for them, may be physical or social. In these inexact sciences, laws take the form of 'quasi-laws', which are not universal but limited generalizations – tendencies – and, consequently, predictions suffice 'to be rendered *more tenable than comparable alternatives*' (italics in the original, 1960: 12). They are like 'inferences to the best explanation', as described in Chapter 5. Here is where the expert enters the picture. In these sciences, statistics is only prima facie evidence that 'must be tempered by reference to background information, which frequently may be intuitive in character' (1960: 20), vague and deficient (1960: 21). They assert:

> The informed expert, with his resources of background knowledge and his cultivated sense of the relevance and bearing of generalities in particular cases, is best able to carry out the application of quasi-laws necessary for reasoned prediction in this field.
>
> (1960: 21)

Helmer and Rescher use the term 'intrinsic expertise' to describe expertise exerted within a theory to assess its hypotheses, and 'extrinsic expertise' as expertise that hypothesizes new laws and constructs new theories (1960: 24). The parallel with abduction is clear. In addition, they propose criteria for the selection of predictive experts: knowledge, his/her relative degree of reliability as compared to that of the average person, his/her degree of accuracy in past predictions, and so on. Finally, they describe means of forming a consensus of judgements in instances where there are several experts available for consultation.

Douglass Walton (1989) links expert reasoning with practical reason and describes the former in a manner that evokes abduction. Walton (1992) analyses the rules of 'plausible reasoning' proposed by Rescher (1976), a kind of reasoning different from deduction and induction, 'based on tentative, *prima facie*, defeasible weights of presumption which can be assigned to the propositions in an argument' (Walton 1992: 33), that is, abduction. This kind of reasoning could be applied when deciding on the course of action to take given the experts' opinions.

In the following passage, Walton (1989: 66) refers to the combined use of abductive reasoning and practical reasoning:

> The theory that an expert's judgment should be taken as a plausible conclusion, rather than as the output of a deductively valid or inductively strong argument, is based on the assumption that to act on expert advice

is to act in a situation where better, more direct evidence is not available within the constraints on reasonable action. One has to act on the best reasons within the known information relative to the given situation [...] an inference based on reasonable expectations, and carefully assessed expert advice, may serve as a kind of reasoned argumentation that may carry justified weight in arriving at a conclusion on how to act.

Boumans and Carlo Martini (2014), for their part, suggest building an 'expert-based consensus' in order to overcome the problems derived from the shortcomings of objectivity. 'Science', they assert, 'is ultimately a product of individual scientists with their own personal backgrounds, and there is [...] no unique methodology to de-personalize and objectify knowledge' (2014: 2). Boumans (2014) proposes a model-based method as a strategy to improve the objectivity of expert consensus. Reiss (2008: 38–39) analyses a specific case and offers some principles to limit the possible expert biases.

Today we find expertise in every field. It is, as Christian Quast and Markus Seidel (2018: 1) say, an 'omnipresent phenomenon'. Harry Collins and Robert Evans (2007 and 2017) have developed arguments about the need for good – in the sense of having real abilities more than a social assignment – scientific experts in democracy. Evans (2014) stresses the relevance of preserving the scientific value of expert institutions to really help decision makers and prevent science from being politicized. Boumans and Martini also draw attention to the role of experts in the interface between science and politics (2014: 5).

In Chapter 4, I explained how the technical aspects of measurement are intertwined with its judgemental practical aspects. The field shares the same characteristics with the subject matter of practical sciences: it is 'context-dependent and sensitive to local conditions', 'much more inexact than a laboratory science' (Boumans 2015: 174); it needs a 'considered judgment' (Elgin 1996), analogous to clinical practice (Boumans 2015: Chapter 5). Boumans often makes reference to the need for expert judgement when measuring and analysing statistics (see, e.g. 2015: 53, 84, 114, 121–123, 146, 176). He eventually concludes: 'the main conclusion is that reliable measurement outside the laboratory is clinical measurement, that is, the combination of model-based procedures of attaining precision and calibration combined with a rational consensus of expert judgments' (2015: 177).

Julian Reiss (2014) deals with economic expertise. He makes some substantive claims in economic expertise. He first shows that the usual foundations of objectivity in economics – product, process objectivities, and value neutrality – have been defeated by facts, such as the 2008 financial crisis. We do not need an expert merely focused on abstract 'objective' economic reasoning, but one embedded in the non-economic dimensions of society that surround economic phenomena.

Carlo Martini (2014b) specifically addresses the role of the expert in regard to the subject matter of this chapter: the art of economics. Martini holds that disregard for the role of the expert in this field is parallel to neglect of the field itself and surmises that it has to do with a 'rationalist' view of expertise, that is the view that its role is merely to interpret and apply theory and evidence. Thus, it has been replaced by actuarial and statistical rules (2014b: 79). However, these are not enough to ensure a successful economic policy: we need evidence, theory, and input gathered from practice, as Duflo's plumber's metaphor illustrates. Martini draws from Jeffrey Sachs a similar metaphor: the apothecary (2014b: 84). In a way that recalls the application of practical reason and abduction, he asserts:

> economics looks a lot more like a 'toolbox science', where different sources of evidence are used for specific prediction problems, and which, in turn, allow practitioners to connect initial conditions and laws with outcomes in policy applications.

He also asserts that experts have 'the ability to contribute to the collective judgment through hunches, speculations, guesses, and so on' (2014a: 7) and recognizes that although they often provide inconclusive evidence (2014a: 13), we should accept expert judgement. Clearly, what we are referring to here is abductive reasoning.

In effect, experts may make mistakes. Abduction is always fallible. However, in a social science such as economics, the probability of error in an expert who combines his/her knowledge of economic theory with available evidence from his/her experience of the historical, psychosociological, ethical, and cultural conditions of his/her environment is less than the probability of error by a theorist. Let us conclude.

Conclusion

The following passage from Duflo adequately expresses my conclusion:

> Many of us chose economics because, ultimately, we thought science could be leveraged to make a positive change in the world. There are many different paths to get there. Scientists design general frames, engineers turn them into relevant machinery, and plumbers finally make them work in a complicated, messy policy environment. As a discipline, we are sometimes a little overwhelmed by 'physics envy', searching for the ultimate scientific answer to all questions – and this will lead us to question the legitimacy of plumbing. This essay is an attempt to argue that plumbing should be an inherent part of our profession: we are well prepared for it, reasonably good at it, and it is how we make ourselves useful. A feature unique to economics is that scientists, engineers, and plumbers all talk to each other (and in fact are often talking to themselves – the same economist wearing different hats). This conversation should continue: it is what will keep us relevant and, possibly, honest.
>
> (2017: 31)

Heikki Patomäki (forthcoming) stresses the self-fulfilling or self-denying character of social processes: the economy influences economics, which, in turn, also influences the economy and so on. In his view, in order to anticipate and provoke outcomes we should use models, informal methods, value-laden extrapolations, leading indicators, expert judgements, timing, and experience.

That is, we need to recover 'the art of economics' which is, as anticipated in the Introduction to this book, a transdisciplinary approach, in the sense that it must integrate all previous economic sciences, insights from other sciences, and input gathered from other sources and from actual implementation of economic policies in order to achieve an adequate practical science.

One final word and warning: the art of economics must exercise prudence and caution upon intervening in the economy. This chapter has often included expressions such as 'make changes in the world', 'design markets', 'apply an engineering approach', 'work as plumbers', and so forth. These actions must be interspersed with a 'leave things alone' disposition, which is sometimes the best thing we can do. The good practitioner of the art of economics should learn and apply this combination.

Notes

1 For a criticism in this regard, see Judith Favereau (2016).
2 https://en.wikipedia.org/wiki/Economic_history_of_Argentina; italics in the original.
3 This article is part of a special collection on 'Argentine Exceptionalism'.
4 See Carlos Alfredo Rodríguez (1994) on fiscal disequilibria and hyperinflation, specifically referring to Argentina's 1989 hyperinflation.
5 See, for example, in the book by Stephan Haggard and Robert Kaufman (1995) about the economic performance of countries living democratic transitions, the close interaction and mutual influence between political affairs, institutions, social events, and economic policies, with a lot of references to Argentina, Brazil, Bolivia, Chile, Korea, México, Peru, the Philippines, Taiwan, Thailand, and Turkey.
6 See, for example, Boumans and Martini (2014) and the collection of articles in *Topoi* 37, 2018.
7 There is a typed edition dated October 13, 1958, as a Rand Corporation paper F-1513 printed in 1960 as R-353.

References

Atkinson, T. and S. Morelli (2011). 'Economic Crises and Inequality', Human Development Research Paper 2011/06, http://hdr.undp.org/sites/default/files/hdrp_2011_06.pdf. Accessed October 2018.

Banerjee, A. V. (2002). 'The Uses of Economic Theory: Against a Purely Positive Interpretation of Theoretical Results', MIT Department of Economics Working Paper No. 02–24, https://papers.ssrn.com/sol3/papers.cfm?abstract_id=315942.57 and https://economics.mit.edu/files/505. Accessed 24 June 2019.

Boumans, M. J. (2014). 'Model-Based Consensus'. In: C. Martini and M. Boumans (eds.), *Experts and Consensus in Social Science*. Dordrecht: Springer, pp. 49–69.

Boumans, M. J. (2015). *Science outside the Laboratory*. Oxford: Oxford University Press.

Boumans, M. J. and C. Martini (2014). 'Introduction: Experts and Consensus in Social Science'. In: C. Martini and M. Boumans (eds.), *Experts and Consensus in Social Science*. Dordrecht: Springer, pp. 1–13.

Buchanan, J. M. (1987). *Economics. Between Predictive Science and Moral Philosophy*. College Station: Texas A&M University Press.

Cavallo, D. (1977). Stagflationary Effects of Monetarist Stabilization Policies, PhD thesis in Economics, Harvard University, www.cavallo.com.ar/wp-content/uploads/2015/08/Tesis-DFC-Harvard.pdf. Accessed 15 November 2018.

Colander, D. (1992). 'Retrospectives: The Lost Art of Economics'. *Journal of Economic Perspectives*, 6/3: 191–198.

Colander, D. (1994). 'The Art of Economics by the Numbers'. In: R. E. Backhouse (ed.), *New Directions in Economic Methodology*. London: Routledge, pp. 35–49.

Colander, D. (2001). *The Lost Art of Economics: Essays on Economics and the Economic Profession*. Cheltenham: Edward Elgar.

Colander, D. (2013). 'The Systematic Failure of Economic Methodologists'. *Journal of Economic Methodology*, 20/1: 56–68.

Collins, H. and R. Evans (2007). *Rethinking Expertise*. Chicago: University of Chicago Press

Collins, H. and R. Evans (2017). *Why Democracies Need Science*. Cambridge: Polity Press.

Díaz Alejandro, C. (1965). *Exchange Rate Devaluation in a Semi-Industrialized Country. The Experience of Argentina, 1955–1961*. Cambridge (MA): MIT Press.

Díaz Alejandro, C. (1970). *Essays on the Economic History of the Argentine Republic*. New Haven (CT): Yale University Press.

Dornbusch, R. and S. Edwards (1991). 'The Macroeconomics of Populism'. In: R. Dornbusch and S. Edwards (eds.), *The Macroeconomics of Populism in Latin America*. Chicago: University of Chicago Press, pp. 7–13.

Duflo, E. (2017). 'The Economist as Plumber', NBER Working Paper Series, Working Paper 23213, www.nber.org/papers/w23213. Accessed 12 May 2019. Published in the *American Economic Review*, 107/5: 1–26.

Elgin, C. Z. (1996). *Considered Judgment*. Princeton: Princeton University Press.

Evans, R. (2014). 'Expert Advisers: Why Economic Forecasters Can Be Useful'. In: C. Martini and M. Boumans (eds.), *Experts and Consensus in Social Science*. Dordrecht: Springer, pp. 233–252.

Favereau, J. (2016). 'On the Analogy between Field Experiments in Economics and Clinical Trials in Medicine'. *Journal of Economic Methodology*, 23/2: 203–222.

Haggard, S. and R. R. Kaufman (1995). *The Political Economy of Democratic Transitions*. Princeton: Princeton University Press.

Helmer, O. and N. Rescher (1958). *On the Epistemology of the Inexact Sciences*. F-1513. Santa Monica (CA): Rand Corporation.

Helmer, O. and N. Rescher (1960). *On the Epistemology of the Inexact Sciences*. R-353. Santa Monica (CA): Rand Corporation.

Keynes, J. M. (1924). 'Alfred Marshall, 1842–1924'. *Economic Journal*, 34/135: pp. 311–372.

Keynes, J. N. ([1890] 1955). *The Scope and Method of Political Economy*. Fourth Edition. New York: Kelley and Millman.

Knight, F. H. (1956). *On the History and Method of Economics*. Chicago: University of Chicago Press.

Koen, B.V. (2003). *Discussion of the Method*. New York: Oxford University Press.

Lagos, M. and J. J. Llach (2011). *Claves del retraso y del progreso de la Argentina*. Buenos Aires: Temas.

Llach, J. J. and M. Lagos (2014). *El país de las desmesuras*. Buenos Aires: Editorial El Ateneo.

Martini, C. (2014a). 'Experts in Science: A View from the Trenches'. *Synthese*, 191/1: 3–15.

Martini, C. (2014b). 'The Role of Experts in the Methodology of Economics'. *Journal of Economic Methodology*, 21/1: 77–91.

Menger, C. ([1883] 1985). *Investigations into the Method of the Social Sciences with Special Reference to Economics*, Ed. Louis Schneider, Transl. Francis J. Nock. New York and London: New York University Press (*Untersuchungen über die Methode der Socialwissenschaften und der Politischen Oekonomie insbesondere*, Leipzig: Ducker & Humblot).

Menger, C. (1960). 'Toward a Systematic Classification of Economic Sciences'. In: Louise Sommer (transl. and ed.), *Essays in European Economic Thought*. Princeton (NJ): D. van Nostrand, pp. 1–38.

Mill, J. S. ([1844] 2006). *Essays on Some Unsettled Questions of Political Economy* (Essay V: 'On the Definition of Political Economy; and on the Method of Investigation Proper to It'). In *Collected Works of John Stuart Mill*, vol. 4. Indianapolis: Liberty Fund.

Mill, J. S. (1882). *A System of Logic, Ratiocinative and Inductive*, Eighth Edition. New York: Harper & Brothers.

Mireles Flores, L. (2016). Economic Science for Use: Causality and Evidence in Policy Making. PhD thesis, Erasmus University Rotterdam.

Patomäki, H. (forthcoming). 'Reflexivity of Anticipations in Economics and Political Economy'. In: R. Poli (ed.), *Handbook of Anticipation. Theoretical and Applied Aspects of the Use of Future in Decision Making*. Berlin: Springer.

Quast, C. and M. Seidel (2018). 'Introduction: The Philosophy of Expertise – What Is Expertise?'. *Topoi*, 37: 1–2.

Reiss, J. (2008). *Error in Economics*. New York and London: Routledge.

Reiss, J. (2014). 'Struggling Over the Soul of Economics: Objectivity Versus Expertise'. In: C. Martini and M. Boumans (eds.), *Experts and Consensus in Social Science*. Dordrecht: Springer, pp. 131–152.

Rescher, N. (1976). *Plausible Reasoning*. Assen-Amsterdam: Van Gorkum.

Robbins, L. C. (1963). *Politics and Economics: Papers in Political Economy*. London: Macmillan and New York: St. Martin's Press.

Rodríguez, C. A. (1994). 'Fiscal Disequilibria and Hyperinflation'. In: W. Easterly, C. A. Rodríguez and K. Schmidt-Hebbel (eds.), *Public Sector Deficits and Macroeconomic Performance*. Oxford: Oxford University Press, pp. 101–151.

Roth, A. E. (1982). 'The Economics of Matching: Stability and Incentives'. *Mathematics of Operations Research*, 7: 617–628.

Roth, A. E. (2002). 'The Economist as Engineer: Game Theory, Experimentation, and Computation as Tools for Design Economics'. *Econometrica*, 70/4: 1341–1378.

Roth, A. E. (2015). *Who Gets What – and Why: The New Economics of Matchmaking and Market Design*. Boston and New York: Houghton Mifflin Harcourt.

Sidgwick, H. (1887). *The Principles of Political Economy*. Second Edition. London: Macmillan.

Taylor, A. M. (2018). 'The Argentina Paradox: Microexplanations and Macropuzzles'. *Latin American Economic Review*, 27/1. https://doi.org/10.1007/s40503-017-0051-8

Wagner, A. (1886). 'Wagner on the Present State of Political Economy'. *Quarterly Journal of Economics*, 1/1: 113–133.

Walton, D. (1989). 'Reasoned Use of Expertise in Argumentation'. *Argumentation*, 3: 59–73.

Walton, D. (1992). 'Rules for Plausible Reasoning'. *Informal Logic*, 14/1: 33–51.

Wicksteed, P. H. (1888). *The Alphabet of Economic Science*. London: Macmillan.

11 Drawing conclusions

The broad and ambitious scope of this book probably created expectations for readers, who will now judge if and to what extent these expectations have been met. In my opinion, given the nature of the subjects tackled, this book remains incomplete and open to further discussions and elaborations. Moreover, many of the proposals discussed require further development: for example, the way of detecting and incorporating final causes in economic theory, the definition of values and objectives involved in the common good, and the formulation of a theory for performing the art of economics. In this conclusion, I will briefly review the findings of the book.

The current heterogeneous state of economic science ignited my writing motivation. Positive economics is in good health, developing new ideas and encompassing new fields. New 'reverse imperialist' currents – behavioural, neuroeconomics, evolutionary, institutional, capability approaches, and so on – are thriving, and some of them are approaching maturity. We are witnessing a growing specialization of different disciplines and dispersed and disconnected new developments in economics. John Davis (2019) concludes, based on research regarding the JEL code and the J. B. Clark Award, that specialization as a 'centrifugal' force in research dominates 'centripetal' forces and that, consequently, economics is becoming increasingly fragmented. At the same time, normative economics seems at least partially set aside, and the art of economics is not actually regarded as a subject of economics. 'L'union fait la force': we need to place the pieces of this jigsaw puzzle in their correct positions to get a coherent picture of economic science. In order to prevent specialization from causing fragmentation, Davis (2019: 289) advocates a complex systems conception in which many cross-cutting relationships lead to multiple influences between the specialized fields. He calls attention to Hans-Michael Trautwein's (2017) considerations about the role of the history of economic thought as a centripetal force that counters centrifugal forces. I have studied philosophy and economics. I trust that philosophical reflection will help dig into the roots of a possible articulated system of economic sciences, albeit without falling in reductionisms. This is what I have tried to do in this book.

I set out endeavouring to discover the essence and define the subject matter of the system of economic sciences: the economy. I reminded the reader what

Uskali Mäki once told me: in his view, this amounts to the most difficult task of the philosophy of economics. I agree, thus probably rendering this conclusion unreliable. However, let's take a look at some authoritative arguments for it. A historical journey in search for the meaning of the economy will identify identifies two main 'literal' meanings of it: one points to the end of the human phenomenon, that is satisfying human material needs (Menger's 'technical-economic' or Neville Keynes' economic activity), and the other points to a way in which this satisfaction can be realized: allocating the disposable means to maximize the attainment of ends, specifically, economic preferences (Menger's 'economizing' or Neville Keynes' 'economic action'). Positive economics deals with the second meaning of the economy (Polanyi's notion of formal economics). However, some ends or motivations cannot be homogenized or explained in terms of the category of preferences, and there are situations in which maximization is unnecessary because there is no scarcity, or in which people simply do not maximize. These two last situations are included in the first meaning of the economy and have to be analysed by economic theory as well (Polanyi's notion of substantive economics).

However, economic theory is not the only approach to the study of the economy. I have postulated five compatible levels or approaches to the economy involved in economic sciences – namely, a) a statistical and historical descriptive level, b) a causal efficient explanatory level, c) a teleological explicative level, d) a normative level, and, finally, e) the art of political economy or applied economics. This book puts forward the idea that, far from being incompatible, these levels are complementary: economic phenomena call for a multilevel approach by a set of economic sciences: statistics, economic history, economic theory (including approaches b) and c)), normative economics, and the 'art of political economy' (as called by Neville Keynes). The different chapters address each of these sciences and show their interactions.

Chapter 4 deals with the first level and group of sciences. History and especially statistics seem to be value-neutral sciences. However, I have exposed the value commitments underlying them. Chapter 5 provides two philosophical concepts which are useful for analysing economic theory: causality and abduction. Chapter 6 describes the work of positive economics, while Chapter 7 argues why and how to cope with ends in economic theory. Hence, values are also included in economic theory. This last chapter in particular remains open, because I am suggesting something that to some extent is new: to analyse the specific content of ends. Chapter 8 upholds the legitimacy of including values in the social sciences and prepares us for Chapter 9 on normative economics. Finally, Chapter 10 explores the most comprehensive of the economic sciences, the art of economics.

In the introduction, I postulate the disciplinary relationships between the different economic sciences. All of them are interconnected. Values are present in different ways – implicitly or explicitly – in all the economic sciences. Their 'material object', that is, their subject matter, is economic phenomena. Their approaches – the 'formal objects' – vary. Thus, economic sciences constitute a multidisciplinary set of sciences. History and statistics describe, but there is no description without theory and values: all data are more or less theory and value-laden. Positive economics addresses the subject matter by restricting it: it deals with the most efficient allocation of means in order to satisfy ends that can be put into the undifferentiated category of 'preferences'. Economic theory complements positive economics by analysing economic phenomena aiming at ends that are not included in preferences: psychological, ethical, sociological. Choice is different from preferences, but preferences are the result of the decision-making process. The task of uniting the different parts of economic theory in a conceptually interdisciplinary way also remains open. Finally, ethics and economics might develop as a transdisciplinary field in normative economics. The art of economics should also be a transdisciplinary science, taking elements from all economic and social sciences, even from non-academic sources.

I hope that I have offered a sufficiently broad picture of economic sciences, encompassing all possible approaches to economic reality. I also hope that my contribution helps those working on each one of these approaches to bear in mind their interrelations in order to avoid inadequate reductivist analyses.

I believe that it is important and urgent to develop a program as delineated in the book. Tupac Amaru II, the last monarch of the Inca empire, was executed in the main plaza of Cuzco (Peru) following a bloody revolt that he himself had promoted. Executioners tried to kill him by tying his legs and arms to four horses that were driven at once towards the four corners of the plaza, pulling his arms and legs from his body. When that failed to dismember him, he was beheaded. This image of Tupac Amaru being dismembered is still evoked today, and often used as a metaphor for someone or something being torn in different directions. I think this metaphor applies to economics. Today, many economic currents are working in isolation from each other, in different directions, as the four horses of Tupac's execution, with the people as victim. In Chapter 1, I hold that working together and considering non-economic social factors that affect economic phenomena are essential to adopting policies that improve people's well-being.

I expect that the (negative) examples from my own country offered in some parts of the book prove instructive. In the last chapter, I mention Rudiger Dornbusch and Sebastian Edwards (1991) and their explanation of how Latin American countries enter into a vicious circle, alternating between populist (often corrupt) governments promoting an economically irrational 'macroeconomics of populism' and governments proposing stabilization plans which are supported by anti-populist sections of society. They explain (1991: 7):

> Latin America's economic history seems to repeat itself endlessly, following irregular and dramatic cycles. This sense of circularity is particularly striking with respect to the use of populist macroeconomic policies for distributive purposes. Again and again, and in country after country, policymakers have embraced economic programs that rely heavily on the use of expansive

fiscal and credit policies and overvalued currency to accelerate growth and redistribute income. In implementing these policies, there has usually been no concern for the existence of fiscal and foreign exchange constraints. After a short period of economic growth and recovery, bottlenecks develop provoking unsustainable macroeconomic pressures that, at the end, result in the plummeting of real wages and severe balance of payment difficulties. The final outcome of these experiments has generally been galloping inflation, crisis, and the collapse of the economic system. In the aftermath of these experiments there is no other alternative left but to implement, typically with the help of the International Monetary Fund (IMF), a drastically restrictive and costly stabilization program. The self-destructive feature of populism is particularly apparent from the stark decline in per capita income and real wages in the final days of these experiences.

A 'drastically restrictive and costly stabilization program' has a strong impact on the economy of people and industries. Hungry people cannot think and thus act irrationally. It is very difficult to create order without affecting people's personal economy, and this leads citizens, time and again, to choose populist alternatives that ultimately perpetuate or even increase impoverishment as, for example, Christina Romer and David Romer (1998) and Michael Gavin and Ricardo Hausmann (1998) have argued.

Behind this bleak scenario there are underlying social and political historical tensions – cracks – between populist and 'rational' sections of the population. Populists often seek power and personal enrichment; 'rationals' honestly attempt to do what is best but fail to communicate well: not only do they not fully capture the consequences of policies for people's lives, but they do not get their messages across effectively. They are convinced that they are doing the right thing and do not worry too much about explaining the reasons for their policies, which can adversely affect the population. In addition, economies in these countries are highly complex. Consequently, getting things right the first time is not easy, and policymakers generally refuse to admit their mistakes. They pack their cabinets with outstanding professionals or academics, but this turns out to be insufficient. Argentina requires a general consensus that it has so far never been able to achieve or implement.

However, it would be simplistic to apply a general paradigm to all Latin America countries (see the criticism of this simplification by Albert O. Hirschman and Mario R. dos Santos 1970). Apparently, Chile, Colombia, Peru, and Uruguay have escaped this vicious circle, but I am not very familiar with the history of these countries. A specific combination of complex social factors will probably determine the road to success or failure. However, success clearly depends on a positive alignment of those factors.

I suppose that Tupac's dismemberment failed due to the difficulty of making the horses pull in the correct directions. In the case of economics, if we fail to prevent economic disciplines from pulling different ways, the effort will succeed and people will suffer. Economists in charge of policies need to perform the art of political economy as explained in the last chapter, as a transdisciplinary science, integrating inputs from the rest of the economic and social sciences, listening and talking to people. The rest of the economic sciences should also work in an integrative way, as recommended in this book.

It is very difficult to predict what will happen with economics. Reverse imperialist currents are actually affecting economics' internal development: this is a good sign. However, the titles and abstracts of papers published in top journals reveal an amazing dispersion. For my part, I am doing what I sincerely think I must do, that is, to call for economic sciences to come together to work in an integrated manner and develop a plurality of approaches.

References

Davis, J. B. (2019). 'Specialization, Fragmentation, and Pluralism in Economics'. *European Journal of the History of Economic Thought*, 26/2: 271–293.

Dornbusch, R. and S. Edwards (1991). 'The Macroeconomics of Populism'. In: R. Dornbusch and S. Edwards (eds.), *The Macroeconomics of Populism in Latin America*. Chicago: University of Chicago Press, pp. 7–13.

Gavin, M. and R. Hausmann (1998). 'Macroeconomic Volatility and Economic Development'. In: S. Borner and M. Paldam (eds.), *The Political Dimension of Economic Growth*. London: Palgrave Macmillan, pp. 97–116.

Hirschman, A. O. and M. R. dos Santos (1970). 'La búsqueda de paradigmas como un impedimento de la comprensión'. *Desarrollo Económico*, 10/37: 3–20.

Romer, C. D. and D. H. Romer (1998). 'Monetary Policy and Well-Being of the Poor', NBER Working Paper No. 6793, https://econpapers.repec.org/paper/nbrnberwo/6793.htm. Accessed 13 September 2019.

Trautwein, H.-M. (2017). 'The Last Generalists'. *European Journal of the History of Economic Thought*, 24/6: 1134–1136.

Index

Printed in the United States
by Baker & Taylor Publisher Services